dBASE III PLUS®
Programming

Programming books from boyd & fraser

Structuring Programs in Microsoft BASIC
BASIC Fundamentals and Style
Applesoft BASIC Fundamentals and Style
Complete BASIC: For the Short Course
Fundamentals of Structured COBOL
Advanced Structured COBOL: Batch and Interactive
Comprehensive Structured COBOL
Pascal
WATFIV-S Fundamentals and Style
VAX Fortran
Fortran 77 Fundamentals and Style
Learning Computer Programming: Structured Logic, Algorithms, and Flowcharting
Structured BASIC Fundamentals and Style for the IBM® PC and Compatibles
C Programming
dBASE III PLUS® Programming

Also available from boyd & fraser

Database Systems: Management and Design
Using Pascal: An Introduction to Computer Science I
Using Modula-2: An Introduction to Computer Science I
Data Abstraction and Structures: An Introduction to Computer Science II
Fundamentals of Systems Analysis with Application Design
Data Communications for Business
Data Communications Software Design
Microcomputer Applications: Using Small Systems Software
The Art of Using Computers
Using Microcomputers: A Hands-On Introduction
A Practical Approach to Operating Systems
Microcomputer Database Management Using dBASE III PLUS®
Microcomputer Database Management Using R:BASE System V®
Office Automation: An Information Systems Approach
Microcomputer Applications: Using Small Systems Software, Second Edition
Mastering Lotus 1-2-3®
Using Enable™: An Introduction to Integrated Software
PC-DOS®/MS-DOS® Simplified

Shelly, Cashman, and Forsythe books from boyd & fraser

Computer Fundamentals with Application Software
Workbook and Study Guide to accompany Computer Fundamentals with Application Software
Learning to Use SUPERCALC®3, dBASE III®, and WORDSTAR® 3.3: An Introduction
Learning to Use SUPERCALC®3: An Introduction
Learning to Use dBASE III®: An Introduction
Learning to Use WORDSTAR® 3.3: An Introduction
BASIC Programming for the IBM® Personal Computer
Workbook and Study Guide to accompany BASIC Programming for the IBM® Personal Computer
Structured COBOL — Flowchart Edition
Structured COBOL — Pseudocode Edition
Turbo Pascal Programming

dBASE III PLUS®
Programming

ROBERT A. WRAY

The Pennsylvania State University

COPYRIGHT 1988
BOYD & FRASER PUBLISHING COMPANY
BOSTON

Credits:

Publisher: Tom Walker
Editor: Sarah Grover
Production Editor: Donna Villanucci
Director of Production: Becky Herrington
Director of Manufacturing: Erek Smith
Book/Cover Design: Becky Herrington
Cover Photography: Mark A. Wiklund
Text Illustration: Mike Broussard and Ken Russo

Registered Trademark Listing:

dBASE II®, dBASE III®, dBASE III PLUS®, dCONVERT®, RUNTIME + ®, dBRUN®, dBCODE®, dBLINKER®,
  Network dBASE III PLUS®, and Multiplan® are registered trademarks of the Ashton-Tate Corporation
UNIX® is a registered trademark of Bell Laboratories
GENIFER® is a registered trademark of the Bytel Corporation
Compaq® is a registered trademark of the Compaq Corporation
IDMS® and IDMS/R® are registered trademarks of the Cullinet Corporation
FoxBASE + ® is a registered trademark of Fox Software
Intel 8086®, Intel 80286®, and Intel 80386® are registered trademarks of the Intel Corporation
IMS®, DL/I®, DB2®, QBE®, SQL®, SQL/DS®, IBM-PC®, IBM/XT®, IBM/AT®, IBM Personal System/2®,
  PC-DOS®, and IBM-PC Network Program® are registered trademarks of International
  Business Machines Corporation
Lotus 1-2-3® is a registered trademark of Lotus Development Corporation
R:BASE SYSTEM V® is a registered trademark of Microrim, Inc.
MS-DOS® and OS/2® are registered trademarks of the Microsoft Corporation
Clipper® is a registered trademark of Nantucket Corporation
NOMAD® is a registered trademark of National CSS, Inc.
Visicalc® is a registered trademark of Software Arts, Inc.
PFS® is a registered trademark of Software Publishing Corporation
TANDY 1000® and TRS-80® are registered trademarks of the Tandy Corporation
Quicksilver® is a registered trademark of Wordtech Systems

Manufactured in the United States of America

Library of Congress Cataloging-in-Publication Data

```
Wray, Robert A.
   dBASE III PLUS programming.


   Includes index.
   1. Data base management.  2. dBASE III PLUS
(Computer program)  3. IBM Personal Computer--
Programming.  I. Title.
QA76.9.D3W73 1988      005.75'65      87-30108
ISBN 0-87835-293-7
```

10 9 8 7 6 5 4 3 2

To Barb

CONTENTS

PART I – THE BASICS

Chapter 1 AN OVERVIEW

Chapter 2 THE dBASE III PLUS ENVIRONMENT

PART II – PROGRAMMING

Chapter 6 THE DO WHILE/ENDDO LOOP

Chapter 7 DECISION MAKING WITH IF/ENDIF

PART III – ADVANCED TECHNIQUES

Chapter 11 CONSTRUCTING SCREENS

Chapter 12 SYSTEM DESIGN USING MULTIPLE FILES

Chapter 13 FUNCTIONS – THE PROGRAMMER'S TOOLKIT

Chapter 14 EFFICIENCY SKILLS

Chapter 15 ADVANCED TOPICS

PREFACE

This text serves a critical need in the contemporary business environment. There is a serious lack of business professionals trained to create microcomputer database systems. Every effort was made to provide all the elements one would expect in an introductory programming course and include required database and structured programming concepts. Students who successfully complete the course will possess a marketable skill that will serve them well for years to come.

OBJECTIVES

1. To describe the use of all of the features of dBASE III PLUS.
2. To teach useful interactive commands to effectively manage and use database files.
3. To present sound structured programming fundamentals using dBASE III PLUS.
4. To develop the ability to design systems.
5. To survey relational aspects of database theory.

Although the book was developed for a one-semester introductory course in dBASE III PLUS programming, it offers maximum flexibility for rapidly changing curriculum needs. There is sufficient support for the solo learner as well. Since it is comprehensive, the text could be used as a component in courses that survey DBMSs. There is enough database theory to satisfy an introduction to the subject. The reading ability and problem level are appropriate for an average freshman or sophomore student with little or no programming experience.

ORGANIZATION

The organization of the book is based on a spiral approach. New concepts and skills build upon the work in previous chapters. This provides reinforcement while motivating the reader with new challenges. The first four chapters introduce the interactive use of dBASE III PLUS. Commands which will be used in programming are emphasized. The student is lead toward writing programs as quickly as possible. The remaining eleven chapters present every aspect of programming required to develop a working business system.

DISTINGUISHING FEATURES

Realistic Business Problem Solving

The concepts and techniques presented in this book have been tested in working systems many times. Examples are based on actual business situations. Mastery will enable the student to "hit the ground running."

Numerous Program Examples

An abundance of figures includes programs, screens, diagrams, and reports. Students can easily see the relationship between the program and its results. Abstract concepts such as nested loops are illustrated by easily understood analogies and drawings.

Introduction to Database Theory

Important aspects of database theory are treated from a practical standpoint. Students are exposed to the normalization of data through a problem. The benefits of the relational model and its comparison with other DBMS types are explored. Many important terms are defined and explained.

In-Depth Coverage of the Control Structures

The DO WHILE/ENDDO, IF/ELSE/ENDIF, and DO CASE/ENDCASE are not merely presented; the structures are analyzed so the student understands how they operate and can predict their behavior.

Free Student Data Disk

All programs and files are contained on a convenient free data disk packaged with each book. This saves the student and the instructor a great deal of time. In a lab setting the students can run the programs to reinforce lecture concepts. The programs and files can be modified for individual study.

Superior Coverage of Multiple File Programming

Chapter 12 provides coverage of an often neglected topic, the programming of multiple file systems. System planning is discussed, and a complex program example clearly illustrates how several database files can be accessed simultaneously.

dBUG dBASE Sections

Most chapters include a dBUG dBASE feature containing valuable hints that relate to the chapter topics. These tips generally originate from practical experience.

Numerous Exercises, Problems, and Projects

Chapters include Self-check Questions that review important chapter material, Try It Yourself exercises that provide hands-on practice of techniques, and Programming Projects that require the student to plan and code comprehensive programs.

Chapter Objectives and Summaries

Following an introduction to motivate further study, students are presented with clearly stated chapter objectives that provide purpose and direction. Each chapter concludes with concise summaries for each section, a list of key terms, and a command summary including definitions. This is convenient for reference while working in the chapter.

Free Educational Version of dBASE III PLUS

A fully functional educational version of dBASE III PLUS is available to adopters of this text. This version is limited to 31 records which is sufficient for class use. The instructions for copying and using the software is included in Chapter 2. Boyd & Fraser will supply adopters with master diskettes for use in class, along with permission to duplicate the diskettes for each student who has purchased a new copy of the text from the publisher.

Structured Principles

The principles of structured programming are presented and constantly reinforced throughout the text. All program examples are documented and indented for emulation by the student.

Complete Case Study

As an optional tool, the text includes a complete, narrative case study. This material includes a working system, with all related programs contained on the Student Data Diskette. Suggestions for using the Case Study are provided in the Instructor's Manual.

Instructor's Manual

An instructor's manual will be provided to all adopters. Lecture notes and hints, answers to exercises, and helpful suggestions will aid the instructor in delivering the course.

ACKNOWLEDGEMENTS

This book includes the valuable ideas and suggestions of several individuals who took the time and interest to review the manuscript. I wish to thank the following educators: Cindy Bonfini-Hotlosz, West Virginia Northern Community College; Helene Chlopan, Lexington Community College; Michael Crews, Pan American University; Julia Hodges, Mississippi State University; Jack Lloyd, Montgomery College; Mike Michaelson, Palomar College; Paul Ross, Millersville University; Mari Ryan, Northeastern University; Pamela Schmidt, Oakton Community College; Bill Strasbaugh, Messiah College; John Zales, Harrisburg Area Community College.

My friends and associates at AMP Inc. have been helpful and supportive in a variety of ways. They were patient while I finished the book, often sacrificing progress on their own projects. I wish to thank Jim Marley, Don Pollard, Don Parrish, Art Rogers, John Trendler, Al Lujan, Ron Schaible, Mike Levan, and the rest of the fine employees of this outstanding organization. I also wish to thank Hank Clay of Digital Business Systems for the excellent photographs in Chapter 1.

The editorial group of Boyd & Fraser is a rare breed. Without the guidance, support and resources that they provided, this book would still be a dream. Peter Gordon shared my vision of a text to formally present dBASE III PLUS as a programming course. Tom Walker backed the project administratively and handled the jib. Donna Villanucci started and finished the editorial work. Arthur Weisbach's editing was an education in pedagogy and style. Matt Loeb contributed his marketing skills and was a lot of help at COMDEX. Toni Rosenberg, a talented and dedicated lady, made certain every comma was properly placed. My editor, Sarah Grover, has contributed more than anyone to the completion of this book. She is considerate, supportive, dedicated, and persistent! I could not ask for a better working relationship than the one that we enjoy. Thank you, Sarah Smile. To the Brea production crew, and in particular to Becky Herrington, I extend a special thanks for all of their hard work. I am deeply appreciative of the faith and hard work of all these special people.

My parents Anthony and Lenore, my brothers, and other friends and relatives have been a rich source of encouragement. I especially wish to thank my mother for her love and inspiration, and her late brother Daniel who taught me to love learning for learning's sake.

My family has sacrificed much in the last two years to allow me to complete my work. This book is dedicated to them. My children, Jennifer and Eric, have been patient and understanding beyond their years. Daddy's done now. I will never be able to thank my wife, Barb, for all her love and support. She shared my frustration and assumed my responsibilities with grace; now she can share my joy.

Robert A. Wray
Mechanicsburg, Pennsylvania
January, 1988

PART I

THE BASICS

AMP Incorporated is a Fortune 200 company with over 20,000 employees worldwide. It is the largest U.S. domestic manufacturer of electronic connectors and terminals. Any business of this size, scope, and complexity naturally relies on a variety of computer systems to remain competitive and to ensure the highest quality of its products and services. In addition to a number of large mainframe systems, AMP currently uses over 900 microcomputers for diverse applications. One of our most widely used database management systems is dBASE III PLUS. Over 600 employees have been trained to use and are currently using dBASE in order to meet the ever increasing need to effectively manage AMP's information. This investment by our corporation is indicative of the value we place on the skills of our employees. Business operations become more complex each year, and we expect that this investment will benefit both ourselves and our customers by meeting our collective needs more efficiently. We encourage business and technical students to develop computer skills and to strive constantly to remain current in those skills so that they may contribute to the advancement of the United States' business interests in an increasingly competitive world market.

James E. Marley, President
AMP Incorporated

1

AN OVERVIEW

LEARNING OBJECTIVES

1. To define a database management system (DBMS) in terms of its capabilities.
2. To define several relevant computer terms.
3. To identify the capacities of dBASE III PLUS.
4. To examine some relevant concepts of database theory.

Chapter

1

AN OVERVIEW

It has been said that information is power. It is certainly true that as society evolves, people are increasingly dependent on timely information to participate in a complex but rewarding environment. The business world recognizes that success often depends on managing information better than the competition does. The computer is widely used to meet this goal. The challenge lies in effectively and efficiently designing the instructions that direct the computer's activities. This chapter will introduce a popular product for meeting that challenge: dBASE III PLUS.

1.1 WHAT IS A DBMS?

These are exciting times in the business world. Recent technological developments, such as superconductivity, promise to improve computers dramatically. Speed and storage capacity will increase, as will the rate at which size and cost continue to diminish. Parallel improvements in software, the instructions that operate the computer, will provide power, flexibility, and ease of use to an increasingly larger segment of society. The businesses that provide these products and services will prosper because they meet a critical need—the effective management of information. Amid these realistically optimistic projections only one deficiency is apparent: an inadequate number of skilled business professionals who are capable of designing systems that can solve complex business problems effectively and profitably.

The combination of a microcomputer system, a powerful software product such as dBASE III PLUS, and a knowledgeable user is all that is required for the effective managemet of astonishing amounts of stored information. This book is designed to help you become a knowledgeable user of this technology. You will learn to manage information and to program in dBASE III PLUS. As you might expect, these abilities are valued highly in the business world. All businesses in contemporary society share a critical dependence on the availability of timely information. Those who are responsible for maintaining that information rely on computers because of the unsurpassable accuracy and efficiency they afford when they are properly programmed.

The statement at the begining of this chapter by James E. Marley, president of AMP, Incorporated, illustrates the value that business places on persons who possess immediately applicable computer skills. Businesses that have made the decision to become automated with computer systems have done so to realize both considerable cost reductions and increases in productivity. It is reasonable to conclude, therefore, that, in general, a job applicant who has already acquired marketable information management skills is more attractive to such businesses than one who will require expensive on-the-job training. Currently, one of the most highly rated of these skills is the ability to develop systems and programs with dBASE III PLUS. This book provides an excellent opportunity to acquire this ability.

FIGURE 1.1   *dBASE III PLUS and a typical microcomputer.*

Businesses use various types of information systems, but no matter which type a particular business has selected, an information system must perform three critical tasks:

1. Collecting information and storing it.
2. Organizing and maintaining the information in a way that will increase its usefulness.
3. Responding to requests for information in a natural and convenient manner.

Any information that has been centralized and organized can be considered a database. Telephone directories, encyclopedias, dictionaries, and card files all store information in a central place in an organized way so that it can be easily retrieved. Since the essence of most business activities can be described as the processing of information, databases are critical to the daily fuctioning of most businesses. Figure 1.2, for example, lists just a few of the functions that are routinely performed by dBASE III PLUS in the area of accounting.

General Ledger	Time and Billing
Accounts Receivable	Personnel
Accounts Payable	Sales Tracking
Inventory	Fixed Asset Manager
Payroll	Customer-Account System

FIGURE 1.2 *Accounting uses of dBASE III PLUS.*

When one is working with computers, information is often referred to as *data*. Data consists of raw facts, such as account numbers, account balances, and dates. Some data is used for calculations, such as gross pay, while other data identifies things, as in names, addresses, and catalog numbers.

Data is organized within several commonly used categories. The smallest of these is the single *character* or symbol. Characters that are grouped together to form a single piece of information, such as a Social Security number, are called *fields*. When several fields are used to represent an entity such as a person, business, product, or city, the grouped fields are called a *record*. A *file* is a collection of records.

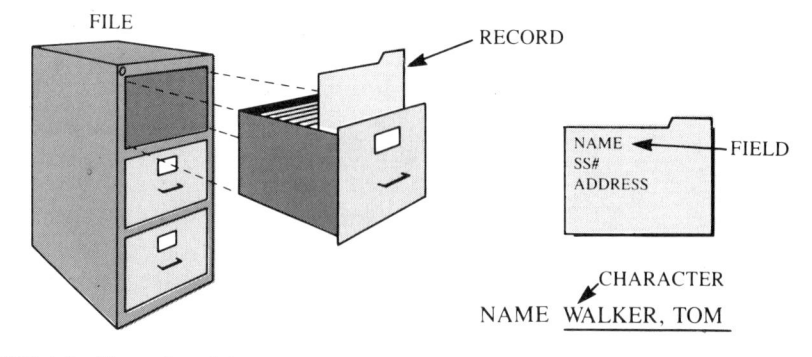

FIGURE 1.3 *Hierarchy of data.*

The terms character, field, record, and file are familiar in the office environment. When data is represented in computer systems, these terms and others are required. A *byte* is a unit of storage in the computer. It usually represents one character of data, such as a number, a comma, or a letter. Files are often measured in terms of the number of *kilobytes* they occupy. A kilobyte contains 1,024 bytes. A *database* is a collection of organized data and other related information which is stored in the computer as a database file. Computer programs that are designed to create, maintain, and use databases are called *database management systems* (DBMSs), the most powerful software products available to manage stored information. These are computer programs that collect, store, retrieve, and report information in an organized way. There are many DBMS products on the market. Some are designed for large computer systems, others for microcomputers such as the IBM Personal System/2. The advantages of a DBMS include the following:

1. It offers rapid access to and flexible use of information. A DBMS uses sophisticated methods of organization and retrieval.
2. The incidence of redundancy (repetition) is limited and information is kept current. This is critical, because there is a direct relationship between the efficiency of a computer program and its ability to avoid storing unnecessary information and to keep the information it does store up-to-date.
3. The cost/benefit ratio is good. The cost of setting up and operating a DBMS is low compared to the value of the benefits it affords.
4. Storage of information is compact, compared to paper storage.
5. Mundane, repetitive tasks such as searching for information and preparing reports can be automated.
6. A DBMS imposes an organized structure that would be difficult to attain manually. Once a DBMS has been established, its maintenance encourages efficiency in office procedures.

The disadvantages of a DBMS include:

1. Operations and programming require skill in the use of the system as well as a knowledge of DBMS concepts.
2. Because information is stored in a complex way, it can be difficult to back up or reconstruct.
3. Information is centralized, and it requires maintenance. Someone must assume responsibility for administering the DBMS.
4. As the power and features of the DBMS are utilized, more complex information management is required, and this generates new administrative problems.

As you can see, the advantages of a DBMS far outweigh its disadvantages. Although some business situations do not require the use of DBMS products, most small businesses and certainly all mid- to large-sized companies use them extensively. In fact, these products pervade the entire spectrum of modern business activity, which suggests that DBMS technology will eventually affect the jobs of most business professionals. Let's take a look now at some of the characteristics of dBASE III PLUS.

1.2 WHAT IS dBASE III PLUS?

Hundreds of thousands of people, in thousands of businesses all over the world, use dBASE III PLUS. It consists of a comprehensive set of programs that is marketed by Ashton-Tate of Torrance, California, and is designed to run on microcomputers. Figure 1.4 lists the contents of a dBASE III PLUS package.

Two-Volume Documentation Set and Several Pamphlets
System Disks 1 and 2
Backup of System Disk 1
Sample Programs and Utilities
Administrator Disks 1 and 2 for Networking
On-Disk Tutorial
Applications Generator Disk

FIGURE 1.4   *Contents of dBASE III PLUS.*

Chapter 2 contains the procedures for using dBASE III PLUS with this book, while later chapters explain the use of the items listed in Figure 1.4. It will be helpful to review these items, since you may not have the opportunity to examine a complete dBASE III PLUS package in class. The success of dBASE III PLUS stems partly from its provision of a comprehensive solution to the need for effective information management. It contains a variety of features that many have found particularly useful, including the following:

1. A set of commands for storing and maintaining organized information.
2. Convenient report- and label-generating programs.
3. The menu-driven Assistant feature to simplify the process of issuing commands.
4. Commands for using dBASE III PLUS in a local area network.
5. A complete programming language including a screen painter and an application generator.

A more complete list of dBASE III PLUS features is shown in Figure 1.5 on the following page.

Features of dBASE III PLUS

Assistant with pull-down menus.

New programming commands and functions (absolute value, modula, highest and lowest number).

HISTORY, RESUME, SUSPEND.

Combined FOR and WHILE.

Capacity to scan keyboard for response without halting execution.

Application generator.

CALL assembly language programs.

LAN programming commands.

   Supports either IBM-PC Network program or Novell Advanced NetWare/86.

   File locking security system with data encryption and password protection.

Commands for working with DOS within a program in the single user or network version.

Screen painter.

SET FIELDS, SET VIEW for interactive use.

Query menu that creates files to filter records.

Enhanced data-sharing capabilities.

Import and export to other programs (Lotus 1-2-3, Multiplan, and PFS).

Interactive debugging commands to suspend execution, perform operations in interactive mode, and resume operation of suspended program.

FIGURE 1.5 *Features of dBASE III PLUS.*

One measurement of the power of a DBMS is the amount of information it is capable of storing. As Figure 1.6 illustrates, dBASE III PLUS has surprisingly large dimensions. In most circumstances, it is the capacity limitations of the microcomputer, not those of dBASE III PLUS, which determine how much information can be managed. (Some of the terms in Figure 1.6 will be defined later in this book.)

1 Billion Records Per File
2 Billion Characters Per File
4,000 Characters Per Record
128 Fields Per Record
254 Characters Per Field
19 Bytes Per Numeric Fields
512,000 Characters Per Memo Field
15 Open Files
10 Open Database Files

FIGURE 1.6 *Capacities of dBASE III PLUS.*

The manner in which dBASE III PLUS stores data varies, depending on how the data is to be used. The table in Figure 1.7 on the opposite page conveys the differences among the types of data, or field types. (Chapter 3 presents more information on this subject.)

Name	Size	Contents
Character	1—254	All Characters
Numeric	1—15	0—9, Decimal Point, +, or -
Date	8	MM/DD/YY, Other Formats Optional
Logical	1	T, F, Y, N, t, f, y, n
Memo	4,000	All Characters

FIGURE 1.7 *dBASE III PLUS field types.*

The evolution of dBASE III PLUS began in the mid-1970s, when a programmer named C. Wayne Ratliff was working on a project for NASA. Over a period of about ten years, Ratliff's work led to the development of dBASE III PLUS. Figure 1.8 traces the emergence of dBASE III PLUS from its origins in earlier products and in dBASE II.

1976. C. Wayne Ratliff gains experience working with data management while programming for the Viking Lander Project at NASA.

1977. Ratliff buys an IMSAI 8800 computer kit (one of the first microcomputers) to track game scores for an office football pool.

1978. Influenced by a program called JPL Display and Information System (JPLDIS), an emulation of an IBM product called Retrieve, Ratliff writes a natural language program to manage data on the IMSAI 8800 and calls it Vulcan.

October 1979. Vulcan is advertised in Byte magazine. Ratliff is overwhelmed with orders for the program.

Summer 1980. The marketing rights for Vulcan are sold to Ashton-Tate. The program is improved through the addition of commands and screens and is renamed dBASE II.

January 1981. dBASE II is introduced, selling over two hundred thousand copies and enjoying worldwide success. It is adapted for machines such as the Osborne, TRS-80, Kaypro, and Intertec, popular business computers at the time.

September 1983. Version 2.4 of dBASE II is released for the IBM-PC, but criticisms of the product include slow processing, small file size, unfriendly screens, and a programming language that is difficult to master and not satisfactory for larger systems.

FIGURE 1.8 *Historical perspective of dBASE III PLUS (Part 1 of 2).*

May 15, 1984. dBASE III Version 1.1, written in C language, is released. It is designed for 16-bit 8088 computers, using the IBM-PC as a standard, and it takes advantage of its increased memory and speed. Help screens and the Assist feature allow users to begin using the product almost immediately, although a considerable learning curve still exists before large applications can be built.

Fall 1985. dBASE III PLUS is introduced.

FIGURE 1.8 *Historical perspective of dBASE III PLUS (Part 2 of 2).*

In *Programmers at Work*, by Susan Lammers (1986), Ratliff compares dBASE to other programs:

dBASE was different from programs like BASIC, C, FORTRAN, and COBOL in that a lot of the dirty work had already been done. The data manipulation is done by dBASE instead of the user, so the user can concentrate on what he is doing, rather than having to mess with the dirty details of opening, reading, and closing files, and managing space allocation.*

— C. Wayne Ratliff, Creator of dBASE

Figure 1.9 summarizes the advantages of dBASE III PLUS.

1. It simplifies and speeds the construction of complicated business systems.
2. An increasingly large community of active users ensures support and continuing product development.
3. Its capacities are more than adequate for most needs.
4. Sets of information can be related in complex ways; for example, the informational needs of personnel and payroll departments can be combined, since they use the same information in different ways.

FIGURE 1.9 *Advantages of dBASE III PLUS.*

Before microcomputers that used sophisticated software became widely available, information management tasks were performed with traditional programming languages like *COBOL* (COmmon Business Oriented Language) on large computers called *mainframes*. Of course, a great deal of work is still done this way today, but, as microcomputers continue to become more powerful and cost-effective and as people acquire the skills needed to use them, products like dBASE III PLUS become an attractive option for information management.

---

*Susan Lammers, *Programmers at Work* (Redmond, WA: Microsoft Press, 1986), 117.

In certain circumstances, dBASE III PLUS is not the appropriate choice for a business. When information needs are so large that the speed and capacity of a large computer system is required, a whole range of products is available. However, dBASE III PLUS enjoys several advantages that languages such as COBOL and BASIC do not.

In comparison to dBASE III PLUS programs, COBOL programs tend to be longer and more complex and require more technical skill and training. Therefore, COBOL users must depend on others to access data, and long backlogs of data requests, measured in months or even years, are common. The disadvantages of other programming languages such as BASIC and FORTRAN are similar to those of COBOL. No function that is needed by a user can be executed unless a program has first been specifically written for it—even, for example, if a single item needs to be removed from a previously existing set of information. In terms of this example and others like it, a program would be difficult to construct and costly to develop. On the other hand, the same task could be accomplished with dBASE III PLUS with two simple commands. This disparity is evident in other areas of system development such as report design and search procedures. Finally, dBASE III PLUS is often preferable to programs written in the named languages for another reason: information can be transferred easily between it and most data-processing environments in common use.

The convenience of use that accounts in part for the popularity of dBASE III PLUS is highlighted in the summary in Figure 1.10.

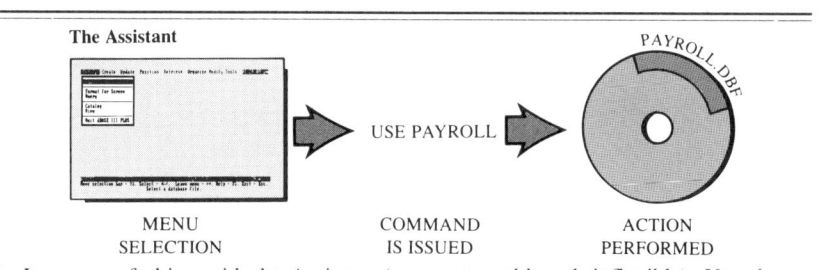

1. In cursory fashion with the Assistant (easy to use although inflexible). You choose the function you want from a menu, and dBASE III PLUS issues the command for you.

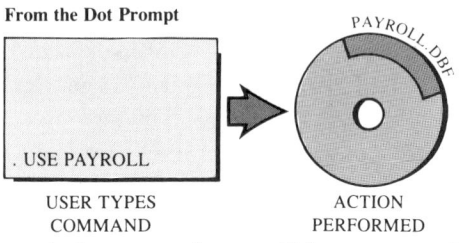

2. You type in the commands yourself from a prompt in the interactive or immediate mode.

FIGURE 1.10 *How dBASE III PLUS is used (Part 1 of 2).*

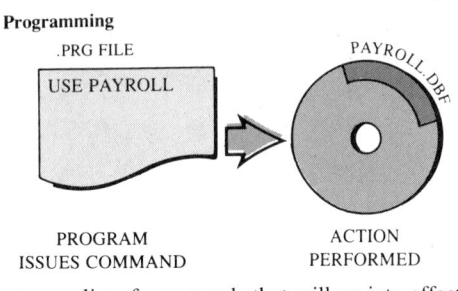

Programming

.PRG FILE

USE PAYROLL

PAYROLL.DBF

PROGRAM
ISSUES COMMAND

ACTION
PERFORMED

3. You type a list of commands that will go into effect at a later time; this is batch mode programming.

FIGURE 1.10   *How dBASE III PLUS is used (Part 2 of 2).*

I.3 DATABASE THEORY

DBMSs provide access to data by responding to requests or *queries*. Besides the ability to manipulate data by appending, retrieving, modifying, and deleting, a DBMS performs other functions including the following:

Data definition, or table creation functions such as CREATE
Programming language
Report writing (formatting and printing data)
File catalogs
Indexing (to locate data)
Views
Security
Integrity
Locking
Database design

As you might expect, users can obtain many products that perform the preceding functions. Most of these products were developed on mainframes, using COBOL. As *minicomputers* (smaller mainframes) and microcomputers became common in business, software developers provided DBMSs to satisfy that market. Like the data itself, DBMSs are often categorized according to the way in which they organize and access that data. The three most common categories are *hierarchical*, *network*, and *relational*. A brief description of each one follows.

Hierarchical DBMSs establish relationships among data items by using sets of pointers, links, and lists. It is as if each piece of data carried a set of directions for access. Because hierarchical DBMSs require large memories and powerful processing units, they are found on mainframe computers, often in a COBOL environment. A good example is IMS, IBM's hierarchical DBMS, and the associated programming language, DL/1.

Network databases are constructed on an underlying foundation of records and relationships. Besides being popular for use on mainframes, they are used extensively on minicomputers, such as the Hewlett-Packard HP-3000. IDMS, by Cullinet, is a network-type DBMS that conforms to an industry standard called the CODASYL model.

In the relational model information is stored in related data tables in separate files. It can be accessed and manipulated interactively or in batch (program) mode. A table organizes data into rows and columns. The rows are records, and the columns are fields. Programmers call the rows *tuples* and the columns *attributes*. Other more complex aspects of a relational database are discussed in Chapter 14.

Since dBASE III PLUS is a relational DBMS, we will explore this type more closely. Imagine a simple table of two columns and four rows. Label the first column NAME and the second column PHONE. Each row will then provide a position in each column for individual records. If we were to add some data, the table might look like the one in Figure 1.11. It is in the ability to access data from either dimension, row or column, that the strength of the relational DBMS resides. In a relational DBMS such as dBASE III PLUS, records are thought of as rows and fields as columns. For example, you could work with only the phone numbers and ignore the names, or vice versa. By positioning yourself at the proper row you can retrieve all the fields in that row.

	Name	Phone
1	Harpo	555-3964
2	Chico	555-9385
3	Groucho	555-9359
4	Zeppo	555-2051
5	↓	↓

FIGURE 1.11 *A sample table.*

The relational DBMS includes the following characteristics:

1. Records must be unique in order to provide access by row.
2. A table does not depend on order in either dimension, because relationships are established through the DBMS structure, not through the physical order of the data. This allows a great deal of flexibility when one is accessing the data.
3. Columns produce consistency in the rows by maintaining a strict format for each field.

DB2, by IBM, is a relational DBMS that is designed for mainframe computers. SQL (the acronym stands for Structured Query Language and is usually pronounced sequel) is an IBM development that is marketed as SQL/DS. SQL is the language used in DB2 and other relational DBMSs. Other examples of relational DBMSs include IDMS/R and R:BASE SYSTEM V.

Chapter 1 has provided an overview of dBASE III PLUS. Chapter 2 will present specific information that you will need to begin working with this important business tool.

CHAPTER SUMMARY

1.1

The effective management of information is critical to businesses. Several terms are associated with the organization of data in a computer system, such as field, record, file, and database. Database management systems, or DBMSs, collect, store, organize, and report information in an organized way. Advantages of a DBMS include rapid access and flexible use of information, relatively low incidence of redundancy, compact storage, and reasonable cost. Its disadvantages include a required level of skill, increased complexity, and the necessity of maintenance for centralized information.

1.2

One of the more popular DBMSs is dBASE III PLUS, which contains useful features and a widely used programming language. It has a very large capacity for storing different types of information. It compares favorably with traditional programming languages like COBOL because it is powerful yet easier to learn and use. It can be used in a variety of information-intensive activities, such as inventory.

1.3

Of the three types of DBMSs, dBASE III PLUS is relational, which means that data is accessed by its relative position in a table containing rows and columns. Data is categorized into characters, fields, records, and files. A DBMS can append, modify, delete, and retrieve data. Other types of DBMSs are hierarchical and network.

KEY TERMS

Database Management System	record	network
DBMS	file	relational
data	database	table
COBOL	structure	tuple
mainframe	byte	attribute
BASIC	kilobyte	SQL
FORTRAN	query	
character	minicomputers	
field	hierarchical	

SELF-CHECK QUESTIONS

1. List three information management functions.
2. What is a DBMS? What does it do?
3. Describe three features of dBASE III PLUS.
4. Name two field types and describe how they might be used.
5. If mainframe computers are more powerful than micros, why are they not used for every business problem? When is it best to use a mainframe?
6. What are some of the disadvantages of using a language like COBOL?
7. Which product would be most suitable for each of the following applications: dBASE III PLUS or a mainframe DBMS?
   a. A major corporation has to handle the payroll for over 8,000 employees.
   b. A health club wishes to keep track of its members.
   c. The business department of a community college wants to schedule fourteen classrooms over a five-day period.
   d. A small consulting firm is trying to keep track of its clients and the various services they use.
8. What features do you think future DBMS products might include to make them more useful?
9. Give some practical examples of a character, a field, a record, and a file.
10. A database file occupies 64 kilobytes. What is the actual number of bytes in the file?
11. What are the four data manipulation functions?
12. Compare the typical features of a DBMS with the dBASE III PLUS features that appear in section 1.2 of this chapter. List the features that are common to both.
13. What are the three types of DBMSs? What type is dBASE III PLUS?
14. Describe how a relational DBMS stores data.

2

THE dBASE III PLUS ENVIRONMENT

LEARNING OBJECTIVES

1. To become familiar with the hardware used with dBASE III PLUS.
2. To properly execute several essential DOS commands.
3. To install, back up, and run dBASE III PLUS.
4. To examine the dBASE III PLUS file types.
5. To configure dBASE III PLUS.
6. To operate the ASSIST and HELP features.

2

THE dBASE III PLUS ENVIRONMENT

Despite their humble appearance, microcomputers are complicated machines. Since the complexity is not mechanical, however, it is difficult to perceive. The sophisticated electronic circuits and their intricate sets of instructions provide the environment in which dBASE III PLUS functions. As a user, and later as a programmer, you will want to make yourself comfortable with this environment in order to take full advantage of the considerable power of dBASE III PLUS.

2.1 HARDWARE CONSIDERATIONS

Any of the IBM personal computers can be used to run dBASE III PLUS, including the IBM-PC, IBM-PC XT, IBM-PC AT, and IBM Personal System/2. In addition, IBM-PC compatible machines such as the COMPAQ and the TANDY 1000 can use dBASE III PLUS.

An understanding of the components and operation of the microcomputer will be useful when you are making programming decisions about problems such as memory capacity and file usage.

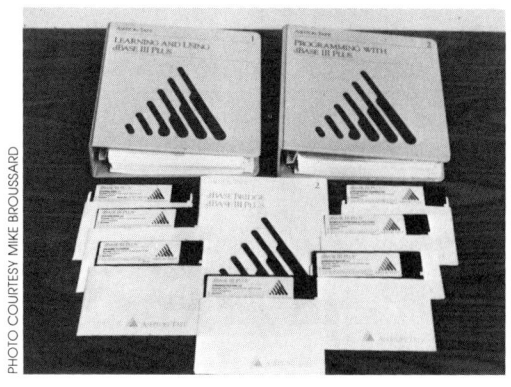

PHOTO COURTESY MIKE BROUSSARD

FIGURE 2.1 *Contents of dBASE III PLUS package.*

There are five components in a microcomputer system, as shown in Figure 2.2.

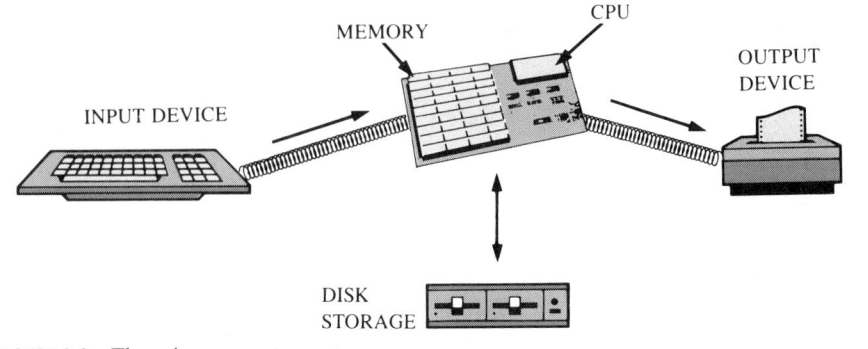

FIGURE 2.2   *The microcomputer system.*

The *central processing unit* (CPU) is contained on a tiny silicon chip and is sometimes called a microprocessor. It performs the arithmetic and logical functions and controls the flow of information through the computer system. Two important factors to consider when you are evaluating a microprocessor are the speed measured in megahertz (MHz) and the number of bits of data processed at one time.

The chart in Figure 2.3 compares some popular computers and their microprocessors. Speeds have increased four times within a six-year period. Microcomputers have advanced from processing 8 bits of data to 32 in approximately the same time. The pace of advancement illustrated by these benchmarks is not likely to decrease. On the contrary, we should witness dramatic increases in hardware development over the next few years. These advances have an effect on software development and usage. For this reason as well, programmers need to be aware of the structure of a microcomputer system.

Computer	Microprocessor	Speed (MHz)
IBM-PC (1981)	Intel 8088	4.77
PC-AT (1984)	Intel 20286	6
PC-AT (1986)	Intel 20286	8
Personal System/2 (1987)		
Model 30	Intel 8086	8
Model 50 and 60	Intel 80286	10
Model 80	Intel 80386	16–20

FIGURE 2.3   *Microprocessor speeds.*

In addition to the microprocessor, the internal electronics contain memory chips that temporarily hold data. Memory is often called RAM, or random access memory. There are also some ROM (read only memory) chips that hold data permanently in the computer. Memory is measured in kilobytes. One kilobyte of data contains 1,024 characters, or bytes. Some typical memory sizes include 256K, 512K, 640K, and 1 megabyte (1 million characters). There are many advantages to installing as much memory as possible in a computer, including speed and flexibility. dBASE III PLUS can make good use of additional memory.

The microcomputer system includes auxiliary storage in the form of disks. There are three types of disks and disk drives.

1. The 5-1/4 inch floppy disk is found on many computers, but its use is declining. The standard capacity for this size disk is 360K.
2. The 3-1/2 inch micro flexible disk is gradually replacing the 5-1/4 inch because of its size, convenience, and capacity. Capacities include 720K and 1.44MB.
3. The hard disk, or hard drive, is an internal device that stores between 5 million to 165 million characters (5MB-165MB) and accesses data much more rapidly than a floppy disk drive.

Input devices include the keyboard, the mouse, the optical reader, the light pen, and, recently, voice command. The keyboard is by far the most common input device. The monitor and the printer are essential output devices.

Your computer should contain least 384K of memory when you are using dBASE III PLUS with DOS Version 3.0 or above. A capacity of 256K is required for DOS Version 2.0 or 2.1. Since improvements in processing speed will be realized when additional memory is installed, 512K to 640K is preferable.

You may use a dual 360K floppy drive system to run dBASE III PLUS, but a hard disk will make usage much more convenient because it will eliminate the need to switch disks constantly, will speed up file access, and will lower the risk of disk damage.

Since dBASE III PLUS provides color capabilities, an RGB, or color monitor, is desirable, although a monochrome monitor can be used. A printer will enhance the use of dBASE III PLUS for reporting and programming. Any printer displaying 80 or more columns may be used.

Other useful hardware items include an internal clock/calendar, which allows dBASE III PLUS to provide the date and time for reports and disk files, and network connecting devices. One of the advanced features of dBASE III PLUS facilitates the use of two popular local area networks (LANs). A network will permit several microcomputers to transfer files and share such resources as hard drives and printers. Chapter 15 explains how dBASE III PLUS works on a network.

It will be helpful to understand how dBASE III PLUS reacts to the keyboard. Figure 2.4 illustrates a typical keyboard divided into several sections. The alphabetic keys and the number row at the top are the most familiar. With them, the computer performs the same tasks as a typewriter does using the standard Qwerty pattern.

FIGURE 2.4   *Common PC keyboards.*

The shift keys are located in the normal typewriter position. They provide the upper symbol on the nonalphabetic keys, or the uppercase letter. The Caps Lock key operates only on the alphabetic keys.

The Return key, which shows a bent arrow pointing left, is often called the Enter key. It is used to execute commands and to perform a carriage return in text editing.

The ten function keys are assigned a purpose by the software currently in control. For example, under DOS, the F1 key will repeat the first character of the previous command, but under dBASE III PLUS the same key issues a HELP command.

With the Num Lock key on, the numeric keypad produces the ten digits; if Num Lock is off the numeric keypad produces the cursor movements.

The Escape key (Esc) is used often in dBASE III PLUS to exit programs or menu options.

On many occasions, the Control key (Ctrl) is used in combination with other keys to perform important functions such as saving a file (Ctrl-End).

The backspace key moves the cursor one position to the left, at the same time erasing the character located there.

The tab key moves left or right several spaces.

Refer to Figure 2.4 and become familiar with the location and function of these keys. Their specific uses will be presented throughout the rest of the text.

2.2 dBASE III PLUS AND DOS

An important part of any computer system is the operating system. This is a set of programs that is designed to allow the user to control the organization and the use of the data that is stored on the disk. The most widely used microcomputer operating system is MS-DOS, also called PC-DOS. The Microsoft Corporation developed the system and sells it as MS-DOS. PC-DOS is the same product, marketed by IBM. The latest version of DOS as of this writing is 3.3, released for the IBM Personal System/2. A powerful new operating system, called OS/2, was introduced for the Model 80 in 1987. For dBASE III PLUS which runs under the MS-DOS operating system, you must use a version of DOS labeled 2.0 or higher.

You will need some knowledge of the MS-DOS commands to perform tasks such as checking the contents of the disk or copying files from one disk to another. An understanding of DOS is essential for the general operation of the computer and for using dBASE III PLUS.

DOS must be read from the default disk drive when the system is turned on or rebooted with the Ctrl-Alt-Del keys. A prompt for the date and time may appear on the screen if the computer has no internal clock/calendar. You can enter the date and time or simply press the Return key twice. DOS will then display a prompt like this:

```
A>
```

The A indicates that the A disk drive is currently active, and all commands will refer to that drive. The greater than sign, >, identifies DOS. You can access another disk drive by typing the letter of the drive and a colon and then pressing Return. Notice that the prompt now shows B as the active drive.

```
A>B:
B>
```

Data is organized and stored on the disk in separate sections called files. A file may contain any kind of information including programs like dBASE III PLUS or the data it uses. A portion of DOS itself is stored in a file called COMMAND.COM. The command DIR (for directory) will display information about all the files on the disk.

A>DIR

```
Volume in drive A is 99999999999
Directory of  A:\

DBASEINL OVL    27648  1-01-1988   4:51p
DBASE    EXE   132608  1-01-1988   4:51p
CONFIG   DB       44   1-01-1988   4:51p
DBASE    MSG    12276  1-01-1988   4:51p
CONFIG   SYS      22   1-01-1988   4:51p
CONFI256 SYS      25   1-01-1988   4:51p
CONFI256 DB      110   1-01-1988   4:51p
INSTALL  BAT     2688  1-01-1988   4:51p
ERRSET   COM      71   1-01-1988   4:51p
UNINSTAL BAT     2560  1-01-1988   4:51p
       10 File(s)    178176 bytes free
```

FIGURE 2.5 *Results of the DIR command.*

DOS will provide the name of the file, its size in bytes, and the time and date when it was created or updated on the disk. It is possible to be selective when referring to files with DIR and other commands. For example, you may type the name of a file after DIR to see if it exists on the disk.

```
        A>DIR COMMAND.COM
Volume in drive A is 99999999999
Directory of  A:\

COMMAND  COM    23210  1-01-88   4:51p
        1 File(s)    154624 bytes free
```

FIGURE 2.6 *Using DIR for a specific file.*

The asterisk may be used as an ambiguous character or "wild card" to group files, as in this example:

```
        A>DIR *.SYS

Volume in drive A is 99999999999
Directory of  A:\

CONFIG   SYS      22   1-01-1988   4:51p
CONFI256 SYS      25   1-01-1988   4:51p
        2 File(s)    154624 bytes free
```

FIGURE 2.7 *Using DIR for a group of files.*

The above command will display all the files with a .SYS as the second section of the file name regardless of the first section of the name.

DIR also provides some useful switches for changing the screen display. To place the file names in columns so that many names may be viewed at once, /W may be used, while /P displays one screenful of names in the normal format. Then you can continue by pressing Return.

```
        A>DIR/W
 Volume in drive A is 99999999999
 Directory of  A:\

 DBASEINL OVL DBASE     EXE CONFIG    DB  COMMAND  COM DBASE    MSG
 DBASE        CONFIG    SYS CONFI256 SYS CONFI256 DB  INSTALL  BAT
 ERRSET    COM UNINSTAL BAT
        12 File(s)     153600 bytes free
```

FIGURE 2.8   *Using the /W with DIR.*

DIR can be executed from dBASE III PLUS.

The COPY command transfers copies of files to other disks. The asterisk (*) can be used effectively with COPY to move groups of files with one command.

```
A>COPY *.DBF B:
```

The above command will write an exact duplicate of all the .DBF files on the A drive to the B drive.

FORMAT is a DOS utility program that will prepare a new disk for use by the disk drive. The process magnetically encodes circular tracks divided into sectors on the disk. The following command will execute the FORMAT program on the A drive, which will prepare the disk in the B drive.

```
A>FORMAT B:
```

A file may be removed from a disk through the use of the DEL or ERASE command.

```
A>DEL TEST.DBF
```

The contents of some files may be displayed with the TYPE command. This is useful with dBASE III PLUS .PRG and .TXT files. However, most files you are likely to encounter will not respond well to this command, because they contain program information that is coded in a special format.

```
        A>TYPE CONFIG.SYS

 files=20
 buffers=15
 Volume 99999999999 created Jan 01, 1988 4:55p
```

FIGURE 2.9   *Contents of CONFIG.SYS.*

^P (Ctrl-P) will toggle on the printer and echo any screen displays. Another ^P will turn if off again.

CLS will clear the screen and place the cursor in the upper left-hand corner.

CHKDSK is a DOS utility program that, like FORMAT, may be found on the DOS disk. It provides the status of the capacities of both the disk and the computer's memory.

```
A>CHKDSK

362496 bytes total disk space
     0 bytes in 1 hidden files
207872 bytes in 11 user files
154624 bytes available on disk

655360 bytes total memory
577792 bytes free
```

FIGURE 2.10   *Results of CHKDSK.*

As computer technology advances and becomes more price-competitive, hard drive systems are more common. Users of hard drives require a means of organizing the large number of files that tend to accumulate. The solution is to partition the drive into subdirectories. Each subdirectory is named, then separated from the other subdirectories on the disk.

In Figure 2.11, MD or MKDIR creates a new subdirectory called DBASE.

```
A>MD DBASE
```

CD or CHDIR changes to the new DBASE subdirectory.

```
A>CD DBASE
A>DIR

Volume in drive A is 99999999999
Directory of   A:\DBASE

.          <DIR>       1-01-88   4:15p
..         <DIR>       1-01-88   4:15p
      2 File(s)    153600 bytes free
```

FIGURE 2.11   *Using the MD and CD commands.*

Files can now be copied in and out of the subdirectory as if it were another disk. RD or RMDIR removes an empty subdirectory:

```
A>RD DBASE
```

The F1 key retypes one character from the last DOS command each time it is pressed in order to duplicate portions of the command. The F3 key displays the complete command.

2.3 SOFTWARE INSTALLATION AND MAINTENANCE

Your instructor will provide you with a copy of dBASE III PLUS on two disks or will allow you to make copies on your disks. This is a special educational version of dBASE III PLUS which you may use in conjunction with this text. It is fully functional, and it performs in exactly the same manner as a commercial version of the program does. However, it permits only thirty-one records to be placed in a database file. You may wish to make backup copies of the disks. An extra disk should be *formatted* for use as a data disk, since there is little remaining space on the dBASE III PLUS disks. It would also be helpful to transfer DOS to System Disk 1 so your computer can be booted directly from the dBASE III PLUS disk.

Procedure for Creating System Disks

1. To format the new disk and to transfer DOS, use the DOS command FOR-MAT B:/S with the DOS disk in drive A and a new disk in drive B. Repeat this process until you have three prepared disks. Figure 2.12 illustrates the results of using the FORMAT command.

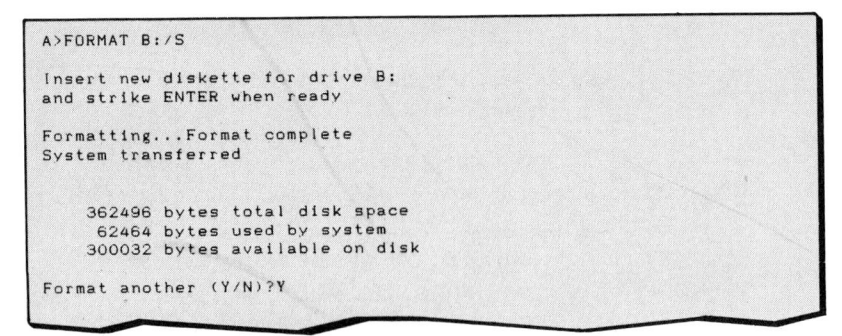

```
A>FORMAT B:/S

Insert new diskette for drive B:
and strike ENTER when ready

Formatting...Format complete
System transferred


    362496 bytes total disk space
     62464 bytes used by system
    300032 bytes available on disk

Format another (Y/N)?Y
```

FIGURE 2.12 *Results of the FORMAT command.*

2. Place your instructor's dBASE III PLUS System Disk 1 in drive A and a formatted disk in drive B, and type the DOS COPY command.

```
A>COPY *.* B:
DBASEINL.OVL
DBASE.EXE
```

```
CONFIG.DB
COMMAND.COM
DBASE.MSG
CONFIG.SYS
CONFI256.SYS
CONFI256.DB
INSTALL.BAT
ERRSET.COM
UNINSTAL.BAT
    11 File(s) copied
```

3. Repeat step 2 with System Disk 2.

```
A>COPY *.* B:
DBASE.OVL
HELP.DBS
ASSIST.HLP
INSTALL.BAT
    4 File(s) copied
```

You can copy dBASE III PLUS to a hard drive by using the utility program INSTALL.

Once your disks have been prepared, you can start dBASE III PLUS.

1. Turn on the computer with DOS in the default drive.
2. You may have to enter the date and time or press Return twice to get the DOS prompt A >.
3. Place System Disk 1 in the A drive and type DBASE.
4. When prompted by dBASE III PLUS, insert System Disk 2 and press Return.
5. You will see either the ASSIST screen or the dot prompt in the lower left corner.

The QUIT command is used to exit dBASE III PLUS properly. The ASSIST screen provides an option to exit, or you can type QUIT from the dot prompt. It is critical to exit dBASE III PLUS with the QUIT command to avoid possible loss of data in the event that files are not properly closed.

Typing a DIR command with System Disk 1 and System Disk 2 will reveal that dBASE III PLUS consists of a number of files. Figure 2.13 on the opposite page and the explanation that follows will provide an overview of the system.

```
            A>COPY *.* B:
            DBASEINL.OVL
            DBASE.EXE
            CONFIG.DB
            COMMAND.COM
            DBASE.MSG
            CONFIG.SYS
            CONFI256.SYS
            CONFI256.DB
            INSTALL.BAT
            ERRSET.COM
            UNINSTAL.BAT
                    11 File(s) copied

       SYSTEM DISK #1

 Volume in drive A is 99999999999
 Directory of   A:\

 DBASEINL OVL      27648    1-01-1988    4:51p
 DBASE    EXE     132608    1-01-1988    4:51p
 CONFIG   DB          44    1-01-1988    4:51p
 DBASE    MSG      12276    1-01-1988    4:51p
 CONFIG   SYS         22    1-01-1988    4:51p
```

```
          CONFI256 SYS         25    1-01-1988    4:51p
          CONFI256 DB         110    1-01-1988    4:51p
          INSTALL  BAT       2688    1-01-1988    4:51p
          ERRSET   COM         71    1-01-1988    4:51p
          UNINSTAL BAT       2560    1-01-1988    4:51p
                   10 File(s)     178176 bytes free

              SYSTEM DISK #2
          Volume in drive A is 99999999999
          Directory of   A:\

          DBASE     OVL    264704    1-01-1988    4:51p
          HELP      DBS     66560    1-01-1988    4:51p
          ASSIST    HLP     17648    1-01-1988    4:51p
          INSTALL   BAT      2688    1-01-1988    4:51p
                   4 File(s)     9216 bytes free
```

FIGURE 2.13 *Directories of System Disks 1 and 2.*

Files on System Disk 1

DBASE.EXE	— Main program.
CONFIG.DB	— Commands to set up dBASE III PLUS environment.
DBASE.MSG	— dBASE III PLUS messages.
CONFIG.SYS	— Commands to set up DOS environment.
CONFI256.SYS	— CONFIG.SYS file for a 256K system.
CONFI256.DB	— CONFIG.DB file for a 256K system.
INSTALL.BAT	— Installs dBASE III PLUS on a hard drive.
UNINSTAL.BAT	— Removes installation of dBASE III PLUS on a hard drive.

Files on System Disk 2

DBASE.OVL	— Main overlay
HELP.DBS	— On-line help feature
ASSIST.HLP	— Assistant feature

2.4 THE FILES

File names in dBASE III PLUS follow the same conventions as those in DOS. The rules for creating names are summarized below.

1. The name must be between 1 and 8 characters long.
2. Acceptable characters include:
   uppercase or lowercase letters A to Z
   numerals 0 to 9
   certain special characters $ & # @ ! % ( ) - { } _ / \
3. Following a dot, a three-character extension may be included.

Things to avoid in names:

1. DOS or dBASE III PLUS commands, file names, or devices.
2. The individual letters A through J, which are used for ALIAS names.

Special characters are usually avoided, with the exception of the hyphen and the underscore. The space is an invalid character. For purposes of simplicity and clarity, it is best to limit file names to the alphanumeric characters and the hyphen. These limitations allow DOS to work with files generated in dBASE III PLUS.

```
ACCT-REC
QRT-1-88
VENDOR
```

The second part of a file name, the extension, contains a dot and three letters. It is assigned by dBASE III PLUS according to the function of the file. Thirteen types of files are used in dBASE III PLUS, as listed below. The .DBF, .PRG, .NDX, and .FMT are the most important file types in the programming environment.

You will be working with these file types as you use dBASE III PLUS in future chapters. For now, it will be helpful to be familiar with their names and functions.

.CAT — The CATALOG file groups dBASE III PLUS files that work together in a system. The names of the files are stored in the .CAT file to facilitate their use.

.DBF — This is the database file. It is the most important file type in dBASE III PLUS because it contains most of the source data in an organized format. A dBASE III PLUS database file contains a header, which is stored in several formats; the data; an end-of-file marker; and a section of scrambled data. The file is loaded into memory and updated occasionally during processing. A final update occurs when the file is closed.

.DBT — The Data Base Text file contains large amounts of text data related to records in the .DBF file through a memo type field. The data would be too bulky to store in the .DBF file, so it is stored in and accessed from the .DBT file.

.FMT — The .FMT, or format file, contains commands to produce a custom data entry screen for use in programs.

.FRM — The Report Generator creates .FRM files to store the specifications, or form, for the formatted printing of data.

.LBL — Labels can be produced easily with the LABEL command. The formatting information for this process is stored in the .LBL file.

.MEM — Information that is generated by programs and is temporarily stored in the computer's memory can be saved in a .MEM file on the disk.

.NDX — Indexing is important for finding data quickly in programs and for displaying data in order. The .NDX file contains the sorting order for the records in the .DBF file.

.PRG — Program files contain dBASE III PLUS commands to perform tasks automatically. MODIFY COMMAND will store a program in a .PRG file.

.TXT — .TXT files contain simple text material stored as in a word processing file. They are important in the transfer of files in or out of dBASE III PLUS.

.QRY — Filtering commands that allow the selective use of data are specified with the CREATE QUERY and are stored in a .QRY file.

.SCR — The Screen Painter feature produces .SCR files to support the .FMT files. .SCR files are internally generated and maintained.

.VUE — These files establish a relationship linking databases that have a field in common. These files can be used to perform powerful functions without programming.

2.5 SETTING A CUSTOM ENVIRONMENT

This section addresses the use of two important files, CONFIG.DB and CONFIG.SYS, and explains how you can use them to customize dBASE III PLUS to meet individual preferences. In addition, exploring the commands involved will help you become more familiar with the general operation of dBASE III PLUS.

The CONFIG.DB file allows you to define a number of settings that will take effect automatically when dBASE III PLUS is started. This is very convenient, since these settings would otherwise have to be typed in before each work session. The CONFIG.DB file that is included with the dBASE III PLUS system disks contains the two commands shown below. They display the status bar at the bottom of the screen and automatically start the ASSIST feature.

```
STATUS = ON
COMMAND = ASSIST
```

Most of the options that are available in the CONFIG.DB file involve the SET TO commands. These commands affect a particular aspect of the operation of dBASE III PLUS. Examples of several common SET commands as they should appear in the CONFIG.DB file are presented below. Notice that the word SET is not included and that the equal sign (=) replaces the word TO when required.

```
DEFAULT = B:
BELL = OFF
TALK = OFF
```

These commands force dBASE III PLUS to access the B disk drive for all file activity. In addition they eliminate the sounding of the bell (actually, a beep on the speaker) and prevent system messages from cluttering the screen.

If you are using a color monitor, you can control the color of many aspects of the display, including the standard characters and background, enhanced characters and background (used for GETs and full screen editing) and the border. Each of these categories may appear in the order above, following COLOR = and separated by commas.

```
COLOR = GR+/B,W/R,B
```

The example above sets the standard display to yellow characters on a blue background; the enhanced display to white characters on a red background; and the border to blue. In this case, the border and the standard background will blend to form a solid background.

Some experimentation may be necessary, since monitors may respond in different ways to the COLOR settings. (Color monitors are sometimes referred to as RGB monitors, since they combine red, green, and blue to achieve a variety of hues.) The letter codes listed below are combinations of these three letters, along with N for black and X for hidden display. The plus (+) sign will produce a higher intensity of the shade selected but may change the hue in some cases. Moreover, an asterisk may be used to cause blinking for special effects.

R — Red	N — Black
G — Green	R+ — Bright Orange
BL — Blue	G+ — Lime Green
RB or BR — Magenta	B+ — Electric Blue
GR or RG — Brown	BG+ — Light Blue
BG — Aqua	GR+ — Yellow
GB — Dull Aqua	RB+ — Bright Magenta
W — White (Grey)	X — Hidden Display
W+ — Bright White	

FIGURE 2.14   *Results of COLOR codes.*

The color display may be modified while dBASE III PLUS is running with a SET command.

```
.SET COLOR TO GR+/B,W/R,B
```

The dot prompt is used as a default by dBASE III PLUS. If you prefer something more friendly, you can indicate your choice in the CONFIG.DB file using PROMPT = dBASE¦, for example. In this case, dBASE III PLUS will display dBASE¦ instead of the dot prompt.

```
dBASE:
```

Programmable Function Keys

```
F2   —  assist;
F3   —  list;
F4   —  dir;
F5   —  display structure;
F6   —  display status;
F7   —  display memory;
F8   —  display;
F9   —  append;
F10  —  edit;
```

FIGURE 2.15   *Typical function key assignments.*

Listed in Figure 2.15 is a set of commands that dBASE III PLUS assigns to each of the function keys when the system is started. You can change these assignments in the CONFIG.DB file by using F2 = MODIFY COMMAND, for example. If you place a semicolon after the command, a Return will be issued and the command will execute automatically. The command must be enclosed in quotation marks. The following commands will cause the F2 function key to issue a MODIFY COMMAND and a Return, and the F4 to issue a DIR without a Return.

```
F2 = "MODIFY COMMAND;"
F4 = "DIR "
```

There are a number of more advanced parameters that may be adjusted only in the CONFIG.DB file.

```
TEDIT      — Selects a word processor for MODIFY COMMAND.
WP         — Selects a word processor for memo fields.
BUCKET     — Sets memory limits.
GETS       — Sets number of input fields in programming.
COMMAND    — Automatically executes a program.
MAXMEM     — Reserves memory when other programs are run.
MVARSIZE   — Sets amount of memory for memory variables.
```

There are thirty-two additional commands that may be included in the CONFIG.DB file. They are listed in Appendix A. As you encounter them in the remaining chapters, you can decide whether you want to specify them in your CONFIG.DB file.

CONFIG.SYS

The CONFIG.SYS file must be present on the disk during a power-up or reboot. DOS will look for it and will make internal settings according to the specifications contained in the file. DOS will allow nine commands in CONFIG.SYS which will control the number of disk drives and the format of the DATE, among other things. However, there are two commands that must be included in order for dBASE III PLUS to operate properly:

```
FILES = 20
BUFFERS = 15
```

Computer systems with 256K must set buffers equal to 4. Failure to set files high enough will produce a "too many files are open" message. Since 8 is the DOS default for FILES, and 2 is the DOS default for BUFFERS, the CONFIG.SYS file will have to be modified before using dBASE III PLUS. The reason for this is that DOS and dBASE III PLUS require seven files to start the program. The thirteen remaining file positions will be occupied by normal processing.

One buffer occupies 512 kilobytes of memory. Reducing the number of buffers will slow down processing time because dBASE III PLUS depends on the transfer of data from the disk to memory for rapid access.

The modification of the CONFIG files may be accomplished by means of one of the following:

1. A word processing program.
2. The MODIFY COMMAND text editor in dBASE III PLUS.
3. The DOS command COPY CON.

MODIFY COMMAND is presented in Chapter 4, but you can use the COPY CON command to write either CONFIG.DB or CONFIG.SYS. COPY CON, which means *copy console*, copies any commands typed at the keyboard to the file named in the command. Type the following commands from the DOS prompt with System Disk 1 in the A drive:

```
A>COPY CON CONFIG.DB
F2 = "MODIFY COMMAND;"
COLOR  = GR+/B,W/R,B
DEFAULT = B:
^Z
     1 File(s) copied
```

FIGURE 2.16   *Changing CONFIG.DB with COPY CON.*

The cursor will move to the next line, where you may type a command and the Return key. The cursor will then be on the next line for another command. When you have completed the file and pressed Return for the last command, hold down the Ctrl key and simultaneously press Z (^Z), then press Return and the file will be written to the disk. The F6 key will also produce a ^Z. Use the TYPE command to view the contents of the file.

```
A>TYPE CONFIG.DB
F2 = "MODIFY COMMAND;"
COLOR  = GR+/B,W/R,B
DEFAULT = B:
```

FIGURE 2.17   *Contents of modified CONFIG.DB.*

One disadvantage of this method is that COPY CON will destroy the existing file when it is used. Therefore, you can't modify a file; you can only rewrite it.

2.6 HELP AND ASSIST

There are three ways of operating dBASE III PLUS, as follows:

1. ASSIST — Commands are automatically issued when choices are made from a menu.

2. Interactive — Commands are typed directly from a prompt and executed immediately upon pressing Return.

3. Programming — Commands are written to a file, which is then executed.

ASSIST is a *front end processor*, in other words, a program that handles tasks for the main system, interprets menu selections, and issues appropriate commands. It is divided into eight sections, or submenus. Each submenu contains a number of functions that can be performed by responding to prompts. Below you will find a brief description of each of the functions as they appear on the screen.

SETUP

Database File — Select the drive and file.

Format for Screen — Select a screen design.

Query — Select a query file to filter records.

Catalog — Select a catalog file to group related files.

View — Select a view file to set up working environment.

Quit dBASE III PLUS — Close files and return to DOS.

CREATE

Database File — Create a new file structure.

Format — Design a new screen.

View — Set up a new view file.

Query — Set up a query file to filter records.

Report — Create a new report format.

Label — Create a new label format.

UPDATE

Append — Add new records to an existing database.

Edit — Modify existing records.

Display — Display the current record.

Browse — View and modify a group of records.

Replace — Globally edit records.

Delete — Mark a record for deletion.

Recall — Remove the delete mark.

Pack — Remove deleted records and rewrite file.

POSITION

Seek — Find a record in an indexed database.

Locate — Find a record without an index.

Continue — Move to next record after locate.

Skip — Move to next record.

Goto Record — Move to a specific record.

RETRIEVE

List — Show all records in a file.

Display — Show the current record.

Report — Activate a report file.

Label — Activate a label file.

Sum — Add numeric fields.

Average — Compute average of numeric fields.

Count — Count the number of records.

ORGANIZE

Index — Establish an index file to order records.

Sort — Change the physical order of records in a new file.

Copy — Duplicate a file.

MODIFY

Database File — Change the database structure.

Format — Change a screen design.

View — Change an existing view file.

Query — Change an existing query file.

Report — Change an existing report format.

Label — Change an existing label file.

TOOLS

Set Drive — Change the default drive.

Copy File — Duplicate a file.

Directory — Show contents of a disk directory.

Rename — Change the name of a file.

Erase — Remove a file from a disk.

List Structure — Display the database structure.

Import — Import PFS file.

Export — Export PFS file.

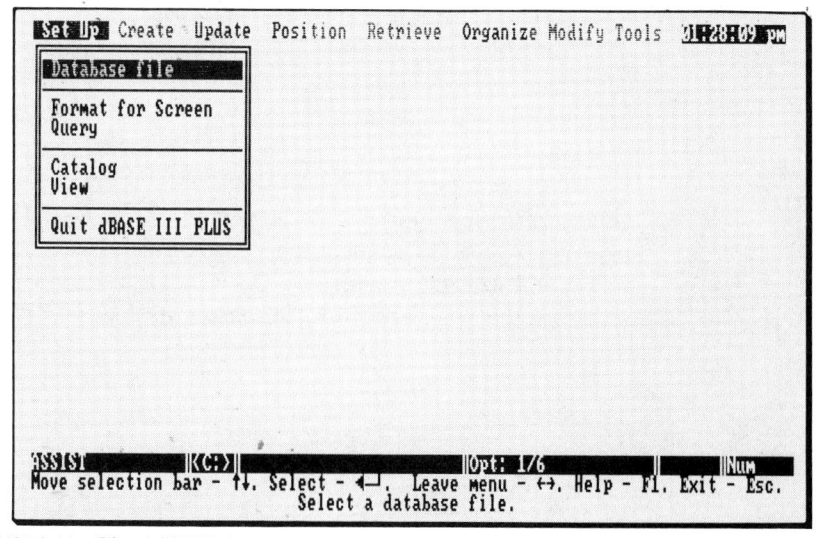

FIGURE 2.18 *The ASSIST Screen.*

The area at the bottom of the screen displays helpful information, as described below.

1. *Status Bar* — displays the active drive and selected database file and current record position.
2. *Action Line* — displays dBASE III PLUS commands that ASSIST executes or you type.
3. *Navigation Line* — explains the functions of the keys.
4. *Message Line* — presents options that are available.

You can switch between ASSIST and the dot prompt by using the F2 and the Esc keys. The right and left arrow keys on the numeric keypad allow movement from menu to menu. The available options are highlighted and may be selected with the up and down arrow keys. The Return key executes the desired action. Options that are not available will not be highlighted. You may execute a command by typing in the first letter of the menu option instead of using the arrow keys and the Return key.

ASSIST is helpful for novices, and experienced users find it convenient when executing elementary commands. However, a person who is interested in learning to program with dBASE III PLUS can learn the form and usage of the commands more efficiently by typing them from the dot prompt.

A few guidelines will help you construct commands correctly. Commands in dBASE III PLUS always start with one of the reserved words, such as LIST, CREATE, or REPLACE. They are limited to a length of 254 characters and are executed by pressing the Return key.

Blanks or spaces are ignored by dBASE III PLUS. You may abbreviate commands to the first four letters or more, but you may not misspell them. You can use the keys described below to edit commands before the Return key is pressed.

The left and right arrow keys will move the cursor one character within the command. The Home and End keys will move one word forward or backward. The up and down arrow keys will redisplay previous commands or move forward to the current command. You may use the backspace, Ins, or Del key to edit commands.

When you are at the dot prompt, the up arrow key will recall the last twenty commands issued in order starting with the most recent. This includes commands issued by ASSIST. The commands may be altered with the editing keys and may be reexecuted with the Return key. On occasion it may be useful to review a work session in this way to uncover the sources of problems.

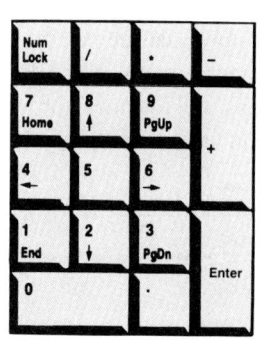

FIGURE 2.19   *Uses of the numeric key pad.*

Commands in dBASE III PLUS are constructed in a pattern. In addition to each verb command itself, you may include optional *scopes*, *expressions*, and *conditions*. Scopes describe the limit of the records affected by the command, such as NEXT 5. Expressions may include fieldnames, constants or literals, variables, and operators or functions. Conditions act as filters to select certain records on the basis of some criterion.

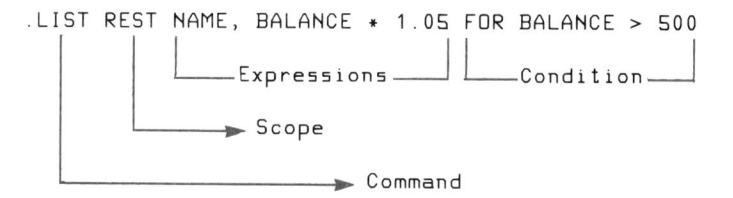

SCOPE

NEXT 5 — The next five records from the current record.
ALL   — The command will affect all the records.
REST   — The remaining records after the current record.

EXPRESSIONS

Any combination of the following:
Field names — from the structure of the database
Variables — the current contents of variables (Chapter 4)
Arithmetic operators — $+, -, *, /, \char`\^$
Logical operators — .AND. , .OR. , .NOT.
Relational operators — = , < , > , <> , # , <= , >=
String operators — + , -
Constants — specific data

CONDITIONS

Conditions compare two or more items to test if a relationship exists or not (True or False). Records will be affected by the command on the basis of this comparison. Chapter 6 contains more explanation of conditions.

A comprehensive set of HELP screens becomes available by pressing the F1 key. The appropriate screen for the current command will display, although you can move to other screens. The HELP screens are also available when an error is made while typing a command. You will be asked by dBASE III PLUS whether you need help. If you answer Y (for yes), the related screen will be displayed.

```
. LOST
*** Unrecognized command verb.
      ?
```

FIGURE 2.20   *Typical error message.*

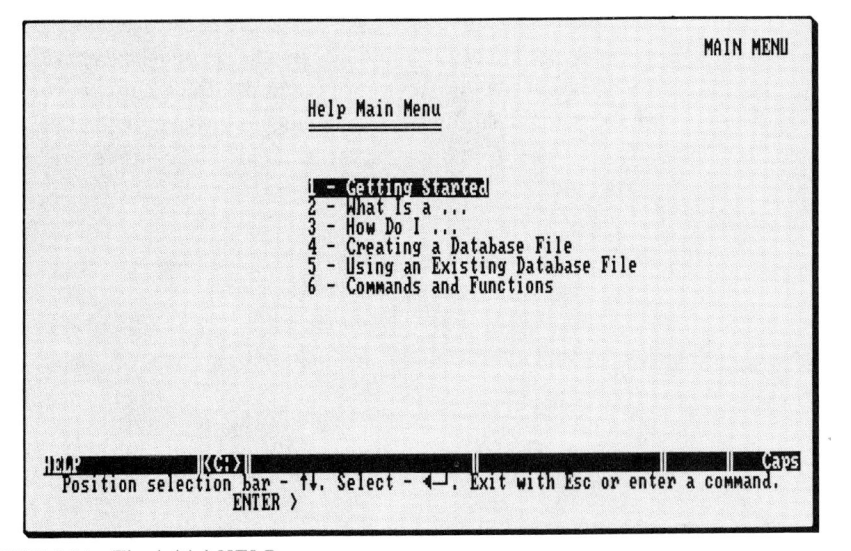

FIGURE 2.21   *The initial HELP screen.*

The HELP screens are divided into six sections as shown in Figure 2.21. A number of topics are presented in each section, as outlined on the following page. Browse through the screens, using the key movements described at the bottom of the display.

1. Getting Started
   General Instructions and use of
   HELP and ASSIST.

2. What is a ...

   0 — Command
   1 — Expression
   2 — Field List
   3 — File
   4 — Key Field
   5 — Memory Variable
   6 — Operator
   7 — Record
   8 — Scope
   9 — Skeleton

3. How Do I ...

   1 — Get Out of dBASE III PLUS
   2 — Turn the Printer On/Off
   3 — Open a Database File
   4 — Save a Database File
   5 — Display the Disk Directory
   6 — Rename a File
   7 — Delete a File
   8 — Copy a File

4. Creating a Database File

   1 — Narrative Description
   2 — Database File Name
   3 — Field Name
   4 — Field Type
   5 — Field Size

5. Using an Existing Database File

   1 — Add New Records
   2 — Edit Records
   3 — Change the Structure
   4 — Extract Data
   5 — Index and Sort
   6 — Locate a Record
   7 — Copy Records
   8 — Delete Record

6. Commands and Functions

   1 — Commands (Starter Set)
   2 — Commands (Advanced Set)
   3 — Functions
   4 — SET TO Commands
   5 — SET ON/OFF Commands

Chapter 3 will present some basic dBASE III PLUS commands that will be typed from the dot prompt. After you have become familiar with most of the commands, you will have to decide which is more convenient when working interactively: using ASSIST or issuing the commands yourself. Of course, when you are programming, the ASSIST feature will be of no use. Since the HELP feature is online and is always available, checking the use or syntax of a command is useful and can save many trips to the manuals.

CHAPTER SUMMARY

2.1

Microcomputer systems consist of a CPU, internal memory, disk drives, input devices, and output devices. Programmers need to be familiar with the configuration and capacity of the system they are using. A number of keys have special uses in dBASE III PLUS, such as the function keys and the Escape and Control keys.

2.2

The operating system MS-DOS performs critical functions both in general use and with dBASE III PLUS. Some DOS commands can be executed within dBASE III PLUS. Important commands include DIR, COPY, DEL, TYPE, and FORMAT.

2.3

It is important to install and operate dBASE III PLUS properly. Formatting disks, transferring DOS, and copying files may be necessary before running the programs. It is useful to be familiar with the files contained on the system disks.

2.4

There are thirteen types of files used in dBASE III PLUS which are identified by a file extension. You must follow DOS rules when assigning the first part of the file name.

2.5

CONFIG.DB and CONFIG.SYS are included on the system disks and may be altered to customize your copy of dBASE III PLUS. Some settings such as FILES and BUFFERS are critical, while others make use more convenient.

2.6

ASSIST will issue commands which are selected from menus. It is convenient for interactive operation, but typing the commands directly will build a command vocabulary useful for programming. dBASE III PLUS commands always contain a verb and may include a scope, expressions, or a condition. The HELP screens are on-line. They briefly explain the commonly used commands and features.

KEY TERMS

CPU	LAN	file name
internal memory	Function key	CONFIG.SYS
disk storage	Escape key	CONFIG.DB
input device	control key	buffer
output device	numeric keypad	interactive
megahertz	operating system	dot prompt
megabyte	MS-DOS	scope
monitor	prompt	expression
local area network	COMMAND.COM	condition

COMMAND SUMMARY

DIR — Display the contents of a directory or disk.

COPY — Copy files.

FORMAT — Format disks.

DEL — Remove a file from a disk.

TYPE — Display contents of a readable file.

CLS — Clear the screen.

CHKDSK — Display disk and memory usage and capacity.

MD — Make a new directory.

CD — Change to another directory.

RD — Remove an empty directory.

INSTALL — Install dBASE III PLUS on a hard disk.

QUIT — Close all files and leave dBASE III PLUS.

ASSIST — Start the ASSISTANT feature.

COPY CON — Copy from the keyboard to a file.

HELP — Start the HELP feature.

SELF-CHECK QUESTIONS

1. Examine your computer system and the manuals and collect specifications on the five components. What type of CPU does your system have? How much memory? What are the disk drive capacities?

2. Which version of DOS are you using? Which version of dBASE III PLUS? Is your computer equipped with enough memory?

3. Write five correct file names for DOS or dBASE III PLUS.

4. Use the HELP screens to answer the following questions:
   a. What is a *scope*?
   b. What is an *expression*?
   c. How do you leave dBASE III PLUS?
   d. What command is used to add new records?
   e. How are records deleted?
   f. What field types are available in dBASE III PLUS?
   g. What is a *memory variable*?
5. Name two factors that are used to measure computer performance.
6. Name three input devices other than the keyboard. Search some computer journals to find out how they work.
7. Is there any disadvantage to increasing the memory of a computer?
8. What is a LAN? What does it do?
9. If Caps Lock is on, what will appear if you press 7?
10. How is the Ctrl key used?
11. How is the computer rebooted?
12. What do the numbers next to the file names mean in a DIR display?
13. What is an ambiguous character?
14. Why is the number of files and buffers important?
15. What do conditions do?

TRY IT YOURSELF

1. Load DOS and issue a command to display all files with a .COM extension.
2. Display all disk files, with a pause for each screen.
3. Format a disk in the B drive (or the A drive on a hard disk system) and copy COMMAND.COM to the new disk. Display the name of the copied file to verify the copy.
4. Delete the file from exercise 3 and check the space usage on the disk and the status of the computer's memory.
5. Make a directory on the new disk called TEST, then change to this directory and display the files. Change back to the root directory.
6. Print the contents of the CONFIG.SYS and CONFIG.DB files from DOS.
7. Start dBASE III PLUS. Use the Escape key to leave the ASSIST feature and quit to DOS. Start dBASE III PLUS again.
8. If the FILES and BUFFERS are incorrectly set, use COPY CON to create a new CONFIG.SYS file. You will have to check the file first.

9. Write a CONFIG.DB file that will do the following:
   a. Assign "DIR *.*" to Function key F4.
   b. Display white letters on a green background.
   c. Change the default to another disk drive.
   d. Start the ASSIST feature when dBASE III PLUS starts.
10. Use the ASSIST feature to do the following:
   a. Change the default drive.
   b. Show the contents of a disk directory.
11. Use CHKDSK to examine disk and memory usage. Display the information on the printer.
12. Change to the TEST subdirectory and copy all the .COM files from the root directory. Display all the file names.
13. Delete all files from the TEST subdirectory. (Caution! Be certain you are not in another subdirectory before deleting.) Return to the root directory and remove the TEST subdirectory.
14. Type a command incorrectly at the dot prompt, then respond "Y" to the HELP prompt. Correct the command in the HELP feature. (Example: DOR, change to DIR.)
15. Using Figure 2.15 as a guide, try each one of the function keys, using the Esc key to cancel the commands as they are issued.

3

INTERACTIVE SKILLS

LEARNING OBJECTIVES

1. To use the CREATE command to establish a database.
2. To use the APPEND command to add records.
3. To modify records with EDIT, BROWSE, and REPLACE.
4. To remove records with DELETE and PACK.
5. To display data using the LIST command and the ? command.

3

INTERACTIVE SKILLS

As you know, the goal of this text is to help you learn to program. Since programs are actually lists of dBASE III PLUS commands, the first thing you need to understand is how each command operates. Some commands, for example, can be executed only from the "dot prompt." Many users who work with data every day use nothing beyond the commands presented here. Mastery of these commands will provide you with an excellent background for the concepts presented in the chapters to follow.

3.1 ESTABLISHING THE DATABASE

Using dBASE III PLUS to establish a database is a simple process. However, using the computer is the last part of this activity. We have all heard the Thomas Edison quote, "Invention is ninety-eight percent perspiration and two percent inspiration." Although the percentages may be somewhat closer together for the creation of a database, the principle is the same. You should spend a reasonable amount of time planning the structure of the database before you begin to enter your specifications into dBASE III PLUS.

You need to have a clear idea of what pieces of information, or data, will be included, such as a name, a Zip Code, or an account balance. These data items are referred to as fields. A field may be as short as one letter (M for male, F for female) or, in the case of a Memo field, as long as 5000 letters or characters. These fields must be in a very rigid format in order for dBASE III PLUS to do its work. This is accomplished by grouping the fields and their individual characteristics into a record. Once the record format has been established, all records with the same characteristics will be stored in the database. Think of the record format as a blank form of some type. Each person has to fill in the same "blanks" because they are preprinted on the form, although the information will certainly vary from person to person. You will be guided through the actual process by dBASE III PLUS, but you must know what you want before you begin.

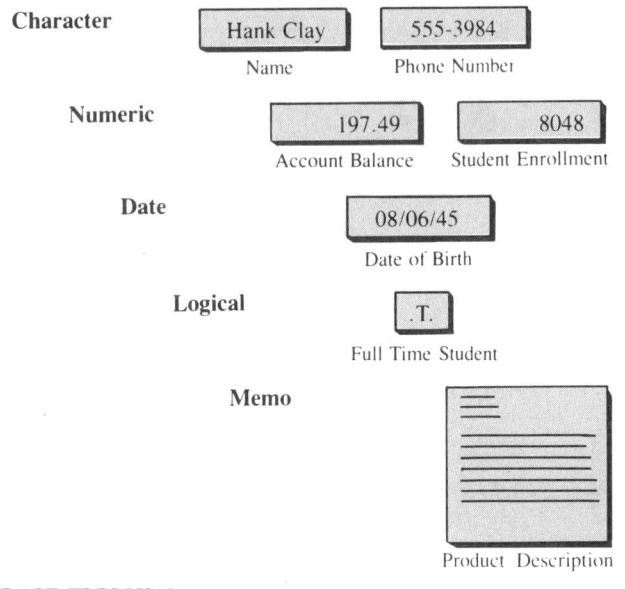

FIGURE 3.1 *dBASE III PLUS data types.*

You will need three or four pieces of information for each field that you plan to include. First, you must give the field a name to which dBASE III PLUS can refer. Before you consider the other requirements, you should know that computers treat numeric values quite differently from character or alphanumeric data. This is because numeric values are used in arithmetic operations and are stored and handled in a special way by the computer and dBASE III PLUS. Other than being sure to identify any fields that might be used for calculation as numeric, you need not be concerned about this. There are three other field types: Date, Logical, and Memo. These will be discussed later in this chapter. What is important for you to know now is that the second piece of information needed by dBASE III PLUS is the field type. Third, you must specify the maximum length of the field. In the event that the field is Numeric, you will also need to specify the number of decimal places to be used by dBASE III PLUS.

It is best to plan this structure on paper first. Figure 3.2 on the opposite page illustrates how this might be done. The example is a design for a database that can store the names of cities and their states and populations for 1982 and 1970.

Field Name	Type	Width	Decimal Places
CITY	Character	20	
STATE	Character	2	
POP_82	Numeric	7	0
POP_70	Numeric	7	0

FIGURE 3.2 *Sample database design.*

The length of the CITY field is an educated guess. There may be some cities with names longer than 20 characters, but you are unlikely to encounter them. You should understand that the extra characters at the end of the name will be truncated (cut off) should the size of the name be larger than the field width. Names shorter than 20 characters will be filled out to 20 with blanks. The STATE field is easy since the state abbreviations used are Zip Code abbreviations, which always contain two letters.

Since numeric fields contain only digits and decimal points, length may be calculated by counting these for the largest numeric value anticipated. Seven digits will represent any value up to 9,999,999, which will be more than enough for any city in the United States. The fields POP_70 and P0P_82 did not require a decimal point, but a position would be needed if one was required. For example, the dollar value 2187.52 also occupies seven positions; four dollar digits, a decimal point, and two digits for cents. Do not include commas or dollar signs in numeric fields, and allow enough positions for the largest possible number. A number that is too large for its established length will not be displayed by dBASE III PLUS.

Now that these specifications have been established, you are ready to instruct dBASE III PLUS to set up or CREATE the file format on your disk. Start dBASE III PLUS by typing DBASE at the DOS prompt after inserting System Disk 1.

```
A>DBASE
```

You will be prompted to insert System Disk 2. Press the Return key to enter dBASE III PLUS and then the Escape key to leave the ASSIST feature. At this point you will see the dot prompt in the lower left corner of the screen. Type the command CREATE and hit the Return key.

```
CREATE
```

Next, dBASE III PLUS will ask you for a file name that can be no longer than eight characters and cannot contain blanks. These are the same rules that are listed for DOS file names in Chapter 2. The file name CITIES will do; however, you may wish to select your own name. When you hit the Return key after typing your file name, dBASE III PLUS will present the following screen:

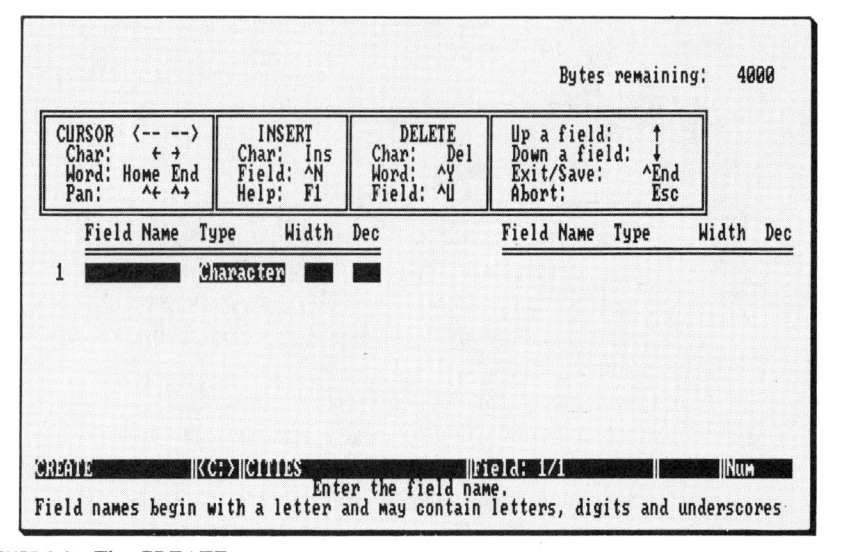

FIGURE 3.3 *The CREATE screen.*

Examine this screen. You will notice that dBASE III PLUS provides some information at the top concerning the use of the keys during the CREATE process. Experiment with these as you enter the field information in the center portion of the screen. Most of the keys are self-explanatory, except for the ˆ sign that means that the Control key (Ctrl) is to be depressed at the same time as the next key. For example, to delete an entire field, hold down the Ctrl key, then hit the U (ˆU). At the bottom of the screen, dBASE III PLUS includes some useful facts and prompts. The name of the screen (CREATE), the active disk drive, the file name, and the current field number are visible above a message area where you are prompted with the task to be performed next. Below the prompt is descriptive information about the task.

You will discover while working with the CREATE screen that you can move easily among the highlighted blocks to enter, edit, or delete your entries. There is little risk of data loss in this operation unless you should inadvertently hit the Escape key or the system should fail. Enter information until your screen looks the same as Figure 3.4 on the opposite page.

1. Type CITY in the Field Name block and press Return.
2. Press the Return key in the Type block.
3. Type 20 in the Width block and press Return.
4. Complete the blocks for STATE as above.
5. Type POP_82 in the third Field Name block.
6. Press the space bar to change the Type to Numeric and press Return.
7. Type 7 in the Width block and press Return.
8. Press Return in the Decimal Places block to accept 0.
9. Complete the blocks for POP_70 as in steps 5 through 8.

Field Name	Type	Width	Decimal Places
CITY	Character	20	
STATE	Character	2	
POP_82	Numeric	7	0
POP_70	Numeric	7	0

FIGURE 3.4 *Completing the CREATE screen.*

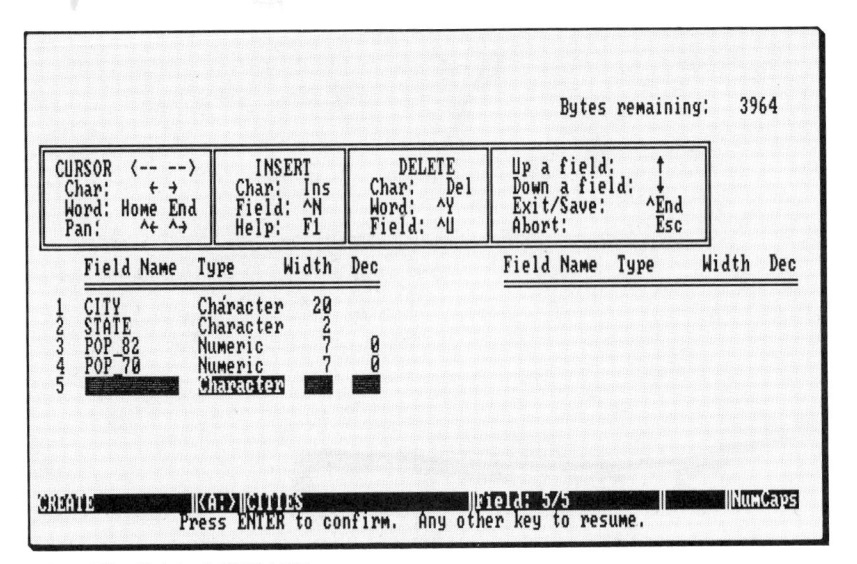

FIGURE 3.5 *The finished CREATE screen.*

After the screen has been completed, you can save the information on your disk by pushing either Ctrl-W (^W) or Ctrl-End (^End). If you hit the Enter key on the Field Name portion of a new field this message will appear:

```
Press ENTER to confirm. Any other key to resume
```

There are several ways to save and exit the CREATE screen. As you will note at the top of the screen the Escape key will abort the operation, as will Ctrl-Q (ˆQ). dBASE III PLUS will also save the file and add an extension .DBF (Data Base File) to your file name, which you can see by typing a DIR command or by pressing F4. The field names and related information are referred to as the STRUCTURE of the database. You will be asked whether you want to input data now. Respond by typing No.

Now that the file CITIES.DBF has been established, you should understand how it can be accessed. Before working with your file, you must "ask permission" or open it by typing:

```
. USE CITIES
```

You will note that the .DBF extension was assumed and not required. The USE command will instruct dBASE III PLUS to position the disk drive on the file and allow access to the data and the STRUCTURE. Once a file is in USE it is vulnerable to unintentional damage. If the system should fail, or if you improperly leave dBASE III PLUS while the file is open, great harm will be done. The best way to prevent this kind of loss is to be sure to leave dBASE III PLUS by means of the QUIT command. Typing a simple USE will properly close your file if you wish to remain in dBASE III PLUS.

Once the CITIES.DBF file is in USE, you can view the structure by hitting the F5 key (DISPLAY STRUCTURE) or by typing:

```
. USE
```

```
                    . USE CITIES

                    . LIST STRUCTURE

        Structure for database: C:CITIES.dbf
        Number of data records:        0
        Date of last update    : 01/01/88
        Field  Field Name  Type        Width     Dec
            1  CITY        Character     20
            2  STATE       Character      2
            3  POP_70      Numeric        7
            4  POP_82      Numeric        7
        ** Total **                     37
```

FIGURE 3.6   *The structure of CITIES.DBF.*

Notice that the total of the lengths of the four fields appears to be overstated by 1 (the total should be 36). This is because one position is reserved in case the record must be marked for deletion later. You will need to become comfortable with the CREATE operation because it is essential to the use of dBASE III PLUS. The exercises at the end of this chapter will help you reinforce these skills.

It may be helpful to think of a database file as a drawer full of record cards in a file cabinet. In order to USE the record cards you will, of course, have to open the drawer. It will also be wise to CLOSE the drawer when you are finished in order to avoid accidental damage to the information.

Three essential tasks keep the file properly updated: APPENDing or adding, EDITing or modifying, and DELETE(ing) record cards. We will consider the order of the record cards later; for now, think of the record cards as being numbered as they are added to the file.

Let's use the analogy of a drawer in a file cabinet to describe the three tasks for updating a file. In order to APPEND, or add, a record card to the file, you might have to allow some room at the end of the drawer and then insert the new record card when the information has been filled in. You could, of course, APPEND a record card that was only partially complete or even empty, then complete it later.

Changing existing information on a record card would require searching through the numbers, then pulling out the proper card and making the change. You could replace the card in its correct numeric position within the file when you finished EDITing.

The records would be easier to work with if they were numbered both sequentially and consecutively; that is, in order with no numbers missing. However, this system of numbering would present a problem anytime you removed a record since that would cause a missing number in the file. The only solution, as difficult as it sounds, would be to renumber the file anytime you DELETEd a record. It might be more convenient to "mark" the records you wished to DELETE, then actually remove them and renumber at a later time.

The tasks that have just been described hypothetically are performed upon your database file in a similar fashion by dBASE III PLUS. In the following sections you will learn to add, modify, and delete records. You will also gain an understanding of how these functions operate for use in programming.

3.2 ADDING RECORDS

The APPEND command provides the means to add records to a database. This command operates only on a .DBF file that has been opened with the USE command. When you ask dBASE III PLUS to APPEND a record, a pointer will be positioned at the next available physical record number. For example, if there are ten records in the .DBF file and you issue an APPEND command, the record pointer will be placed at eleven. You will then be presented with another screen which will reflect the structure CREATEd earlier.

```
. USE CITIES
. APPEND
```

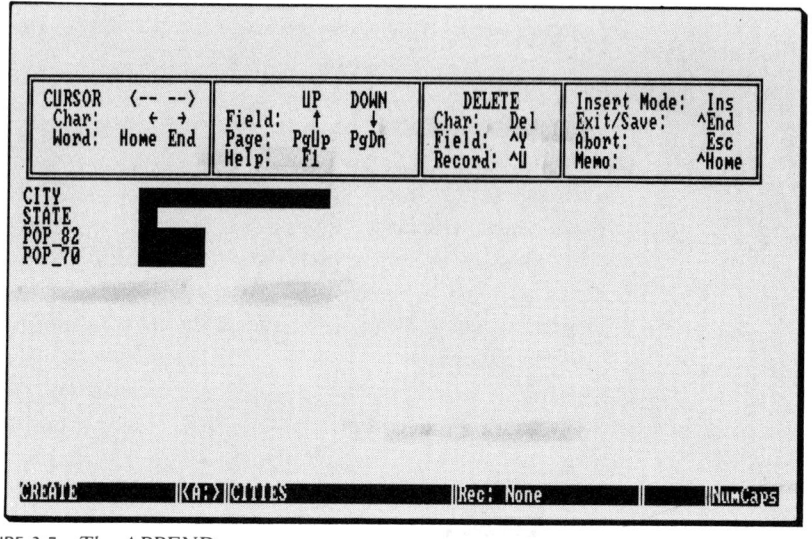

FIGURE 3.7   *The APPEND screen.*

You will find that cursor movement and editing in this screen are accomplished by the same keys as in the CREATE screen, with a few exceptions that are noted at the top of the display. Your field names are listed to the left of the highlighted blocks. You may now enter data in the fields and modify the data using the keys as described in the top section of the screen. When you either fill in the last character of POP_82, the last field on the screen, or press the Return key, APPEND will store that record, advance to the next record number, and present a fresh screen for data entry. At this point you may either enter data or press the Return key on the first character of the first field to exit the procedure. Since the file is still open, you can LIST the records by typing LIST from the dot prompt.

```
. LIST
```

Record#	CITY	STATE	POP_70	POP_82
1	SAN FRANCISCO	CA	715674	691637
2	PHILADELPHIA	PA	1949996	1665382
3	DALLAS	TX	844401	943848
4	SAN DIEGO	CA	697471	915956
5	HOUSTON	TX	1233535	1725617
6	MIAMI	FL	334859	558869
7	CLEVELAND	OH	750879	558869
8	PITTSBURGH	PA	520089	414936
9	LOS ANGELES	CA	2811801	3022247
10	JACKSONVILLE	FL	504265	556370
11	COLUMBUS	OH	540025	564871

FIGURE 3.8   *Result of the LIST command.*

APPEND the records in Figure 3.8 to your file. The exercises at the end of this chapter will help you gain the skills needed to perform the APPEND function. However, you will eventually write dBASE III PLUS programs that will automate this process.

It may become necessary, on occasion, to change the structure of the .DBF file. Perhaps a new field will be required or one will have to be deleted. You may need to increase or decrease the length of a field or change the number of decimal positions. These changes can be accomplished with the MODIFY STRUCTURE command. If a .DBF file is in USE, when you type the command a screen similar to CREATE will allow you to make any changes. The data is preserved in a separate file while this operation is performed, and rewritten to the original but changed structure. Avoid changing the name of a field, since the data will not properly copy back to the file.

CREATE a .DBF file with the following structure, then use MODIFY STRUC-TURE to make the appropriate changes.

```
. CREATE STOCKS
. LIST STRUCTURE
```

```
Structure for database: C:STOCKS.dbf
Number of data records:        3
Date of last update   : 01/01/88
Field  Field Name  Type      Width    Dec
    1  COMPANY     Character    15
    2  SHARES      Numeric       3
** Total **                    19
```

FIGURE 3.9   *Structure for STOCKS.DBF.*

Use APPEND to add the following records to the file:

```
. LIST
```

```
Record#  COMPANY       SHARES
      1  XYZ CO          150
      2  ABC CO           50
      3  DEF CO           75
```

FIGURE 3.10   *Data in STOCKS.DBF.*

Change the length of COMPANY to 10, increase the length of SHARES to 4, and add the PRICE field with MODIFY STRUCTURE.

Type the following two commands at the dot prompt to check the accuracy of your work.

```
. MODIFY STRUCTURE
3 records added.
```

```
      . LIST STRUCTURE

Structure for database: C:STOCKS.dbf
Number of data records:        3
Date of last update   : 01/01/88
Field  Field Name  Type       Width   Dec
    1   COMPANY     Character      10
    2   SHARES      Numeric         4
    3   PRICE       Numeric         6

** Total **                       21

         . LIST

Record#  COMPANY    SHARES  PRICE
    1    XYZ CO        150
    2    ABC CO         50
    3    DEF CO         75
```

FIGURE 3.11   *Results of MODIFY STRUCTURE.*

The next section will explain how to use BROWSE in order to add the data shown below to the PRICE field.

```
. LIST
```

```
Record#  COMPANY    SHARES  PRICE
    1    XYZ CO        150   25.00
    2    ABC CO         50   34.75
    3    DEF CO         75  120.50
```

FIGURE 3.12   *New data in the PRICE field.*

Modifying the structure of a .DBF file, like CREATE, is a process that must be executed from the dot prompt and cannot be effectively programmed. You should, therefore, be quite familiar with these and the other operations that will follow.

3.3 RECORD MODIFICATION

Several methods are provided by dBASE III PLUS to modify the data in existing records. These include EDIT, BROWSE, REPLACE, and GET/READ. However, the only commands used in programming are REPLACE and GET/READ. All of these commands act upon records that are already part of the database, or .DBF file. Remember that each record has a unique record number, which you will need for the EDIT command. Activate the CITIES database with the USE command.

```
. USE CITIES
```

It would be best to USE a copy of the database while working with the next few commands in order to preserve the original data in CITIES. Type the following two commands:

```
. COPY TO TEMP
. USE TEMP
```

LIST the data in TEMP.DBF to reassure yourself that this copy of your file is identical to the original. You may access a specific record by including the proper record number in the EDIT command:

```
. EDIT 3
```

After you press the Return key, you will be presented with a screen like the one below:

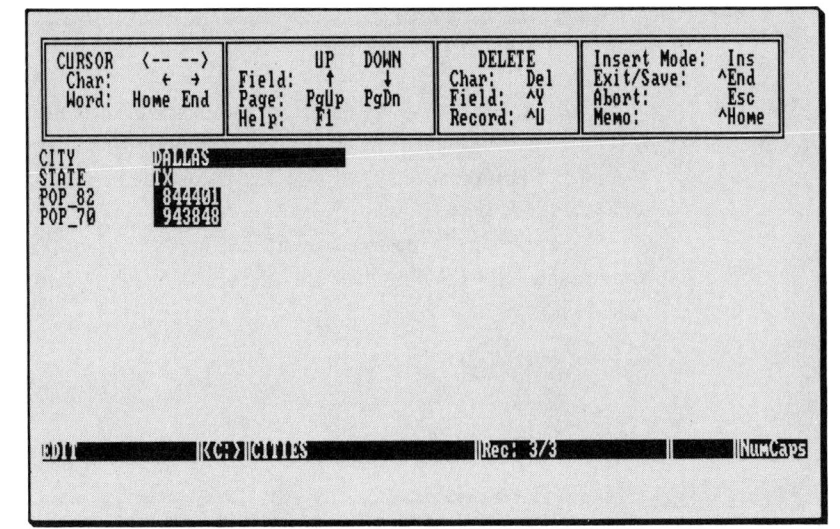

FIGURE 3.13   *The EDIT screen.*

You will now be able to change the existing data in any field, using the same keys as in APPEND. When you are finished EDITing, you can press the Ctrl and the End keys simultaneously to save the changes. Check the results with LIST.

BROWSE will display many records with any number of fields and, like EDIT, will allow changes to the data. You can use the editing keys and the Ctrl-B and Ctrl-Z to pan left and right if there are too many fields to fit on the screen. Use the Ctrl-End keys to save the changes. USE the STOCKS database and enter the PRICE data from Figure 3.12 using BROWSE.

```
. USE STOCKS
. BROWSE
```

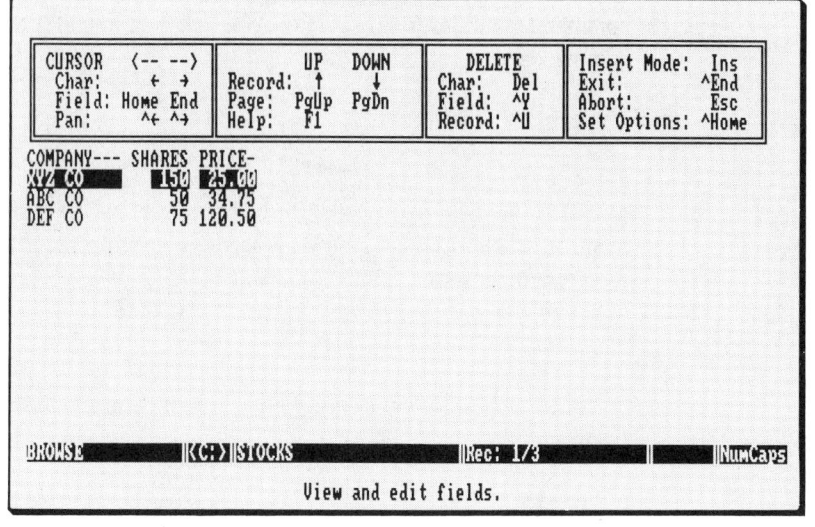

FIGURE 3.14   *The BROWSE screen.*

REPLACE and GET/READ are more useful to the programmer than EDIT or BROWSE because they can be used with memory variables. They do not require special key combinations, and they make custom data entry screens possible, as you will see in Chapter 10.

Open the TEMP database again and access record 6 by positioning the record pointer and DISPLAYing the data. Type GO 6, followed by a DISPLAY command, as shown in Figure 3.15.

```
. USE TEMP
. GO 6
. DISPLAY
```

FIGURE 3.15   *Using the DISPLAY command.*

REPLACE the CITY field with some new data and DISPLAY again.

```
        . REPLACE CITY WITH 'GREATER MIAMI'

   1 record replaced

        . DISPLAY

Record#  CITY                      STATE  POP_70  POP_82
      6  GREATER MIAMI             FL     334859  558869
```

FIGURE 3.16 *Result of the REPLACE command.*

The REPLACE command is especially useful in programming when it is combined with memory variables, which are addressed in Chapter 4. Work with EDIT and BROWSE until you are comfortable using them to modify data from the dot prompt; however, they are of no use when programming in dBASE III PLUS.

3.4 REMOVING RECORDS

For safety reasons removing records is a four-step task in dBASE III PLUS since the record numbers must not contain any gaps. The following steps are necessary:

1. Mark unwanted records with DELETE.
2. Copy the file structure to a temporary file.
3. Copy unDELETEd records to the new file in order.
4. Rename the temporary file and delete the original.

The records are first marked with an asterisk through the use of the DELETE command. Then the file is recreated and renumbered. This is similar to the way in which wooded areas are cleared. Workers will mark the less desirable trees with paint before actually felling them, perhaps on another day.

The process is not really difficult, because steps 2, 3, and 4 are performed with the PACK command. Since you are working with TEMP.DBF, which is a copy of the original file, no risk is incurred by removing record 6 with the following commands:

```
        . DELETE RECORD 6

   1 record deleted

        . DISPLAY

Record#  CITY                      STATE  POP_70  POP_82
      6  *GREATER MIAMI            FL     334859  558869
```

FIGURE 3.17 *Result of the DELETE command (Part 1 of 2).*

```
        . LIST

Record#  CITY                STATE  POP_70   POP_82
      1  SAN FRANCISCO        CA     715674   691637
      2  PHILADELPHIA         PA    1949996  1665382
      3  DALLAS               TX     844401   943848
      4  SAN DIEGO            CA     697471   915956
      5  HOUSTON              TX    1233535  1725617
      6  *GREATER MIAMI       FL     334859   558869
      7  CLEVELAND            OH     750879   558869
      8  PITTSBURGH           PA     520089   414936
      9  LOS ANGELES          CA    2811801  3022247
     10  JACKSONVILLE         FL     504265   556370
     11  COLUMBUS             OH     540025   564871
```

FIGURE 3.17   *Result of the DELETE command (Part 2 of 2).*

Notice that record 6 contains an asterisk. Now, actually remove the record with the PACK command.

```
        . PACK

    10 records copied

        . LIST

Record#  CITY               . STATE  POP_70   POP_82
      1  SAN FRANCISCO        CA     715674   691637
      2  PHILADELPHIA         PA    1949996  1665382
      3  DALLAS               TX     844401   943848
      4  SAN DIEGO            CA     697471   915956
      5  HOUSTON              TX    1233535  1725617
      6  CLEVELAND            OH     750879   558869
      7  PITTSBURGH           PA     520089   414936
      8  LOS ANGELES          CA    2811801  3022247
      9  JACKSONVILLE         FL     504265   556370
     10  COLUMBUS             OH     540025   564871
```

FIGURE 3.18   *Result of the PACK command.*

You can remove the asterisk ($*$) from a deleted record by means of the RECALL command. This will prevent the record from being deleted during the PACK operation.

```
        . DELETE RECORD 3

    1 record deleted

        . DISPLAY

Record#  CITY                STATE  POP_70   POP_82
      3  *DALLAS              TX     844401   943848

        . RECALL RECORD 3

    1 record recalled

        . DISPLAY

Record#  CITY                STATE  POP_70   POP_82
      3  DALLAS               TX     844401   943848
```

FIGURE 3.19   *Using RECALL.*

Notice that the "Greater Miami" record is now missing and that the records that had followed it have changed their position in the file to eliminate the gap. This is the *only* method available in dBASE III PLUS to remove records permanently from a file. Always be cautious in its use, because the data cannot be retrieved after the PACK, and it may be a time-consuming process under some circumstances.

3.5 DISPLAYING DATA

You have seen how the LIST command was used earlier in this chapter to display all the data in a .DBF file on the screen. Although LIST is more flexible and powerful than earlier examples indicate, like EDIT, it is of no use to the programmer. It is helpful to be skilled in the use of LIST from the dot prompt, as the following examples illustrate.

Open the original CITIES.DBF file.

```
. USE CITIES
```

You can specify the fields you want to LIST.

```
          . LIST STATE, CITY

Record#   STATE  CITY
      1   CA     SAN FRANCISCO
      2   PA     PHILADELPHIA
      3   TX     DALLAS
      4   CA     SAN DIEGO
      5   TX     HOUSTON
      6   FL     MIAMI
      7   OH     CLEVELAND
      8   PA     PITTSBURGH
      9   CA     LOS ANGELES
     10   FL     JACKSONVILLE
     11   OH     COLUMBUS
```

FIGURE 3.20 *Using the LIST command.*

Performing an arithmetic operation on numeric fields while LISTing can produce interesting results. For example, you can compare the population growth of all the cities. You will find that you can LIST fields in any combination.

```
        . LIST CITY, POP_82 - POP_70

Record#  CITY                POP_82 - POP_70
      1  SAN FRANCISCO             -24037
      2  PHILADELPHIA            -284614
      3  DALLAS                    99447
      4  SAN DIEGO                218485
      5  HOUSTON                  492082
      6  MIAMI                    224010
      7  CLEVELAND               -192010
      8  PITTSBURGH              -105153
      9  LOS ANGELES              210446
     10  JACKSONVILLE              52105
     11  COLUMBUS                  24846
```

FIGURE 3.21   *Arithmetic operation with LIST.*

If you wish to be selective while LISTing records, specify a criterion by placing one of the relational operators between a field name and a specific expression. The expression will contain a piece of data to be used by dBASE III PLUS for comparison. Character (alphanumeric) data must be placed within a set of quotation marks (' ' or " "). Never use quotes with numeric information, and avoid nonnumeric symbols such as the dollar sign and the comma. Effectively writing these comparison expressions, or conditions, is a skill that you will use frequently when programming. Here are the relational operators:

=	Equal To
<	Less Than
>	Greater Than
<=	Less Than or Equal To
> =	Greater Than or Equal To
# or <>	Not Equal To

FIGURE 3.22   *The relational operators.*

Notice how the conditions in the next few examples are constructed, and observe the results on the displayed data.

```
        . LIST FOR CITY = 'SAN DIEGO'

Record#  CITY                STATE  POP_70  POP_82
      4  SAN DIEGO           CA     697471  915956

        . LIST FOR CITY = 'SAN'

Record#  CITY                STATE  POP_70  POP_82
      1  SAN FRANCISCO       CA     715674  691637
      4  SAN DIEGO           CA     697471  915956
```

FIGURE 3.23   *Using conditions with LIST.*

In the previous example, dBASE III PLUS tested the first three characters of the CITY field of each record and displayed the records that matched, regardless of what is contained in the following characters. Sometimes this kind of test may be helpful, but a more specific comparison may be required on occasion. The SET EXACT ON command allows only those fields which match perfectly to be displayed.

```
    . SET EXACT ON

    . LIST FOR CITY = 'SAN'

Record#  CITY                  STATE  POP_70  POP_82

. SET EXACT OFF
```

FIGURE 3.24 *Result of SET EXACT ON.*

Since none of the city names matched 'SAN' *exactly*, no records were displayed.

Here is an example of a numeric comparison:

```
    . LIST FOR POP_82 < 1000000

Record#  CITY                  STATE  POP_70  POP_82
      1  SAN FRANCISCO         CA     715674  691637
      3  DALLAS                TX     844401  943848
      4  SAN DIEGO             CA     697471  915956
      6  MIAMI                 FL     334859  558869
      7  CLEVELAND             OH     750879  558869
      8  PITTSBURGH            PA     520089  414936
     10  JACKSONVILLE          FL     504265  556370
     11  COLUMBUS              OH     540025  564871
```

FIGURE 3.25 *Result of a numeric comparison.*

Notice that only cities with a 1982 population of fewer than 1,000,000 are displayed. If you were interested in Pennsylvania cities in this category, you might do another LIST and compare.

```
    . LIST CITY FOR STATE = 'PA'

Record#  CITY
      2  PHILADELPHIA
      8  PITTSBURGH
```

FIGURE 3.26 *Comparison using the STATE field.*

A more convenient way to accomplish the same result is to combine the two tests with .AND. , a logical operator. This will prove to be a useful technique in Chapter 6.

```
        . LIST CITY FOR STATE = 'PA' .AND. POP_82 > 1000000

Record#  CITY
      2  PHILADELPHIA
```

FIGURE 3.27   *Combining conditions with .AND.*

Position the record pointer at record 3 with the GO command, then try displaying the data in the CITY field, combined with a message. The ? will allow you to print almost any type of expression or field.

```
    . GO 3

      . ? 'METROPOLITAN AREA IN RECORD 3 - '.CITY

METROPOLITAN AREA IN RECORD 3 -   DALLAS
```

FIGURE 3.28   *Using the ? command.*

It is even possible to perform calculations with the ? .

```
      . ? '10% GROWTH OF POPULATION IN 1982 = '.POP_82 * 1.10

10% GROWTH OF POPULATION IN 1982 =   1038232.80
```

FIGURE 3.29   *Performing calculations with ? .*

Perhaps you are wondering what .80 of a person would look like! The fraction appeared because of the two decimal places in the multiplier, 1.10. You will learn to round or remove fractions in a later chapter.

Fields may be printed in any order as shown in the example below. The ? displays data only from the record pointer's current location.

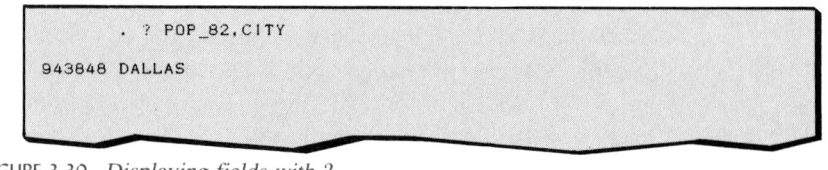

FIGURE 3.30 *Displaying fields with ? .*

The exercises at the end of this chapter are designed to develop your ability to use ? and LIST. These skills will be applied again when you begin to program in dBASE III PLUS.

CHAPTER SUMMARY

3.1

After you have planned the format of the database, including the name, type, and length of each field, the structure of the .DBF file can be established with CREATE. A convenient screen is used to set up the specifications for each field. A .DBF file must be opened with USE before the data can be accessed.

3.2

The APPEND command allows the addition of records to a .DBF file that has been opened with USE. A screen is employed to prompt the user to enter data into each field. The structure of a .DBF file can be altered with the MODIFY STRUCTURE command, which displays a screen similar to CREATE. The data is rewritten to the file following the alterations.

3.3

Existing records may be modified\ with several commands, including EDIT, BROWSE, REPLACE, and GET.EDIT will allow any changes to the data in an individual record. If many records require modification, the BROWSE command is more convenient. REPLACE changes the data in the current record from the dot prompt. REPLACE and GET are useful for programming, while EDIT and BROWSE are not.

3.4

The removal of a record is a two-command process using DELETE and PACK. The DELETE command marks the record with an asterisk, while PACK actually removes the marked record and rewrites the file.

3.5

LIST is a flexible command that will display any combination of fields from selected records. Comparative expressions using relational operators can be linked logically to perform the selection. The ? will display fields from the current record and messages. LIST is useful from the dot prompt, and ? is used in programs.

KEY TERMS

character type	logical type
alphanumeric	memo type
numeric type	.DBF
date type	relational operator

COMMAND SUMMARY

CREATE — Establish a database file.

USE — Open a database file for use.

DISPLAY STRUCTURE — Show the structure of a database file.

LIST STRUCTURE — Show the structure of a database file.

APPEND — Add a record to a database file.

MODIFY STRUCTURE — Change the structure of a database file.

LIST — Display the data in a database file.

EDIT — Modify the data in a record.

BROWSE — Change the data in several records.

REPLACE — Substitute the data in the fields.

PACK — Remove deleted records.

RECALL — Unmark a record for deletion.

LIST FOR — Display data with a condition.

SET EXACT ON — Display data that matches a condition exactly.

? — Display data or literals.

SELF-CHECK QUESTIONS

1. Why is it important to consider the characteristics of a field such as length?
2. What is the difference between numeric data and character data?
3. How does one determine the length of a numeric field?
4. What does a Ctrl-U (^U) do? How is this done on the keyboard?
5. What happens when you USE a file?
6. What happens when an APPEND command executes?

7. What piece of information is required in order to EDIT a record?
8. Why is the deletion process done in two steps?
9. Provide a field name and determine the type and length (include decimal positions if appropriate) for each of the following examples:
   a. A Social Security number with hyphens.
   b. The hourly pay rate at a fast-food restaurant.
   c. The price of a new car.
   d. The date on which an employee was hired.
   e. A product description.
   f. A code for marital status.
   g. An interest rate, such as 9.25%.
10. When would SET EXACT ON be useful?

TRY IT YOURSELF

1. Plan a database structure for the following body of information. Consider the name, type, and length of each field.

   A charity wishes to record the name of the contributor, the amount of the contribution, and the date on which the contribution was made. Amounts of 1000 or more are not included, but change (a cents figure) is often given. Only last names are required.

2. Use CREATE to establish and name a .DBF file for the previous exercise. Display the structure.
3. APPEND these records to your file:

   Garcia, 21.50, March 8, 1988
   Nelson, 120, January 12, 1988
   Gordon, 58.75, April 19, 1988
   Zucco, 325, February 3, 1988

   LIST the records.

4. Make the following modifications to the appropriate records:
   a. Nelson's name is incorrect. Change it to Neilson.
   b. Gordon contributed 158.75, not 58.75.
   c. The contribution shown for February 3 was actually made on February 13.
5. Remove the Gordon record from the file. LIST the records and note the change in record numbers. Add a record for Norton's contibution of 34.50 on March 15, 1988.
6. LIST the records with the following conditions:

    a. The dates first and then the amounts without the names.

    b. The original amounts and then the amounts increased by 10%.

    c. The names that begin with 'N' and the dates of those records.

    d. The names of those who contributed more than $100.

    e. The entire record of those whose names begin with 'N' and who gave more than $100.

7. Place the record pointer at record 3. Display this message:

LAST NAME IS — ZUCCO

8. Modify the structure of the database in exercise 1 so that it includes a field to represent the status of the contributions (P — pledged, R — received). Use REPLACE to place a P in all the records.

9. Print a LIST of the names of the cities whose population in 1970 was 600,000 or less.

10. Print a list of the city name and the difference in population between 1982 and 1970 if the city is in California.

11. Modify the structure of the CITIES database to add a 10-character field called TIME_ZONE. Use BROWSE FIELDS to add the data to the new field.

12. Print the city, the state, and a population projection that is based on a 10% increase over the 1982 population.

13. CREATE a daily log database, including the date and a 20-character field for the event. Add several records from your daily life during the last week.

14. Using the database in exercise 13, edit several records, delete one record, and PACK.

WORKING FROM
THE DOT PROMPT

LEARNING OBJECTIVES

1. To use the report and label generators.
2. To use utility commands such as COPY, DIR, and ERASE.
3. To learn the characteristics of the date-, memo-, and logical-type fields.
4. To control the record pointer with GOTO and SKIP.
5. To place data in order with the INDEX command.

4

WORKING FROM THE DOT PROMPT

Now that you have begun to experience dBASE III PLUS, you will want to take advantage of some of the powerful commands and features that are available from the dot prompt. For example, you can easily produce attractive reports and useful labels by means of convenient generator programs. You will also find that a knowledge of the various utility commands will be helpful when you are maintaining files. Further, you will learn to move through the database and place records in order. As you become competent in the use of these and other commands, you will be acquiring an excellent preparation for programming, which is presented in Chapter 5.

4.1 USING THE REPORT GENERATOR

The report generator is an automatic report writer. It can be mastered quickly, and produces attractive reports from the data in the .DBF file. There are two principal disadvantages of this feature: it lacks flexibility, and it will operate on only one database. These shortcomings limit the use of the report generator in programming. However, the ability to generate reports from the dot prompt is often useful.

REPORT FORM will prompt you for your specifications through a set of menus that are similar to those in the assistant. These details will be saved by dBASE III PLUS in an .FRM file, which can then be used to generate reports when they are required. Before using REPORT FORM, open the .DBF file, select a name for the .FRM file, and sketch the format you want on paper.

On the following page is how a report might appear using CITIES.DBF.

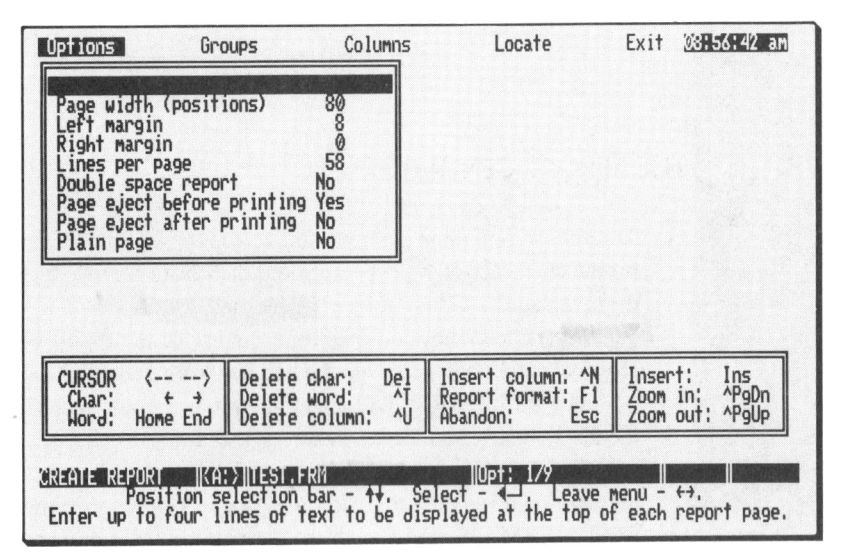

Page 1
01/1/88

Report of U.S. Cities

San Francisco   CA   691637
Philadelphia   PA   1665382
Dallas   TX   943848
San Diego   CA   915956
Houston   TX   1725617
Miami   FL   558869
Cleveland   OH   558869
Pittsburgh   PA   414936
Los Angeles   CA   3022247
Jacksonville   FL   556370
Columbus   OH   564871

*** Total ***   11618602

FIGURE 4.1   *Design for a report.*

Start REPORT with the following command and the Report Options menu will appear. FIRST will become the name of the .FRM file.

```
. CREATE REPORT FIRST
```

```
Options      Groups        Columns        Locate      Exit  03:56:42 am

   Page width (positions)     80
   Left margin                 8
   Right margin                0
   Lines per page             58
   Double space report        No
   Page eject before printing Yes
   Page eject after printing  No
   Plain page                 No



CURSOR   <-- -->   Delete char:   Del  Insert column: ^N  Insert:     Ins
Char:      + +     Delete word:   ^T   Report format: F1  Zoom in:  ^PgDn
Word:    Home End  Delete column: ^U   Abandon:       Esc  Zoom out: ^PgUp

CREATE REPORT    |KA:>|TEST.FRM              |Opt: 1/9
          Position selection bar - +↓.  Select - ↵.  Leave menu - ↔.
     Enter up to four lines of text to be displayed at the top of each report page.
```

FIGURE 4.2   *The Report Options menu.*

Four other menus are listed at the top of the screen. You can select them with the left and right arrow keys. You will also notice a set of four boxes that list actions performed by various keys. Located below the boxes are status lines that provide instructions.

By moving the up and down arrow keys, you can make selections from the nine choices in the Options Menu box. Select Page Title and press Return. You may type up to four lines, which will appear at the top of the page. Press the Ctrl and the End keys simultaneously to accept the title.

Move to the Columns menu and select the field that will appear in the first column. You can type in your choice after pressing Return or you can choose from the fields by pressing F10. Place CITY in the space provided, using either method. You will find that the width of the CITY field, 20, is automatically displayed. To allow extra space in the report for this field, change the width to 25 by pressing the up arrow key after selecting the option with the Return key. Use the Page Down key to move to the next column, and repeat the process, setting STATE to 5 and POP_82 to 8. Finally, use the Save option in the Exit menu to finish the report.

You may now generate the report with this command:

```
. REPORT FORM FIRST
```

```
Page No.        1
01/01/88
                            REPORT OF U. S. CITIES


        SAN FRANCISCO         CA       691637
        PHILADELPHIA          PA      1665382
        DALLAS                TX       943848
        SAN DIEGO             CA       915956
        HOUSTON               TX      1725617
        MIAMI                 FL       558869
        CLEVELAND             OH       558869
        PITTSBURGH            PA       414936
        LOS ANGELES           CA      3022247
        JACKSONVILLE          FL       556370
        COLUMBUS              OH       564871
        *** Total ***
                                     11618602
```

FIGURE 4.3 *Result of the report generator.*

Not all the features that are available in the report generator have been addressed here. You will find that the status lines at the bottom of the screens will be helpful when you are exploring theses other options.

Your experience with the report generator will be helpful in learning to produce paper labels with the label generator, since both features use pull-down menus and input screens for the sake of convenience. The first screen, Options, allows you to define the size and spacing of the labels, as in Figure 4.4. The Contents screen will accept field names from the active database to appear on the five positions on the label. In Figure 4.6, the CITIES database is used to provide an example.

The label generator is started with the CREATE LABEL command. As with the report generator, a valid file name for the label file must be provided. The file will appear on your disk with an .LBL extension. A .DBF file must be open; if it isn't, you will be prompted. Finally, you will be presented with the Options screen. Pressing Return on the predefined size option will display one of five common sizes that you may accept or modify as necessary.

Figure 4.5 illustrates the Contents screen. Pressing Return on one of the label contents positions will allow you to select a field from a list produced with the F10 key. When all the desired fields have been selected, use the Save option in the final menu. The labels can be produced on the screen with the LABEL FORM CITIES command. The clause TO PRINT can be added in order to direct the output to the printer. The SAMPLE option displays a facsimile of a label, using an X for each character. It is then possible to adjust the printer before starting to print the labels.

```
. USE CITIÉS

. CREATE LABEL CITIES
```

FIGURE 4.4   *Using the label generator.*

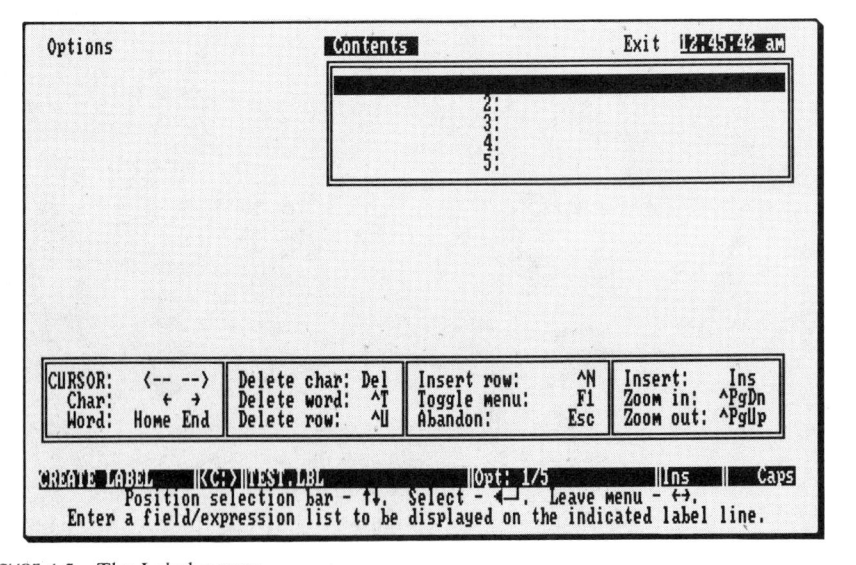

FIGURE 4.5   *The Label screen.*

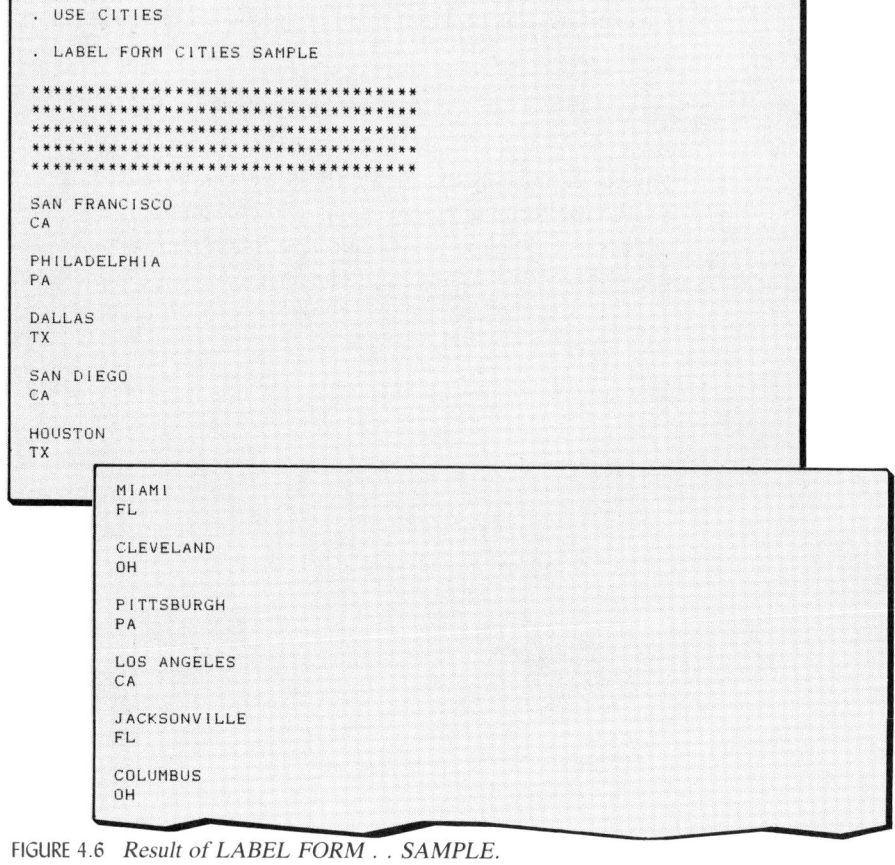

```
. USE CITIES

. LABEL FORM CITIES SAMPLE

************************************
************************************
************************************
************************************
************************************

SAN FRANCISCO
CA

PHILADELPHIA
PA

DALLAS
TX

SAN DIEGO
CA

HOUSTON
TX

           MIAMI
           FL

           CLEVELAND
           OH

           PITTSBURGH
           PA

           LOS ANGELES
           CA

           JACKSONVILLE
           FL

           COLUMBUS
           OH
```

FIGURE 4.6   *Result of LABEL FORM . . SAMPLE.*

You learned how to use the LIST command with a FOR clause in Chapter 3. The same clause can be used with the LABEL FORM command to print labels on the basis of a condition. The example in Figure 4.7 will print labels only for cities that are in Pennsylvania.

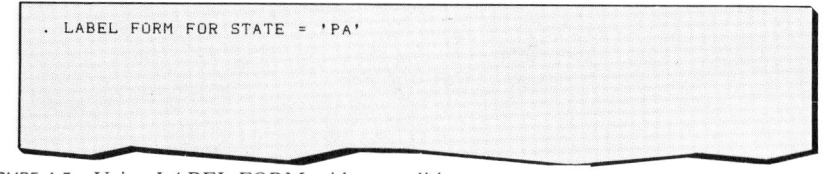

```
. LABEL FORM FOR STATE = 'PA'
```

FIGURE 4.7   *Using LABEL FORM with a condition.*

Both the report generator and the label generator are useful, convenient features. However, some business projects require programming because they are too complex for the REPORT generator. Chapter 5 will introduce programming and Chapters 12 and 14 will present programs that produce reports.

4.2 UTILITY COMMANDS AND OTHER FIELD TYPES

Several commands in dBASE III PLUS can be used to save time and effort when you are performing housekeeping chores with your files. Some of these commands are presented below, with brief descriptions and examples. Try each of these with the TEMP.DBF file in order to understand how they operate.

COPY TO

This command is used to produce an identical copy of the .DBF file currently in use.

```
         . USE TEMP

         . COPY TO TEMP2

     10 records copied

         . LIST FILES

Database Files      # Records      Last Update      Size
CITIES.DBF                 11      01/01/88          606
TEMP.DBF                   10      01/01/88          569
TEMP2.DBF                  10      01/01/88          532

    1707 bytes in    3 files.
```

FIGURE 4.8 *Using COPY TO.*

COPY STRUCTURE

The COPY STRUCTURE command can be used to copy the structure of a .DBF file without the records.

```
. COPY STRUCTURE TO TEMP3

. USE TEMP3
```

```
         . LIST STRUCTURE

  Structure for database: C:TEMP3.dbf
  Number of data records:       0
  Date of last update   : 01/01/88
  Field  Field Name Type       Width    Dec
     1     CITY       Character    20
     2     STATE      Character     2
     3     POP_70     Numeric       7
     4     POP_82     Numeric       7
  ** Total **                      37
```

FIGURE 4.9 *Using COPY STRUCTURE.*

COPY FILE

If you need to perform a COPY on other types of files, use the COPY FILE command.

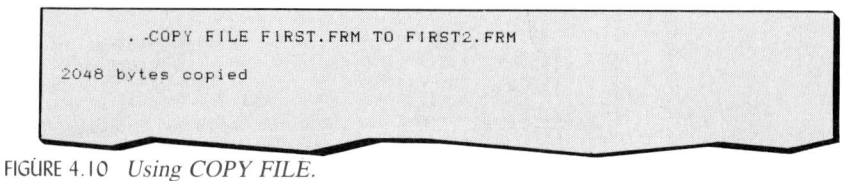
```
    . COPY FILE FIRST.FRM TO FIRST2.FRM
2048 bytes copied
```

FIGURE 4.10   *Using COPY FILE.*

COUNT

The COUNT command is combined with a condition to return the number of records that satisfy the criteria.

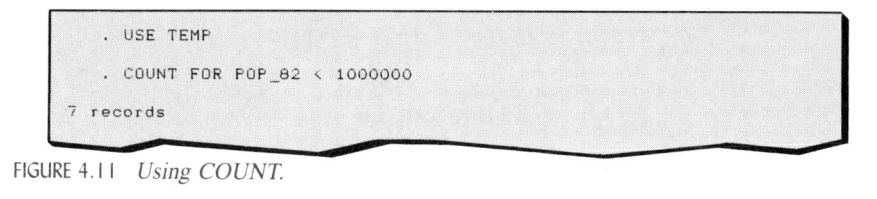
```
. USE TEMP
. COUNT FOR POP_82 < 1000000
7 records
```

FIGURE 4.11   *Using COUNT.*

SUM

If there are numeric fields in the .DBF file, they can be totaled with the SUM command.

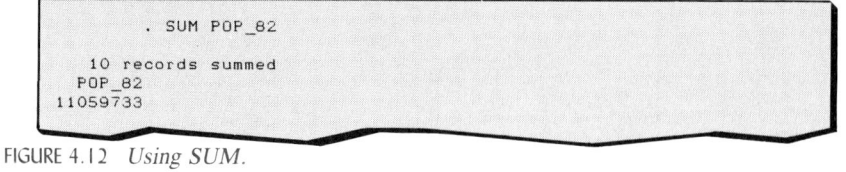
```
. SUM POP_82
  10 records summed
  POP_82
11059733
```

FIGURE 4.12   *Using SUM.*

AVERAGE

The AVERAGE command will calculate an average on any or all numeric fields.

```
. AVERAGE POP_82
   10 records averaged
 POP_82
1105973
```

FIGURE 4.13   *Using AVERAGE.*

DIR

This is a DOS command that will check the directory of the disk and display any .DBF files. The names of other files can also be displayed by means of the *.

```
     . DIR

Database Files      # Records     Last Update      Size
CITIES.DBF              11        01/01/88          606
TEMP.DBF                10        01/01/88          569
TEMP2.DBF               10        01/01/88          532
TEMP3.DBF                0        01/01/88          162

    1869 bytes in      4 files.


          . DIR *.FRM

FIRST.FRM            FIRST2.FRM

    4038 bytes in      2 files.
```

FIGURE 4.14   *Using DIR.*

DISPLAY STATUS or LIST STATUS

This command provides a variety of useful information about the files being used and about dBASE III PLUS itself.

```
      . DISPLAY STATUS

Currently Selected Database:
Select area:   1. Database in Use: C:TEMP.dbf     Alias: TEMP

Alternate file:
File search path:
Default disk drive: C:
Print destination:  PRN:
Margin =      0
Current work area =     1


Press any key to continue...

ALTERNATE   - OFF    DELETED     - OFF    FIXED       - OFF    SAFETY     - ON
BELL        - ON     DELIMITERS  - OFF    HEADING     - ON     SCOREBOARD - ON
CARRY       - OFF    DEVICE      - SCRN   HELP        - ON     STATUS     - OFF
CATALOG     - OFF    DOHISTORY   - OFF    HISTORY     - ON     STEP       - OFF
CENTURY     - OFF    ECHO        - OFF    INTENSITY   - ON     TALK       - ON
CONFIRM     - OFF    ESCAPE      - ON     MENU        - ON     TITLE      - ON
CONSOLE     - ON     EXACT       - OFF    PRINT       - OFF    UNIQUE     - OFF
DEBUG       - OFF    FIELDS      - OFF

      Programmable function keys:
      F2  - assist;
      F3  - list;
      F4  - dir;
      F5  - display structure;
      F6  - display status;
      F7  - display memory;
      F8  - display;
      F9  - append;
      F10 - edit;
```

FIGURE 4.15   *Using DISPLAY STATUS.*

DISPLAY HISTORY

This command will display the most recent commands which have been typed. The up arrow key will display them one at a time. Pressing the Return key will allow a command to be executed again without retyping.

```
          . DISPLAY HISTORY

COPY FILE FIRST.FRM TO FIRST2.FRM
COPY STRUCTURE TO TEMP3
USE TEMP3
LIST STRUCTURE
USE TEMP
COUNT FOR POP_82 < 1000000
SUM POP_82
AVERAGE POP_82
Press any key to continue...
DIR
DIR *.FRM
DISPLAY STATUS
DISPLAY HISTORY
```

FIGURE 4.16   *Using DISPLAY HISTORY.*

SKIP

The SKIP command will move the record pointer to the next record.

```
          . SKIP

Record No.      4

          . DISPLAY

Record#  CITY              STATE  POP_70  POP_82
      4  SAN DIEGO         CA     697471  915956
```

FIGURE 4.17   *Using SKIP.*

RENAME

The DOS directory name of a file can be changed with this command. Make certain that the file is closed before using RENAME. In this case, the old file name, TEMP2.DBF, is changed to NEW.DBF.

```
            . RENAME TEMP2.DBF TO NEW.DBF

            . LIST FILES

Database Files      # Records      Last Update      Size
CITIES.DBF               11        01/01/88          606
TEMP.DBF                 10        01/01/88          569
NEW.DBF                  10        01/01/88          532
TEMP3.DBF                 0        01/01/88          162

    1869 bytes in      4 files.
```

FIGURE 4.18   *Using RENAME.*

ERASE

Use the **ERASE** command to remove files from the disk.

```
. ERASE TEMP3.DBF

File has been deleted.
```

```
            . LIST FILES

Database Files      # Records      Last Update      Size
CITIES.DBF               11        01/01/88          606
TEMP.DBF                 10        01/01/88          569
NEW.DBF                  10        01/01/88          532

    1707 bytes in      3 files.
```

FIGURE 4.19   *Using ERASE.*

ZAP

ZAP is useful when the structure of a .DBF file is to be retained but the data is no longer wanted.

```
            . USE NEW

            . ZAP

Zap C:NEW.dbf? (Y/N) Yes

            . LIST
```

FIGURE 4.20   *Using ZAP.*

You have seen only a selection of the commands that are available in dBASE III PLUS. However, you will find that the ones you have seen are those which are most frequently used. As you become skilled in their use, take note of those commands which are identified as useful for programming and those which are not. In order to fully use the considerable power of dBASE III PLUS, you must be competent both as an interactive user (typing commands from the dot prompt) and as a programmer. In Chapter 5 you will begin to write programs with many of the commands that were presented here.

In Chapter 3, you learned the critical difference between character- and numeric-type data fields. Although these two types will work well with most of the data you will encounter, you need to be familiar with the three other data types that are used in dBASE III PLUS. The first, date, is a convenient way to handle the type of data it is named for. Exactly six numeric digits are required to fill in a date-type field, with two extra positions provided for the slashes. To be certain that they are reasonable, dBASE III PLUS checks the digits. For example, since there are only twelve months in a year, you cannot enter the number 13 in the month position. Date fields accept data in the following format:

```
MM/DD/YY

01/01/88 represents January 1, 1988
```

FIGURE 4.21   *Format of date-type fields.*

If you enter an invalid date during an APPEND or EDIT, dBASE III PLUS will sound a beep that prompts you to press the space bar in order to correct the data. Date fields also enable you to calculate the number of days between dates, information that you find useful when programming.

Memo fields, which require special handling, are used when large fields of character-type data are needed in records. When you use dBASE III PLUS, you are permitted to include as many as 5000 characters in memo fields. If you define a field as a memo in the CREATE operation, you will have to use the Ctrl and End keys to input data during APPEND or EDIT. This data will be stored in a separate file on your disk with a .DBT extension. Unfortunately, these and other factors limit the practical use of memo fields during programming.

The final dBASE III PLUS field type is the logical field, which is also of limited value to the programmer. The letters T or t (true), and F or f (false), are used to represent a generic status or condition that the user must interpret. The letters Y or y, and n or N may also be used. It is frequently more useful to include a character-type field with a length of 1 in this case. Some examples would be:

O — overdue   A — active
C — current   R — retired

In conclusion, most data that you will encounter can be stored effectively in numeric-, character-, or date-type fields. On occasion, the memo and logical fields will be useful when you are working from the dot prompt.

4.3 GETTING AROUND IN THE DATABASE

As you learned in Chapter 3, all .DBF files contain a record pointer. This is an internal "bookmark" that can be moved from record to record. For example, after a USE command has been issued, the record pointer is positioned at the first record. Since the DISPLAY command always references the current record, it is useful for examining the behavior of the record pointer, as Figure 4.22 illustrates. Try each of the commands to become familiar with the behavior of the record pointer, because its use will be critical in later chapters.

Several commands enable you to move the record pointer to any location in the file. A specific record number can be placed after the GOTO command to position the record pointer on that record. In Figure 4.22, the commands GOTO 6, GO 3, and 5 place the record pointer on the sixth, third, and fifth records. As you can see, this command has three variations. GO BOTTOM moves the pointer to the last record in the file, record 11. GO TOP returns the pointer to the first record. The SKIP command moves the record pointer a specified number of records away from the current location. The SKIP in Figure 4.22 moves the record pointer from the current location, record 1, to record 6. Other numbers such as 5 and –3, can be used with the SKIP, as the figure illustrates.

The GOTO command requires the user to know which record number contains the desired data. It is unlikely that the record numbers would be useful, since they bear no relevance to the data but are simply sequential numbers. The LOCATE command will position the record pointer on the basis of selected data placed in the command. For example, if you issued the LOCATE command in Figure 4.23, the record pointer would be positioned at the first record that met the condition CITY = 'PHILADELPHIA'. If the specified condition could be true for more than one record, the CONTINUE command could be used to advance to the next record that satisfied the condition. Since three California cities are in the database, the CONTINUE command can be used to display the second and third in Figure 4.23.

```
        . USE CITIES

        . DISPLAY

Record#  CITY                   STATE  POP_70  POP_82
     1   SAN FRANCISCO          CA     715674  691637

        . GOTO 6

        . DISPLAY

Record#  CITY                   STATE  POP_70  POP_82
     6   MIAMI                  FL     334859  382726

        . GO 3

        . DISPLAY

Record#  CITY                   STATE  POP_70  POP_82
     3   DALLAS                 TX     844401  943848

        . 5

        . DISPLAY

Record#   CITY                  STATE  POP_70   POP_82
     5    HOUSTON               TX     1233535 1725617

        . GO BOTTOM

        . DISPLAY

Record#   CITY                  STATE  POP_70   POP_82
    11    COLUMBUS              OH     540025   570588

        . GO TOP

        . DISPLAY

Record#   CITY                  STATE  POP_70   POP_82
     1    SAN FRANCISCO         CA     715674   691637

        . SKIP

Record No.        2

        . DISPLAY

Record#   CITY                  STATE  POP_70    POP_82
     2    PHILADELPHIA          PA     1949996  1665382

        . SKIP 5

Record No.        7

        . DISPLAY

Record#   CITY                  STATE  POP_70   POP_82
     7    CLEVELAND             OH     750879   558869
```

FIGURE 4.22 *Moving the record pointer.*

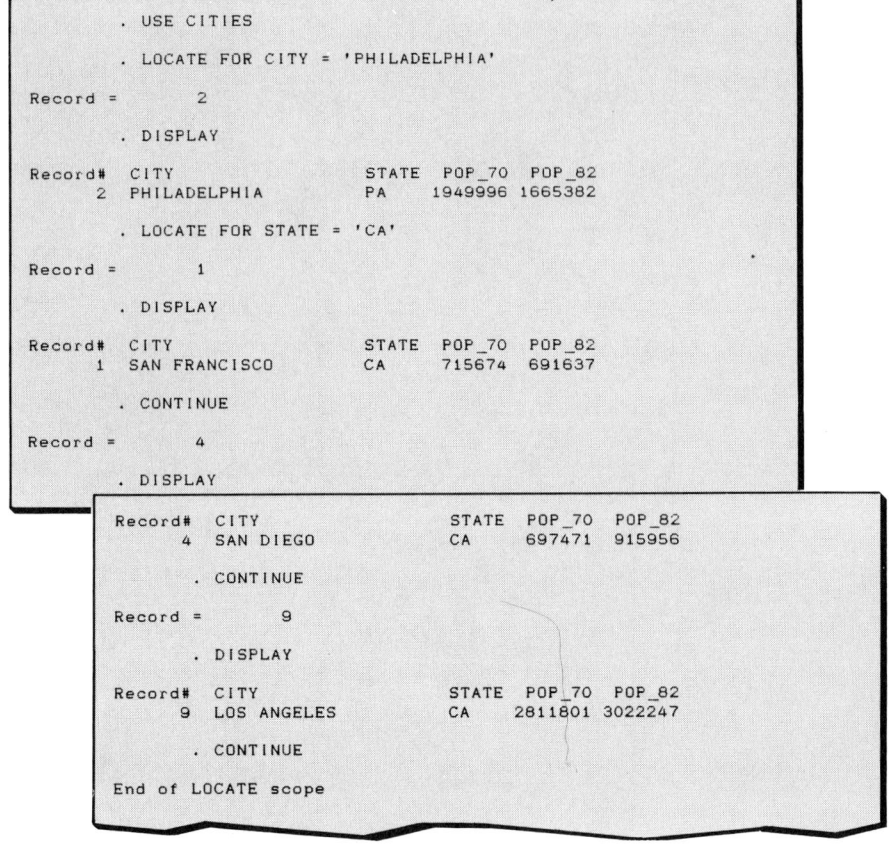

```
. USE CITIES

. LOCATE FOR CITY = 'PHILADELPHIA'

Record =        2

. DISPLAY

Record#  CITY                    STATE  POP_70   POP_82
     2   PHILADELPHIA            PA     1949996  1665382

. LOCATE FOR STATE = 'CA'

Record =        1

. DISPLAY

Record#  CITY                    STATE  POP_70   POP_82
     1   SAN FRANCISCO           CA     715674   691637

. CONTINUE

Record =        4

. DISPLAY

Record#  CITY                    STATE  POP_70   POP_82
     4   SAN DIEGO               CA     697471   915956

. CONTINUE

Record =        9

. DISPLAY

Record#  CITY                    STATE  POP_70   POP_82
     9   LOS ANGELES             CA     2811801  3022247

. CONTINUE

End of LOCATE scope
```

FIGURE 4.23   *Using LOCATE and CONTINUE.*

4.4 USING INDEX TO PUT DATA IN ORDER

You may have noticed that the data you have been using never appears in alphabetical order. The fields all seem to be in random order. This is the way most databases are maintained. The records are left in the same order in which they were appended to the .DBF file. Of course, it is possible to order data on the basis of any field. The CITIES database could appear in order by CITY or STATE, for example. A field that is used for this purpose is often called the *key field*. This is accomplished by means of a special file that is related to the .DBF file. This special file is called an index file. The command in Figure 4.24 will produce an index file whose order is determined by the contents of the CITY field. Notice that the LIST command displays the records in alphabetical order by CITY. The record numbers appear scrambled because the file is still in the original *physical* order.

In Figure 4.25, the records appear in alphabetical order by state as a result of the INDEX command. Figure 4.26 shows how a numeric field as well as a character field may be used for an index. Notice that the DIR command displays the names of the three .NDX files created with the INDEX command.

```
        . USE CITIES

        . INDEX ON CITY TO CITY

100% indexed           11 Records indexed

        . LIST

Record#  CITY                 STATE  POP_70   POP_82
      7  CLEVELAND            OH      750879   558869
     11  COLUMBUS             OH      540025   570588
      3  DALLAS               TX      844401   943848
      5  HOUSTON              TX     1233535  1725617
     10  JACKSONVILLE         FL      504265   556370
      9  LOS ANGELES          CA     2811801  3022247
      6  MIAMI                FL      334859   382726
      2  PHILADELPHIA         PA     1949996  1665382
      8  PITTSBURGH           PA      520089   414936
      4  SAN DIEGO            CA      697471   915956
      1  SAN FRANCISCO        CA      715674   691637
```

FIGURE 4.24 *Using INDEX with the CITY field.*

```
        . INDEX ON STATE TO STATE

100% indexed           11 Records indexed

        . LIST

Record#  CITY                 STATE  POP_70   POP_82
      1  SAN FRANCISCO        CA      715674   691637
      4  SAN DIEGO            CA      697471   915956
      9  LOS ANGELES          CA     2811801  3022247
      6  MIAMI                FL      334859   382726
     10  JACKSONVILLE         FL      504265   556370
      7  CLEVELAND            OH      750879   558869
     11  COLUMBUS             OH      540025   570588
      2  PHILADELPHIA         PA     1949996  1665382
      8  PITTSBURGH           PA      520089   414936
      3  DALLAS               TX      844401   943848
      5  HOUSTON              TX     1233535  1725617
```

FIGURE 4.25 *Using INDEX with the STATE field.*

```
            . INDEX ON POP_70 TO POP_70

    100% indexed              11 Records indexed

        . LIST

Record#   CITY                    STATE   POP_70   POP_82
      6   MIAMI                   FL      334859   382726
     10   JACKSONVILLE            FL      504265   556370
      8   PITTSBURGH              PA      520089   414936
     11   COLUMBUS                OH      540025   570588
      4   SAN DIEGO               CA      697471   915956
      1   SAN FRANCISCO           CA      715674   691637
      7   CLEVELAND               OH      750879   558869
      3   DALLAS                  TX      844401   943848
      5   HOUSTON                 TX     1233535  1725617
      2   PHILADELPHIA            PA     1949996  1665382
      9   LOS ANGELES             CA     2811801  3022247

        . DIR *.NDX

CITY.NDX            STATE.NDX              POP_70.NDX

    1040 bytes in    3 files.
4227072 bytes remaining on drive.
```

FIGURE 4.26   *Using INDEX with the POP_70 field.*

Once an index has been established, it can be made active again by means of the SET INDEX TO command. It is then possible to use a number of .NDX files, utilizing different key fields when you so desire. The ordering effect of the index file can be used in combination with other features, such as the report generator. Once the CITY.NDX file has been activated, the record display of the FIRST.FRM file will be in order by city, as Figure 4.27 illustrates.

```
    . SET INDEX TO CITY

    . REPORT FORM FIRST

    Page No.      1
    01/01/88
                          REPORT OF U. S. CITIES


    CLEVELAND             OH      558869
    COLUMBUS              OH      570588
    DALLAS                TX      943848
    HOUSTON               TX     1725617
    JACKSONVILLE          FL      556370
    LOS ANGELES           CA     3022247
    MIAMI                 FL      382726
    PHILADELPHIA          PA     1665382
    PITTSBURGH            PA      414936
    SAN DIEGO             CA      915956
    SAN FRANCISCO         CA      691637
    *** Total ***
                                 11448176
```

FIGURE 4.27   *Using REPORT FORM with an INDEX.*

If an index does not appear to be working properly — for example, if it is not displaying certain records — simply recreate it with another INDEX ON command. You will be asked if you wish to overwrite the file. Respond with a Y and the file will be replaced with a correct version. This sort of correction becomes necessary when the records in the database are changed with APPEND or EDIT, for example, but the .NDX file is not updated as well. Indexing is obviously quite useful, and it will be addressed in much more detail in Chapter 10. The summary in Figure 4.28 will help you to work with indexes until you have an opportunity to learn more about them.

Using INDEX

1. Use INDEX ON < field name > TO < file name > to establish the index, which becomes an .NDX file on the disk.
2. Activate the index, if necessary, with the SET INDEX TO command.
3. You can index on any type of field except memo.
4. The records remain in their original physical order but appear to be in order by the selected field.
5. Commands such as REPORT FORM and LIST will be affected by the index.
6. An index file can be recreated if it does not work properly.

FIGURE 4.28 *Guidelines for using INDEX.*

CHAPTER SUMMARY

4.1

Attractive reports can be generated from the dot prompt by means of the report generator, a dBASE III PLUS feature that allows the user to place specifications in an .FRM file.

4.2

A number of commands make dBASE III PLUS easier to use. Among these are COPY, DIR, DISPLAY STATUS, DISPLAY HISTORY, RECALL, SKIP, ERASE, and ZAP. Dates may be stored in date-type fields. Although they are employed infrequently in programs, memo- and logical-type fields are used, respectively, to store large amounts of text and true/false conditions.

4.3

The record pointer can be used to DISPLAY a particular record. The GOTO command positions the record pointer when a record number is specified. The SKIP command moves the record pointer a specified number of records away from the record pointer's current location. The LOCATE command positions the record pointer by matching the data to a specified condition. The CONTINUE command moves to other records that match the condition.

4.4

An index file can be used to display records in alphabetical or numerical order on the basis of a selected field. The INDEX ON command establishes an .NDX file that can be reactivated with the SET INDEX TO command. Records will be displayed in order with commands such as REPORT FORM and LIST. An index can be recreated easily if it is not working properly.

COMMAND SUMMARY

CREATE REPORT — Establish a REPORT format.

MODIFY REPORT — Change a REPORT format.

REPORT FORM — Produce a report.

CREATE LABEL — Establish a LABEL format.

MODIFY LABEL — Change a LABEL format.

LABEL FORM — Produce labels.

COPY TO — Copy a .DBF file.

LIST FILES — Display .DBF file names.

COPY STRUCTURE — Copy the structure of the active .DBF file.

COPY FILE — Copy any file.

COUNT — Count the number of records that meet a condition.

SUM — Sum numeric fields.

AVERAGE — Average numeric fields.

DIR — Display file names.

DISPLAY STATUS — Show statistics concerning environment.

DISPLAY HISTORY — Show recently executed commands.

DELETE RECORD — Mark a record for deletion.

SKIP — Move the record pointer.

DISPLAY — Show the contents of the current record.

RENAME — Change a file name.

ERASE — Remove a file from the disk.

ZAP — Remove all records from a file.

GOTO — Move the record pointer.

GOTO TOP — Place the record pointer at the top of the file.

GOTO BOTTOM — Place the record pointer at the bottom of the file.

LOCATE — Place the record pointer after meeting a condition.

CONTINUE — Move to the next record that meets a condition.

SELF-CHECK QUESTIONS

1. Why is it important to be familiar with DOS commands?
2. Is it possible to have more than one .FRM file per .DBF file?
3. Why is the SAMPLE option in the LABEL FORM command useful?
4. When is it helpful to use the COPY STRUCTURE command?
5. What is the difference between DISPLAY STATUS and LIST STATUS?
6. Why would you want to recall a record?
7. What are the disadvantages of the MEMO-type field?
8. Is it useful to be able to move around the database by record number? Why?
9. Can a LOCATE command be used with a numeric field?
10. Under what conditions could an index file be corrupted?
11. How can an index file be useful when you are using the label generator?
12. Is it a good idea to create index files for all the fields in a database just in case they are needed? Why?
13. Can the LOCATE command be employed with a file that is utilizing an index?
14. What would happen if you issued the following two commands while a .DBF file was open?

```
. GOTO BOTTOM
. SKIP
```

15. Some accounting procedures require the aging of accounts, which means calculating the number of days between the current date and a due date. Which feature of dBASE III PLUS could be used for this purpose?

TRY IT YOURSELF

1. Produce a report that is similar to the one below from the CHARITY database in the Try It Yourself exercises in Chapter 3.

```
Page No.        1
01/01/88                        DONATIONS

DATE                NAME OF PATRON          AMOUNT

03/08/88            GARCIA                   21.50
01/12/88            NEILSON                 120.00
02/13/88            ZUCCO                   325.00
03/15/88            NORTON                   34.50

*** Total ***                               501.00
```

2. Execute the following commands:
   a. COPY the .FRM file from Try It Yourself Exercise 8 in Chapter 3 to a file called PATRON.FRM.

    b. COPY the structure of the .DBF file CREATEd in Try It Yourself Exercise 2 in Chapter 3 to a file named TEMP.DBF.

    c. COUNT the number of records with contributions over $25. Then SUM and AVERAGE the contributions.

    d. Show a directory of all .FRM files.

    e. Display the settings for the programmable function keys.

3. Print a set of labels for the data in Try It Yourself Exercise 2 in Chapter 3. Include only the name of the patron in alphabetical order. Print a sample first.

4. Produce labels, as in the preceding exercise, for those patrons who contributed more than $100. Make a copy of the label file under a different name.

5. Display a list of all the commands you have issued while completing these exercises.

6. Erase the file copy you made in Exercise 4 above.

7. Make a copy of the CITIES database. Add a date-type field called FOUNDED. Practice putting data in the new field by means of BROWSE.

8. Add a logical field called INCORP and add data the way you did in the previous exercise.

9. Use the CITIES database. Move the record pointer in the following ways:

    a. Move to record 4.

    b. Skip to record 7.

    c. Move to the top of the file.

    d. Skip backward one record.

10. Move the record pointer to any city in Pennsylvania. Move the record pointer to all other Pennsylvania cities.

11. Index the CITIES database by state, and LIST. Are the cities in alphabetical order within each state?

12. Attempt to index by the FOUNDED field, and LIST.

13. Append your city to CITIES.DBF. Reactivate the state index and LIST. Does your city appear? Attempt to LOCATE your city by name.

14. Move the record pointer to the bottom of the file and DISPLAY. What appears on the screen? Why?

15. Attempt to index by the logical field in Exercise 8, and LIST. Can you LOCATE by INCORP?

PART II

PROGRAMMING

5

INITIAL
PROGRAMMING SKILLS

LEARNING OBJECTIVES

1. To understand the procedures and advantages of programming.
2. To use the features of MODIFY COMMAND.
3. To use pseudocode and debugging procedures in program development.
4. To examine the principles of structured programming.
5. To use the STORE command in order to create and use memory variables.
6. To identify the differences between numeric and character-type data.

Chapter

5

INITIAL PROGRAMMING SKILLS

You have learned a great deal about dBASE III PLUS in the last four chapters. All the powerful functions and operations you have performed have been in the interactive mode or from the dot prompt. All your experience may make it difficult to believe the fact that programming will increase the range of tasks you can perform and at the same time make dBASE III PLUS easier to use. Besides these benefits, programming offers others. You will learn to approach problems in a more effective way and to plan in a logical sequence. Finally, you will have the satisfaction of creating something useful and the enjoyment of watching it perform.

5.1 ADVANTAGES OF PROGRAMMING

In Chapter 3, you operated at command level, or from the dot prompt. This means that commands that are typed execute immediately after you press the Return key. The command must be retyped for each repetition. You also learned that the Assist option will relieve you of the necessity of typing any commands at all. You can use menus that prompt you for your intentions; your responses then issue the commands automatically. Although many people regularly work with their data in this way, you will surely want to take advantage of the power and flexibility of the extensive programming capability of dBASE III PLUS.

Programming in dBASE III PLUS is the process of grouping normal dBASE III PLUS commands in a special file that contains a .PRG extension. This file can then be run so that the commands it contains will execute one at a time, in order. Once the .PRG file is saved on the disk, it can be executed with the DO command as often as you wish. This is like making a list of chores and performing the listed tasks in order every Saturday morning, rather than doing one chore, then trying to decide which chore to do next, and repeating this random process indefinitely.

This chapter will explain how to plan, code, revise, and debug programs in dBASE III PLUS. In later chapters, you will see how several programs can be organized into a system to perform a number of useful functions.

Let's return now to the .PRG file. The commands stored in it will be read and executed one at a time by dBASE III PLUS. The computer will be operating in batch mode at this point. This means that predefined tasks are being performed in a set order. As an analogy, you might think of a player piano. When a set of instructions, encoded on the piano roll, is inserted and run, the player piano appears to play itself. But the roll must be encoded with music that the listener wishes to hear. Similarly, if the instructions are correct and the needs of the user are met, the computer program will be successful.

Some formal methods and procedures associated with the proper construction of programs will be addressed later in this chapter. For now it may be more helpful to use the following strategy for your first efforts.

1. List the actions you wish to perform, step by step, in plain English.
2. Translate the actions into dBASE III PLUS commands that you already know.
3. Type the commands into a file using the text editor, MODIFY COMMAND (see section 5.2).
4. Test the program by running it with a DO command.
5. Evaluate the performance and consider modifications.
6. Use MODIFY COMMAND to change the program.
7. Repeat steps 4, 5, and 6 until you are satisfied.

An experienced programmer once made the comment that a good program is never finished. Step 7 seems to reinforce this idea, which expresses the essence of what programmers do much of the time. You will find that adjusting to this cycle of development is a familiar process. You did something very similar when you learned how to use note cards, outlines, drafts and, of course, revisions, to write a term paper. In the next few pages you will see how a programmer, faced with the need to perform a series of steps over and over again, designs and codes programs in dBASE III PLUS.

First, though, you need to learn about the text editor in dBASE III PLUS, which is called MODIFY COMMAND.

5.2 USING MODIFY COMMAND

The purpose of MODIFY COMMAND is to allow you to create programs, which are sometimes called command files. It can also be used as an elementary word processor for other tasks. MODIFY COMMAND operates from the dot prompt. It should include the name of the file you wish to create or modify. If you do not specify a file, dBASE III PLUS will prompt you for a name. If you do not include a DOS extension, .PRG will be assigned to your file name on the disk. Study the following examples:

```
. MODIFY COMMAND TEST
or
. MODIFY COMMAND
ENTER FILE NAME: TEST
```

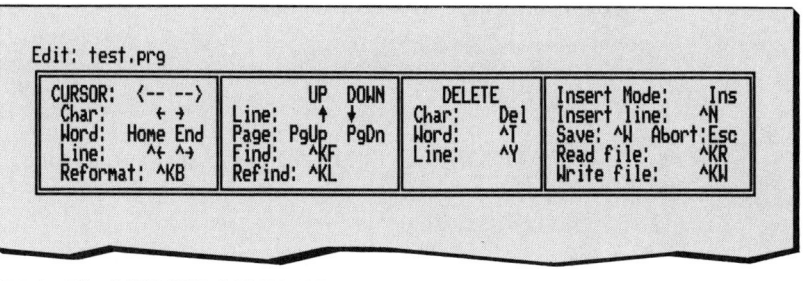

Edit: test.prg

CURSOR: <-- -->	UP DOWN	DELETE	Insert Mode: Ins
Char: ← →	Line: ↑ ↓	Char: Del	Insert line: ^N
Word: Home End	Page: PgUp PgDn	Word: ^T	Save: ^W Abort:Esc
Line: ^← ^→	Find: ^KF	Line: ^Y	Read file: ^KR
Reformat: ^KB	Refind: ^KL		Write file: ^KW

FIGURE 5.1   *The MODIFY COMMAND screen.*

You will be presented with a blank work area and a Help menu that contains available key functions. The Help portion of the screen can be turned on or off with the F1 key. Although the most frequently used keys are described below, it would be useful to experiment with all the listed keys.

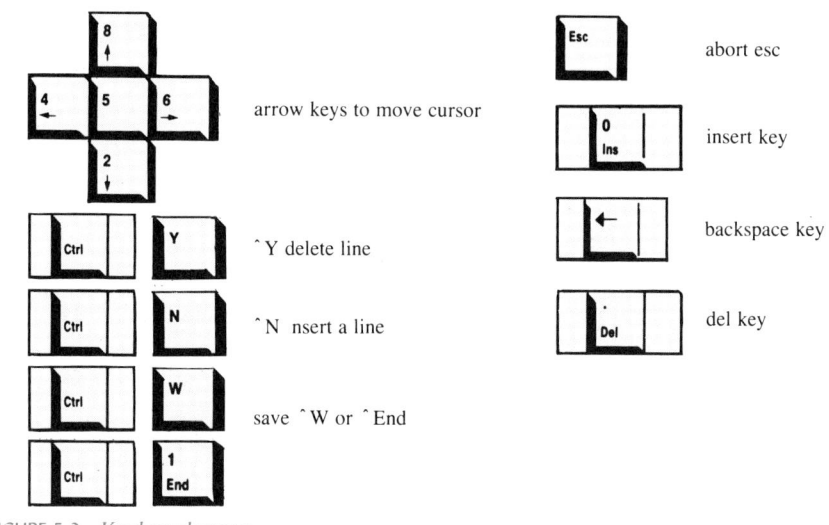

arrow keys to move cursor

^Y delete line

^N nsert a line

save ^W or ^End

abort esc

insert key

backspace key

del key

FIGURE 5.2   *Keyboard usage.*

You must press the Return key at the end of each command. When you do, a < symbol will appear at the end of the line. You may type in uppercase or lowercase; however, uppercase will be used for dBASE III PLUS commands in this text. Spaces can be placed anywhere in the line, but the length of a line cannot exceed 256 characters. As you begin to type near the right margin, MODIFY COMMAND will automatically wrap around to the next line. As long as you do not press the Return key at the end of the line, dBASE III PLUS will correctly process a command that is split in this way. If you wish to place a return at the end of a split command, end it with a semicolon.

```
LIST CITY, POP_82 FOR
  STATE = 'CA'
```

Use MODIFY COMMAND to type in the following program:

```
* Test.prg
        DIR *.PRG
```

The first line of the program begins with an asterisk (*) that identifies the line as a comment or note. Get in the habit of placing such lines in your programs to identify and document what is occurring. Comments can be placed in a .PRG file by preceding the line with an asterisk, two ampersands, or NOTE. The asterisk is easier to type and is therefore less prone to error than && or NOTE. However, the && may be placed at the end of a command line, while the * declares the entire line a comment.

```
* Test.prg
        DIR *.PRG
        *          This is a comment
        &&         So is this
        NOTE       and this
```

Save the program on your disk by pressing and holding the Ctrl key, pressing the End key, and releasing both keys simultaneously. The program will be stored on the disk as TEST.PRG. Execute the program with the DO command. As you might expect, the program does nothing with the comment lines but does display a directory of .PRG files.

```
              .  DO TEST

TEST.PRG

       30 bytes in      1 files.
13443072 bytes remaining on drive.
```

FIGURE 5.3 *Execution of a .PRG file.*

Changes can be made to the program by typing MODIFY COMMAND TEST again. When the screen appears, you can add, delete, or change commands at will, then save the .PRG file again with the Ctrl-End keys. Add two commands to the program that will turn on communications with the printer before the DIR and then turn them off after the command. Make certain that the printer is ready before executing the program with the DO command.

```
* Test.prg
        SET PRINT ON
        DIR *.PRG
        SET PRINT OFF

        *      This is a comment
        &&     So is this
        NOTE  and this
```

FIGURE 5.4 *Modifying a .PRG file.*

If you enter MODIFY COMMAND and decide not to change the program, press the Escape key (Esc) to exit without saving. This procedure of changing, saving, and testing is repeated until the programmer is satisfied with the perform- ance of the program. Become comfortable with the procedure by adding, deleting, and changing comment lines in the TEST.PRG file and experimenting with the keys in the MODIFY COMMAND menu.

It is sometimes helpful to have a hard copy of your program for study when you are away from the computer. If the program is less than one full screen, simply press the shift and the PrtScr keys simultaneously. A snapshot of the screen's con- tents will print, providing the printer is on and is correctly set. Longer programs may be printed through the use of either of the following command sequences:

```
.  TYPE TEST.PRG TO PRINT
or
.  SET PRINT ON
.  TYPE TEST.PRG
.  SET PRINT OFF
```

Notice that the .PRG extension was required in the TYPE command. This is because TYPE can be used to print other types of files. DOS, which actually exe- cutes the command, requires the full file name.

The steps outlined on the previous page are only the means for putting commands in the file. A great deal more than this is involved in building a program. Before the computer is turned on, complete a clear and effective plan.

5.3 PLANNING A PROGRAM

After you have written a number of programs (and made a few mistakes), you will begin to develop both a style and an organized way of working. Some techniques and structures that provide programming standards and guidance are presented below and in Chapter 9.

A convenient way to begin planning a program is to briefly state in plain language the tasks that the program must perform. Although it may be necessary to add, delete, or change some steps later, you should be able to specify most of the required tasks. A list of tasks in logical order is often called *pseudocode*. The example below illustrates how pseudocode might be written.

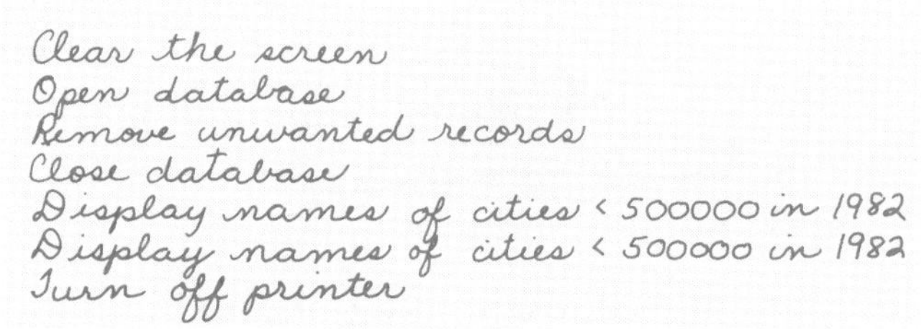

> Clear the screen
> Open database
> Remove unwanted records
> Close database
> Display names of cities < 500000 in 1982
> Display names of cities < 500000 in 1982
> Turn off printer

FIGURE 5.5   *Example of pseudocode.*

Figure 5.5 is an example of pseudocode for a program that will attempt to clean up a database by PACKing it and that will then display some data on the printer. The programmer thought through the pseudocode and made the following changes which are shown in the pseudocode in Figure 5.6.

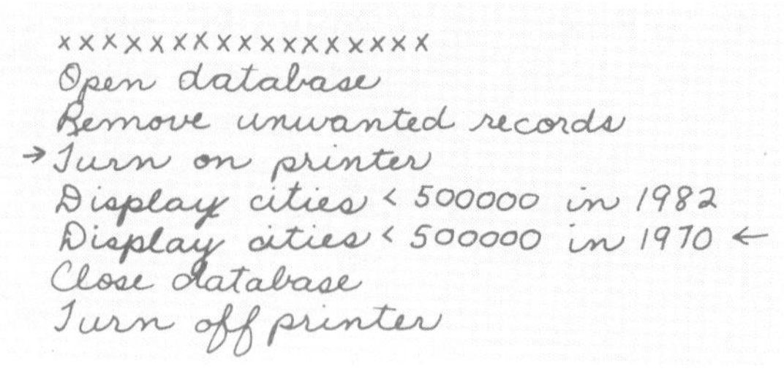

> x x x x x x x x x x x x x x x x x
> Open database
> Remove unwanted records
> → Turn on printer
> Display cities < 500000 in 1982
> Display cities < 500000 in 1970 ←
> Close database
> Turn off printer

FIGURE 5.6   *Modifying pseudocode.*

Figure 5.6 shows how easily pseudocode can be changed. Steps can be added, deleted, moved, or modified until the purpose of the program appears to be satisfied. Then the pseudocode must be translated into acceptable dBASE III PLUS commands and tested. Figure 5.7 illustrates the translation, and Figure 5.8 shows a test run of the commands.

x x x x x x x x x x x x x x x x	
Open database	USE CITIES
Remove unwanted records	PACK
Turn on printer	SET PRINT ON
Display cities < 500000 in 1982	LIST FOR POP_82<500000
Display cities < 500000 in 1970	LIST FOR POP_70<500000
Close database	CLOSE
Turn off printer	SET PRINT OFF

FIGURE 5.7 *Converting pseudocode to commands.*

The dBASE III PLUS commands in Figure 5.7 can be placed in a .PRG file with MODIFY COMMAND and can be executed with a DO from the dot prompt. This step in the process is referred to as *coding*. That the commands are typed into the computer does not mean that the resulting program is complete or correct. It is simply your best first effort, and it must be tested. As you will discover, programs very rarely run correctly the first time. When the program in Figure 5.7 is executed, an error is detected by dBASE III PLUS, as shown in the following figure.

```
* TEST2.PRG
  USE CITIES
  PACK
  CLOSE
  SET PRINT ON
  LIST FOR POP_82<500000
  LIST FOR POP_70<500000
  SET PRINT OFF

        . DO TEST2.PRG

     11 records copied
Unrecognized phrase/keyword in command.
        ?
    CLOSE
Called from - C:TEST2.PRG
Cancel, Ignore, or Suspend? (C, I, or S) Cancel
Do cancelled
```

FIGURE 5.8 *Example of a syntax error.*

TEST2.PRG will have to be changed by means of MODIFY COMMAND and then tested again. Because this program is not complicated, it will not require many revisions. As you work through the process of finding errors, correcting them, and retesting, you will notice that some errors are the result of mistyping or misunderstanding the *syntax* (rules) of a command. This is what happened in Figure 5.8.

The command CLOSE must be written as CLOSE ALL or CLOSE DATA-BASES. When the program was executed, dBASE III PLUS detected the error, paused, and asked if you would prefer to cancel, ignore, or suspend the execution of the .PRG file. Press C to cancel. The printer is still responding to any commands you type, because the SET PRINT OFF command never executed. Type the command from the dot prompt to stop it. Type MODIFY COMMAND TEST2 to change the CLOSE to CLOSE ALL, and run the program again. The results of this rerun are shown in Figure 5.9.

```
* TEST2.PRG
  USE CITIES
  PACK
  CLOSE ALL
  SET PRINT ON
  LIST FOR POP_82<500000
  LIST FOR POP_70<500000
  SET PRINT OFF


        . DO TEST2

     11 records copied
No database is in USE. Enter file name: CITIES
Record#  CITY                    STATE  POP_70  POP_82
      6  MIAMI                   FL     334859  382726
      8  PITTSBURGH              PA     520089  414936
Record#  CITY                    STATE  POP_70  POP_82
      6  MIAMI                   FL     334859  382726
```

FIGURE 5.9 *Correcting a syntax error.*

Although dBASE III PLUS detected no errors this time, there does appear to be a problem. When a program runs but does not perform as expected, a logic error has probably been committed. This means that a command is missing, has been misplaced, or has not been used effectively. In this case, the .DBF file was closed after the PACK, and the LIST commands could not operate. The user (you, in this case) must type in the name of the .DBF file in order to complete the execution of the program. The obvious solution is to move the CLOSE ALL command to a more appropriate location, and Figure 5.10 shows this correction.

```
* TEST2.PRG
  USE CITIES
  PACK
  SET PRINT ON
  LIST FOR POP_82<500000
  LIST FOR POP_70<500000
  CLOSE ALL
  SET PRINT OFF


           . DO TEST2

     11 records copied
Record#  CITY                    STATE  POP_70  POP_82
      6  MIAMI                   FL     334859  382726
      8  PITTSBURGH              PA     520089  414936
Record#  CITY                    STATE  POP_70  POP_82
      6  MIAMI                   FL     334859  382726
```

FIGURE 5.10 *Correcting a command position error.*

Logic errors can be very difficult to find when programs are complicated. dBASE III PLUS provides a way to obtain a step-by-step listing of the commands in your program as they execute. This listing can be compared with the program in order to study its behavior. SET ECHO ON will display each command in the .PRG file as it executes. If SET PRINT ON was previously typed, the commands will be sent to the printer as well. As you can see from Figure 5.11, you will have to separate the commands from the results of the program.

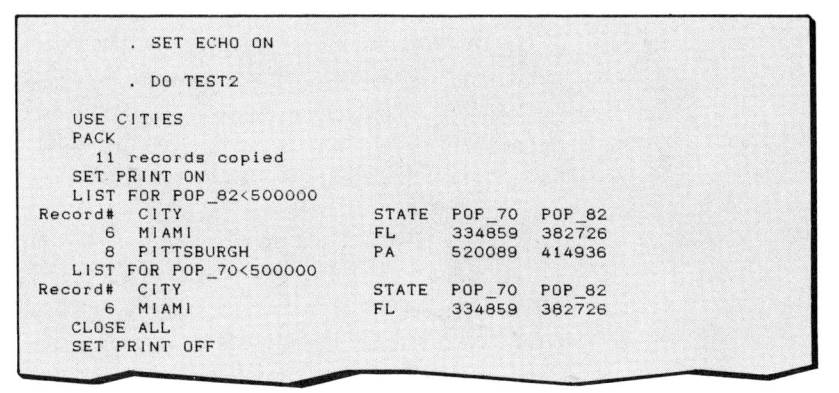

```
. SET ECHO ON

. DO TEST2

USE CITIES
PACK
    11 records copied
SET PRINT ON
LIST FOR POP_82<500000
Record#   CITY                STATE   POP_70   POP_82
     6    MIAMI               FL      334859   382726
     8    PITTSBURGH          PA      520089   414936
LIST FOR POP_70<500000
Record#   CITY                STATE   POP_70   POP_82
     6    MIAMI               FL      334859   382726
CLOSE ALL
SET PRINT OFF
```

FIGURE 5.11 *Using SET ECHO ON.*

Consider some of the potential advantages and benefits of this brief program, now that it is working as expected.

1. Future executions of the program will accurately reflect any changes in the data, including APPENDs, DELETEs, and EDITs.
2. A person who is not familiar with dBASE III PLUS can run the program and produce results with very little instruction.
3. As the needs of the user change, modifications can be made to the existing program; it is not necessary to begin all over again.
4. Time is wasted on typing errors and on incorrect syntax when commands are typed interactively (from the dot prompt), especially if the same commands are used on a regular basis. Once the program is correct, this is no longer a problem.
5. The data in the files is safer if the standardized and tested procedures in the program are used instead of haphazard or poorly chosen interactive commands.

5.4 PROPER FORM

The work of innovators such as Edsger W. Dijkstra, Larry L. Constantine, Edward Yourdon, and others has produced some programming principles that enjoy wide acceptance among data processing professionals. These principles define what is known as structured programming. The general goals of structured programming are to ensure that programs will operate in an organized and predictable manner and that programmers can understand each other's work.

Although much can be said for individuality and creativity in programming, the business environment requires accountability. This means that projects must be completed in a cost-effective manner. It is difficult, if not impossible, to estimate the amount of time and money a program will consume if the programming methods to be used are understood by the programmer alone. Structured programs are developed in less time and are more easily maintained than those which are written freestyle.

Large organizations depend on structured programming because teams of programmers are often assigned to one project. With respect to programs that can be universally understood, one programmer can substitute for another if necessary. It has also been demonstrated that structured programs require less "debugging" than programs that are written in a loose, haphazard manner.

Common Features of Structured Programs

Comments	— It is always preferable to include enough comments so that the reader can follow the logic of the program, without the listing being cluttered.
Indention	— Since dBASE III PLUS ignores spaces, indent where appropriate and include blank lines between sections.
Design	— The primary consideration is the design of the program, which must be complete before coding can begin. If the design is flawed, the program can never perform satisfactorily.
Top-down Design	— Proceed from the general to the specific when designing the program. Large tasks should be broken down into subtasks.
Modularity	— Each section should be a freestanding module that can be tested and that can function on its own.

No Direct Branching — Since dBASE III PLUS has no direct branching statement such as the GOTO in BASIC
or COBOL, and since it uses block structured commands, it encourages structured
programming.

No Infinite Loops — Looping must be controlled by a structure of
some type.

Some of these features may not be clear to you at this time; they will be
discussed in later chapters. Other features such as the use of comments, indention,
and top-down design, can become part of your programming practice immediately.

5.5 MEMORY VARIABLES

An essential part of any programming environment is the capability to store data in
the computer's *random access memory* (RAM) for temporary use while a program is
executing. The way in which this storage is accomplished is the same in most
programming languages. The data is STOREd in a memory location, which must be
labeled. The name provided will allow the program to reference the data location by
the memory variable name regardless of what specific data happens to be STOREd
there at the moment. The STORE command is used for this purpose in programs.
Memory variable names may be between one and ten characters long. They should
follow the same restrictions as DOS file names (Chapter 2). You can use the underscore (_) in the name.

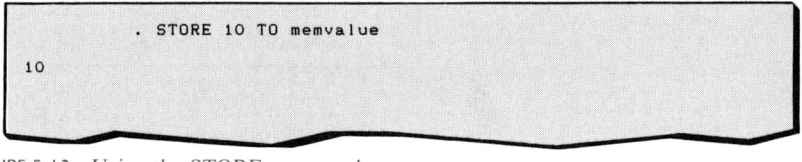

FIGURE 5.12 *Using the STORE command.*

Figure 5.12 illustrates how the STORE command can be used to place a
numeric value in a memory variable. By displaying the contents, dBASE III PLUS
verifies the operation. LIST MEMORY or DISPLAY MEMORY will provide the
current status of all memory variables that are currently active. Either command is
useful for studying how memory variables operate, and either can be used as a
debugging tool.

```
     . LIST MEMORY

MEMVALUE          pub   N           10  (          10.00000000)
    1 variables defined,            9 bytes used
  255 variables available,       5991 bytes available

     . DISPLAY MEMORY

MEMVALUE          pub   N           10  (          10.00000000)
    1 variables defined,            9 bytes used
  255 variables available,       5991 bytes available
```

FIGURE 5.13   *Viewing the contents of memory.*

The contents of a memory variable can be redefined with a second STORE command.

```
     . STORE 10 + 12 TO memvalue

  22

     . STORE 15 + memvalue TO memvalue

     37

     . LIST MEMORY

MEMVALUE          pub   N           37  (          37.00000000)
    1 variables defined,            9 bytes used
  255 variables available,       5991 bytes available
```

FIGURE 5.14   *Redefining a memory variable.*

If several memory variables must be assigned the same value, separate the names with commas, as in Figure 5.15.

```
     . STORE 16 TO memfirst, memsecond, memthird

  16


     . LIST MEMORY

MEMVALUE          pub   N           37  (          37.00000000)
MEMFIRST          pub   N           16  (          16.00000000)
MEMSECOND         pub   N           16  (          16.00000000)
MEMTHIRD          pub   N           16  (          16.00000000)
    4 variables defined,           36 bytes used
  252 variables available,       5964 bytes available
```

FIGURE 5.15   *Assigning multiple memory variables.*

A memory variable's type is determined by the data that is being STOREd. In the example on the opposite page, a character literal defines the type of the memory variable "capitol". Programmers often use lowercase letters for memory variables in order to distinguish them from commands. The prefix m or mem is also used for this purpose.

```
        . memcapitol = "JEFFERSON CITY"

JEFFERSON CITY

        . LIST MEMORY

MEMVALUE      pub    N           37  (         37.00000000)
MEMFIRST      pub    N           16  (         16.00000000)
MEMSECOND     pub    N           16  (         16.00000000)
MEMTHIRD      pub    N           16  (         16.00000000)
MEMCAPITOL    pub    C   "JEFFERSON CITY"
    5 variables defined,        52 bytes used
  251 variables available,    5948 bytes available
```

FIGURE 5.16 *Character-type memory variables.*

The ? can be used to print the contents of memory variables on the screen or the printer (with SET PRINT ON). If the + sign is used between character variables, the two will be "pasted" together; this is a process known as *concatenation*. Of course, when the + sign is used between numeric variables, addition is assumed.

```
        . ? memcapitol + ', MISSOURI'

JEFFERSON CITY, MISSOURI

        . ? memfirst + memthird

        32

        . LIST MEMORY

MEMVALUE      pub    N           37  (         37.00000000)
MEMFIRST      pub    N           16  (         16.00000000)
MEMSECOND     pub    N           16  (         16.00000000)
MEMTHIRD      pub    N           16  (         16.00000000)
MEMCAPITOL    pub    C   "JEFFERSON CITY"
    5 variables defined,        52 bytes used
  251 variables available,    5948 bytes available
```

FIGURE 5.17 *Using the ? command.*

Data that is stored in memory variables is easily lost, since it is in the computer's memory rather than in a file on a disk. If you leave dBASE III PLUS or turn off the power, memory variables are erased.

5.6 NUMERIC VERSUS CHARACTER

Although there are five data or field types available in dBASE III PLUS, character and numeric are used most frequently. It is essential that you understand the purpose of and the differences between these two data types.

In Chapter 3, you learned that fields that might be used in an arithmetic operation should be declared numeric during CREATE. In a business environment, this generally means either money or an inventory of items. It may be difficult on occasion to decide which type a certain field should be. Below are some examples of fields followed by explanations of the proper choice of field type.

```
111-11-1111      Social Security number
```

Although this field contains no letters, it does contain hyphens. These would not be accepted by dBASE III PLUS as negative (minus) signs because they do not precede the field and because there is more than one of them. Further, a Social Security number would probably not be used in a calculation. Given these reasons, the field should be declared as character.

```
12/88            December 1988
```

Dates are always stored in date-type fields that include the month, day, and year. (Chapter 13 will explain how to do arithmetic with dates.)

```
SKU-101-24636    Furniture Inventory Number
```

The letters SKU and the hyphens require this to be a character-type field.

```
22               Person's age
```

It is usually best to record age as the date of birth in a date-type field. However, it would be possible to store 22 as a numeric field and use it in a calculation, such as the average age of a group.

```
.007             Tolerance in a manufacturing process
```

This field would probably be useful for calculation and should be declared numeric.

```
200000.00        Salary of the president of the United States
```

Money is almost always declared as numeric. It is primarily because the last three examples could be used in an arithmetic operation that they should be numeric-type fields. Consider which type would be most appropriate for fields as you encounter data in daily life.

When specific data is used in dBASE III PLUS, some rules must be followed for expressing it. A specific piece of character data, which may be referred to as a *string*, a *label*, an *alphanumeric literal*, or an *alphanumeric constant*, must always be enclosed in a matched set of quotation marks. You can use single or double quotes if the same symbol is placed before and after the data. Square brackets may also be used.

```
'SOUTH DAKOTA'
"Wayne Ratliff"
[dBASE III PLUS]
```

If the symbols surrounding a string do not match, dBASE III PLUS will generate an error.

```
        . ? "1600 Pennsylvania Avenue'

Unterminated string.
                                ?
? "1600 Pennsylvania Avenue'
Do you want some help? (Y/N) No


        . ? "1600 Pennsylvania Avenue"

1600 Pennsylvania Avenue
```

FIGURE 5.18 *Result of unmatched quotation marks.*

Conversely, when specific numeric data is being referenced, it is never enclosed in quotation marks or square brackets. This type of data is sometimes called a *value*, a *numeric constant*, or a *numeric literal*. Care must be taken not to include stray symbols such as letters, dollar signs, or commas in numeric data.

```
        . ? 12 * "3"

Data type mismatch.
              ?
? 12 * "3"
Do you want some help? (Y/N) No
```

FIGURE 5.19 *Data type mismatch.*

The quotation marks in the example above express the character symbol "3", not the numeric value 3. The problem was detected by dBASE III PLUS, which could not perform the calculation. The corrected statement follows.

```
        . ? 12 * 3

   36

        . ? 2 + $4,500.00

Syntax error.
        ?
? 2 + $4,500.00
Do you want some help? (Y/N) No
```

FIGURE 5.20 *Effect of $ and , in numeric fields.*

Usually dollar signs and commas are included when one is dealing with money, but these characters are not permitted in numeric fields. The value should be expressed as 4500.00.

```
        . ? 2 + 4500.00

   4502.00
```

FIGURE 5.21 *Corrected numeric field.*

Although pi is often used in mathematics, it is not recognized by dBASE III PLUS (a number of arithmetic functions are discussed in Chapter 13). You must provide the actual value of pi to perform the operation.

```
        . ? 45 * PI Variable not found.
                ?
? 45 * PI
Do you want some help? (Y/N) No

        . ? 45 * 3.14159

   141.37155
```

FIGURE 5.22 *Unrecognized arithmetic functions.*

Being careless with data types when expressing field names, memory variables, or specific data in programs will produce annoying errors. Figure 5.23 lists some key combinations that will be helpful for correcting errors when using MODIFY COMMAND. Mastering them now will save a great deal of time when you are writing longer programs in the chapters to follow.

Alternate Key Combinations

ˆG	Del—Delete character above cursor.
ˆV	Ins—Toggle between overwrite and insert.
ˆC	Pg Dn—Move down one screen or page.
ˆR	Pg Up—Move up one screen or page.
ˆE	Up Arrow—Move up one line.
ˆX	Down Arrow—Move down one line.
ˆS	Left Arrow—Move one position to the left.
ˆD	Right Arrow—Move one position to the right.
	Home—Move one word to the left.
	End—Move one word to the right.
	Ctrl-Q or Esc—Abort operation without saving.
	Ctrl-W or Ctrl-End—Save and exit.
ˆY	Delete a line.
ˆN	Insert a line.
ˆKB	Reformat block.
ˆKW	Write current file to a specified file.
ˆKR	Read in a specified file (added at cursor location).

FIGURE 5.23 *Alternate key combinations.*

CHAPTER SUMMARY

5.1

Sets of dBASE III PLUS commands that are saved on the disk with a .PRG extension and that can be executed with the DO command are called programs. Programs increase efficiency, flexibility, and power, and they are an effective way of solving complex business problems. An organized method of modifying and testing programs is essential.

5.2

MODIFY COMMAND is a text editor that facilitates the creating and modifying of programs. A variety of key combinations is available to manipulate commands within the .PRG file. Comments can be included by preceding the line with *, &&, or NOTE. TYPE < file name > TO PRINT will display a program on the printer.

5.3

Programs should be written in pseudocode before the actual dBASE III PLUS commands are coded. Doing this will help prevent logic errors caused by misplaced or missing commands. Commands must be spelled and expressed correctly or the program will stop, owing to a syntax error. SET ECHO ON displays the commands as they execute; this is helpful in debugging.

5.4

Structured programming is a set of principles that encourages the development of clear, well-organized programs. Comments, indention, and top-down design are some of the features of this important concept.

5.5

Memory variables are used to hold data temporarily during the execution of a program. They may be examined with LIST MEMORY or DISPLAY MEMORY. The STORE command requires a name and a specific piece of data in order to establish the memory·variable.

5.6

Data should be declared numeric if it is going to be used in an arithmetic operation. Numeric data can contain digits, commas, and a negative sign. Character data is always enclosed in a matched set of quotation marks, while numeric data is not.

KEY TERMS

pseudocode	label
coding	alphanumeric constant
syntax	alphanumeric literal
random access memory (RAM)	value
concatenation	numeric constant
string	numeric literal

COMMAND SUMMARY

MODIFY COMMAND — Edit a file with the MODIFY COMMAND text editor.
* — Comment.
&& — End-of-line comment.
NOTE — Comment.
CLOSE ALL — Close all open files.
SET ECHO ON — Display commands as they execute.
SET PRINT ON — Activate the printer.
STORE — Place a value in a memory variable.
LIST MEMORY — Display the contents of memory.

dBUG dBASE

- Debugging is the process of finding errors in a program and correcting them. Since the debugging of a program can consume as much as half of the programmer's development time, it is wise to learn to use the available techniques and features. You will find helpful dBUG dBASE sections at the end of most of the remaining chapters.
- It is very important to keep backup copies of your programs in case something should happen to your work disk. Making a backup copy takes only a few minutes with the COPY FILE in dBASE III PLUS or with the COPY command in DOS. Many hours of work can be lost in an instant as the result of having no backup.
- When a program is not working as expected, you can examine a "play-by-play" listing of the commands as they executed by using LIST HISTORY as an alternative to SET ECHO ON. The default is twenty commands, but you can increase the size of the HISTORY buffer with SET HISTORY TO 100, for example. Use SET PRINT ON to obtain a printed copy.
- Get in the habit of constantly monitoring the dBASE III PLUS environment with the following commands. You can often spot an unanticipated problem simply by frequently checking the disk, memory, structure, and status.

DIR	DISPLAY STRUCTURE
DISPLAY FILES	LIST STRUCTURE
DISPLAY MEMORY	LIST FILES
DISPLAY STATUS	LIST STATUS

SELF-CHECK QUESTIONS

1. What are some of the advantages of programming?
2. Is writing a program always the best way to use dBASE III PLUS?
3. How can you tell when a program is finished?
4. Why are comment lines important?
5. Why would you want to exit MODIFY COMMAND without saving the file?
6. Why is a printed copy of a program useful?
7. Why is pseudocode useful? Wouldn't it be easier to immediately type the program into the computer?
8. If a program has a significant number of syntax errors, is it fair to say that it was poorly designed? Would you say that a program containing many logic errors had been poorly designed?
9. Why is data safer when it is maintained and accessed by good programs as opposed to interactive use?

10. What is the danger in planning bottom-up rather than top-down, in other words, in programming details first and then moving on to the larger aspects of the program?

11. Why might overuse of a direct branching statement, such as the GOTO in BASIC, be harmful to program design?

12. Why is it important to be aware of the data type when working with memory variables?

13. What is the danger in holding data in memory variables?

14. Is there a way to include quotation marks when printing a character string (Example: "Garbage In, Garbage Out")?

TRY IT YOURSELF

1. Use MODIFY COMMAND to create the .PRG file below.

```
* EX.PRG
* This will illustrate how MODIFY COMMAND is used.
```

After saving EX.PRG on your disk, use MODIFY COMMAND and the available key functions to change the program, as shown below:

```
* EX.PRG
* This is a program modification.
* This program will illustrate how MODIFY COMMAND is used.
```

2. Use the DIR command to display all .PRG files on your disk. Display a copy of the program in Exercise 1 on the screen and then on the printer.

3. Use the memory variables memrate and memhour to STORE 4.75 and 37, respectively. Write another STORE statement to calculate the product in memgross. List the memory variables. Change memrate to 5.25, and calculate memgross again.

4. Here is a section of pseudocode. Study the sequence of the tasks and determine whether the pseudocode will execute properly when converted to dBASE III PLUS commands. Make corrections if necessary.

   Open the database.
   Display cities in California.
   Turn off the printer.
   Display names of .DBF files.
   Clear the screen.

5. Write a dBASE III PLUS program on paper, using the pseudocode in Exercise 4. Evaluate and modify the program until you are satisfied that it works properly.

6. Write a short program that consists of several comment lines and that utilizes all three symbols for comment lines. Try all the features displayed in the Help panel, including deleting and inserting lines and characters, and moving around the file by line, word, and character.

7. Using the program in Exercise 6, try word-wrap and the use of the semicolon to break a line. Print a copy of the program.

8. Store your first name to one memory variable and your last name to another. Display them together on the screen. Store both names to a single memory variable.

9. Store 28 in memone and 32 in memtwo. Store the sum in memtot. If you now store 15 in memone, will memtot change?

10. Store the perimeter and the area of a 9 by 12 feet room in two memory variables.

11. Using the ˆ sign for exponentiation, store increasingly larger values in a memory variable in order to test the limits of dBASE III PLUS and your system (example: memval = 10 ˆ 20).

PROGRAMMING PROJECT

Write a program that will STORE your last name to the memory variable memlast and that will assign the first names of other members of your family to memfirst1, memfirst2, and so on. Include ? statements to print a list of the full names of the family members on the printer.

THE
DO WHILE/ENDDO
LOOP

LEARNING OBJECTIVES

1. To construct and use the DO WHILE/ENDDO loop.
2. To examine the effect of the DO WHILE/ENDDO on program control.
3. To code and test several types of DO WHILE/ENDDO loops.

Chapter

6

THE DO WHILE/ENDDO LOOP

Since computers are machines, they never become bored with their work. If you were asked to repeat the same menial task a hundred or a thousand times you would probably not be pleased. The capability of computers to repeat operations is one of the features that make them so valuable to the business world. As you have learned, computers cannot operate without specific instructions for all activity, including repetition. This chapter presents the DO WHILE/ENDDO, the commands that control repetition, or looping, in dBASE III PLUS. The ability to construct looping structures effectively is vital to a programmer's success.

6.1 CONSTRUCTING THE DO WHILE/ENDDO

The DO WHILE/ENDDO loop is the primary control structure in dBASE III PLUS programming. Since it is, at minimum, a two-command structure, it can be used only in a program, not interactively (from the dot prompt).

Think of this structure as a sandwich. The DO WHILE statement is the upper slice of bread and the ENDDO is the lower slice. The most important part of the sandwich (the meat, cheese, etc.) will consist of normal dBASE III PLUS commands that you wish to repeat a certain number of times. These commands will be placed between the DO WHILE and ENDDO.

```
DO WHILE.....
    ?   CITY, STATE
    SKIP
ENDDO
```

FIGURE 6.1 *The DO WHILE/ENDDO sandwich.*

Notice that there is a space between the DO and the WHILE command but none in the ENDDO command. Another important thing to know is that these commands are always used as a pair (no open-faced sandwiches, please).

Before attempting to construct a DO WHILE loop, you should understand how it operates. Some sort of qualifying expression has to be placed after the command DO WHILE. This expression will determine how many times the loop will execute or under what conditions the loop will cease to operate.

College students might express a spring vacation this way:

```
DO WHILE not in Florida

        Drive a mile

ENDDO

        Enjoy the beach
```

This example would obviously not work in dBASE III PLUS, but the same logic would apply in an actual program. The action placed between DO WHILE and ENDDO, "Drive a mile," must be repeated until the expression after DO WHILE, "not in Florida," is no longer true. This would mean that the students would have to be in Florida for the action following the ENDDO, "Enjoy the beach," to occur.

You will find that the expression following the DO WHILE is often stated in the negative, because you want the action statements to continue to execute as long as the test to leave the loop is not true. It is also important to note that this exit test is always at the top of the structure. This is an aspect of structured programmming, and it also follows from common sense. Before commencing an activity one needs to decide whether the activity is appropriate. This is the reason why a structure should not execute unless the test condition is satisfied first.

A good illustration of the DO WHILE loop is a counting loop. Use MODIFY COMMAND to create a .PRG file called LOOP. Your first step will be to initialize, or establish a value for, a variable called counter.

```
STORE 1 TO counter
or
counter = 1
```

You can then specify how many times you wish the loop to execute in the DO WHILE statement. In this case, you will express the test to exit the loop in a positive way.

```
DO WHILE counter < 11
```

What this means is that the loop will continue to operate as long as the variable called counter contains a value that is less than (<) 11. It should be apparent that you will require some means of incrementing or increasing the value of counter each time the loop executes. This can be accomplished by including another STORE command. Although this command appears to be a formula, it is actually a means of assigning a value to the "new" counter by incrementing the value of the "old" counter.

```
STORE counter + 1 TO counter
or
counter = counter + 1
```

Before this command, however, you should include a statement that will demonstrate that the loop is actually operating.

```
? 'Counter value is ', counter
```

The ? will print the literal, 'Counter value is ', on the screen, followed by the current value of counter (1, 2, 3, etc.). The comma separates the two parts of the print display. There will be a number of spaces between the two parts in order to display larger numbers.

Finally, all DO WHILE loops always conclude with an ENDDO command. The complete program follows:

```
* LOOP.PRG    demonstrates the DO WHILE loop
counter = 1
DO WHILE counter < 11
       ? 'Counter value is ', counter
       counter = counter + 1
ENDDO
```

FIGURE 6.2 A counting loop.

Press the Ctrl and the End keys simultaneously to save the program and exit MODIFY COMMAND, then execute the program by typing DO LOOP from the dot prompt.

The following display should appear on the screen:

```
1
Counter value is           1
       2
Counter value is           2
       3
Counter value is           3
       4
Counter value is           4
       5
Counter value is           5
       6
Counter value is           6
       7
Counter value is           7
       8
Counter value is           8
       9
Counter value is           9
      10
Counter value is          10
      11
```

FIGURE 6.3   *Execution of LOOP.PRG.*

The DO WHILE loop operates by testing the condition following the DO WHILE first. If the condition is logically true (counter is less than 11) then all the statements between the DO WHILE and the ENDDO are executed. This execution will continue until the ENDDO is encountered. Think of the ENDDO as a trampoline bouncing program control back up to the DO WHILE, where the condition must be tested again. The extra numbers that you see between each line display the value of counter each time it is changed with the counter = counter + 1 statement. You can remove this "system chatter" with the command:

```
. SET TALK OFF
```

In a properly constructed DO WHILE loop, the condition being tested will eventually not be true (counter will not be less than 11; it will be equal to 11). At that point, rather than executing the statements inside the loop, as it did previously, control will pass to the statement following ENDDO.

Since nothing follows the ENDDO in the LOOP program, you will have to add a command to test the action of exiting the loop. Type in the command MODIFY COMMAND LOOP from the dot prompt, and add the following statement after the ENDDO:

```
? 'Exit value of counter is ', counter
```

Save this modified version of the program by typing the Ctrl and End keys as usual, and DO the program. This time you will see the following display after 'Counter value is 10':

```
Exit value of counter is  11
```

One of the fundamentals of structured programming is that programs must be *self-documenting*. Two ways to accomplish this with DO WHILE/ENDDO loops are indention and the use of comments following the ENDDO. Indention of the commands placed between the DO WHILE and the ENDDO is essential for clarity. Chapter 9 will discuss *nesting*, a technique that places one loop within another. Without indention, it becomes very difficult to determine which commands are part of which structure.

Comments that are placed after the ENDDO are ignored by dBASE III PLUS. This is another effective way to self-document a program, because it establishes a visual connection between the DO WHILE and the ENDDO. The following two examples will illustrate how effective these techniques can be.

```
* STRUCTURED EXAMPLE

DO WHILE .NOT. EOF()
    DO WHILE row < 58
        ? 'CITY - ', CITY
        ? 'STATE - ', STATE
        ? '1970 POPULATION - ', POP_70
        ? '1982 POPULATION - ', POP_82
        ?
        SKIP
    ENDDO row < 58
ENDDO .NOT. EOF()
```

FIGURE 6.4 *Example of structured style.*

Notice how evident the two DO WHILE/ENDDO structures are in Figure 6.4. The indentions and the comments after the ENDDO contribute to the clarity of form.

In the following example it is very difficult to determine how the commands are related. The missing comments contribute to the ambiguity. If an ENDDO is forgotten, dBASE III PLUS executes the loop only once, while a missing DO WHILE will cause an endless loop.

```
DO WHILE .NOT. EOF()
DO WHILE ROW < 58
? 'CITY - ', CITY
? 'STATE - ', STATE
? '1970 POPULATION - ', POP_70
? '1982 POPULATION - ', POP_82
?
SKIP
ENDDO
ENDDO
```

FIGURE 6.5 *Example of unstructured style.*

It is important to be experienced in the proper construction of DO WHILE loops if you are to solve complex business problems. Very rarely does a program of any significance or value not use DO WHILE loops extensively.

Most DO WHILE commands require the use of a comparative expression. The effective construction of this portion of the DO WHILE/ENDDO is an essential skill. A comparative expression consists of two data items, which may be stored in memory variables or field names, separated by a relational operator. Once the expression has been established, dBASE III PLUS can evaluate it and decide whether it is logically true or false. This true or false condition will then be the basis for the continued execution of the DO WHILE/ENDDO.

The relational operators are used in mathematics and were presented in earlier chapters, so most of them will be familiar. The following signs will be accepted by dBASE III PLUS as valid:

=	equal to
<	less than
>	greater than
<=	less than or equal to
>=	greater than or equal to
<>	not equal to
#	not equal to

Never place a space between any of the combined relational operators such as < = .

The following examples illustrate the variety of expressions that can be constructed.

Memory variable compared to a literal (specific data):
```
memcount > 100
```

Field name compared to a literal:
```
CITY = 'KANSAS CITY'
```

Memory variable compared to a memory variable:
```
row <= max_row
```

Any comparative expression is allowed in dBASE III PLUS as long as the items on either side of the relational operator are of the same type. LOOP.PRG from Figure 6.2 has been modified in the following examples to illustrate how dBASE III PLUS reacts to mismatches of data types in comparative expressions. Figure 6.6 on the opposite page initializes the memory variable counter to a character literal '1' rather than the numeric value 1. Once counter has been established as a character-type variable with the quotes around '1', it cannot be compared to the numeric literal 11 in the DO WHILE. In response, dBASE III PLUS indicates a Data type mismatch error.

```
* LOOP.PRG
counter = '1'
DO WHILE counter < 11
    ? 'Counter value is ',counter counter = counter + 1
ENDDO counter < 11


        . DO LOOP


1
Data type mismatch.
                              ?
DO WHILE counter < 11
Called from - C:LOOP.prg
Cancel, Ignore, or Suspend? (C, I, or S) Cancel
Do cancelled
```

FIGURE 6.6 *Data type mismatch error.*

A more obvious example may be found in the following modification of LOOP. PRG. Although counter has been initialized as numeric, the DO WHILE is comparing it to the character literal 'ELEVEN'. The Data type mismatch error is generated by dBASE III PLUS in this case as well.

```
* TEST_ LOOP.PRG
  counter = 1
  DO WHILE counter < 'ELEVEN'
      ? 'Counter value is ',counter
  counter = counter + 1
ENDDO counter < 'ELEVEN'


        . DO LOOP 1

Data type mismatch.
                            ?
DO WHILE counter < 'ELEVEN'
Called from - C:LOOP.prg
Cancel, Ignore,or Suspend? (C, I, or S) Cancel
Do cancelled
```

FIGURE 6.7 *Another Data type mismatch error.*

Another common problem encountered in the construction of comparative expressions is inaccuracy in the use of the relational operator. Part of the difficulty is that the same comparison may often be made in several different ways. Consider the following examples:

```
AGE >= 18
AGE >  17

BALANCE <  500.01
BALANCE <= 500.00
```

People usually understand that when someone says, "You must be over 18 to vote," he or she means that you must be 18 or older to vote. We adjust to idiomatic usage of this type in everyday speech, but dBASE III PLUS evaluates an expression quite literally. In general discourse it may not be essential to mean what you say, but when you are programming you must be certain to say what you mean.

6.2 THE DO WHILE/ENDDO AND PROGRAM CONTROL

Effectively writing the expression that is placed after the DO WHILE is the key to using the structure for program control. Study the following examples and their effect on the execution of the program.

In Chapter 3, the logical .T. and .F. were introduced as field types. In the next example, the .T. is used to create a type of loop that is usually considered to be undesirable by programmers. Because the condition to end the loop is being preset as logically true (.T.), the DO WHILE loop will never end by itself. As you can see, you must press the Escape key (Esc) to interrupt, then the C key to cancel the program's execution.

```
      * ENDLESS.PRG
      DO WHILE .T.
                ? 'PLEASE PRESS THE ESCAPE KEY TO STOP THIS MADNESS!'
      ENDDO WHILE .T.


      . DO ENDLESS

PLEASE PRESS THE ESCAPE KEY TO STOP THIS MADNESS!
PLEASE PRESS THE ESCAPE KEY TO STOP THIS MADNESS!
PLEASE PRESS THE ESCAPE KEY TO STOP THIS MADNESS!
PLEASE PRESS THE ESCAPE KEY TO STOP THIS MADNESS!
*** INTERRUPTED ***
Called from - C:ENDLESS.prg
Cancel, Ignore, or Suspend? (C, I, or S) Cancel
Do cancelled
```

FIGURE 6.8 *Cancelling an endless loop.*

In Chapter 7, you will learn how to exercise some control over an endless loop by providing a "back door," or exit, within the program, and in Chapter 8, you will discover some practical applications of this technique. What is important to understand in the preceding example is that the DO WHILE/ENDDO can have a powerful effect on how a program behaves.

It is often necessary to go through a .DBF file, record by record, until all the records have been accessed. By checking for a special character that is found after the last record, dBASE III PLUS is able to determine when the end of the file has been reached. The EOF() function can be used to control a DO WHILE loop when this is the case. The logical operator .NOT. will be used to test for a false condition.

```
* TEST_EOF.PRG
USE CITIES
DO WHILE .NOT. EOF()
        ? ST, CITY
ENDDO .NOT. EOF()


. DO TEST_EOF

CA SAN FRANCISCO
CA SAN FRANCISCO
CA SAN FRANCISCO
CA SAN FRANCISCO
CA SAN FRANCISCO
*** INTERRUPTED ***
Called from - C:TEST_EOF.prg
Cancel, Ignore, or Suspend? (C, I, or S) Cancel
Do cancelled
```

FIGURE 6.9 *Result of a missing SKIP command.*

It appears that this program is behaving like the endless loop example, ENDLESS.PRG. The reason is that although the USE command set the file at the first record, there is no command in the program to advance to the next record. In previous chapters LIST did this automatically, but now you will have to place a SKIP command in the program for this purpose. The modified version of TEST_ EOF.PRG also includes a message to be printed when the DO WHILE loop is finished and a CLEAR ALL command to close CITIES.DBF.

```
* TEST_EOF.PRG
USE CITIES
DO WHILE .NOT. EOF()
        ? ST, CITY
        SKIP
ENDDO .NOT. EOF()
? 'END OF FILE HAS BEEN REACHED'
CLEAR ALL

. DO TEST_EOF

CA SAN FRANCISCO
PA PHILADELPHIA
TX DALLAS
CA SAN DIEGO
TX HOUSTON
FL MIAMI
OH CLEVELAND
PA PITTSBURGH
CA LOS ANGELES
FL JACKSONVILLE
OH COLUMBUS
END OF FILE HAS BEEN REACHED
```

FIGURE 6.10 *Proper use of the SKIP command.*

This program effectively accesses all the records in the file, because the comparative expression in the DO WHILE will not branch to the statement after the ENDDO (? 'END OF FILE HAS BEEN REACHED') until EOF() is true (.T.).

This actually means that the EOF() function will be set to true when dBASE III PLUS detects a special marker, control-Z (˄Z), that always follows the last record in the file. When this marker is detected by dBASE III PLUS, the EOF() function is set, but the programmer has the responsibility of testing for the condition. You also observed that dBASE III PLUS must be instructed to move to the next record in the file when the current record has been processed.

The combination of the *test* to exit the loop in the DO WHILE and the *changing of factors* within the loop affecting that condition allows the DO WHILE loop to work properly. In Figure 6.11, the DO WHILE .NOT. EOF() is the test to exit the loop, and the SKIP is the factor that affects the condition. Being aware of these two aspects of the DO WHILE loop will reveal its purpose and will allow you to predict its behavior. An additional consideration with this type of DO WHILE/ENDDO is that commands such as LIST, SUM, and COUNT go through all the records in a file one at a time. While these commands are very useful from the dot prompt, they slow down processing considerably when they are included in a loop.

```
* TEST_EOF.PRG
USE CITIES
DO WHILE .NOT. EOF() ◄──────── Test to exit loop
          ? ST, CITY
            SKIP ◄──────── Factor affecting test
ENDDO .NOT. EOF()
? 'END OF FILE HAS BEEN REACHED'
CLEAR ALL
```

FIGURE 6.11 *Analysis of a DO WHILE/ENDDO.*

The test expression after the DO WHILE is actually "remembered" by dBASE III PLUS and recalled when the ENDDO has been reached. You can observe the resulting loop action through the use of the SET ECHO ON command. This command will display each line from the program as it executes. The lines that would normally be displayed on the screen by the program have been offset in Figure 6.12 so that the program commands may be studied. Remember to SET ECHO OFF after the program has been run.

```
    . SET ECHO ON

    . DO TEST_EOF

USE CITIES
SET TALK OFF
DO WHILE .NOT. EOF()
? STATE,CITY
            CA SAN FRANCISCO
```

FIGURE 6.12 *Studying loop execution with SET ECHO ON (Part 1 of 2).*

```
SKIP
ENDDO .NOT. EOF()
? STATE,CITY
          PA PHILADELPHIA
SKIP
ENDDO .NOT. EOF()
? STATE,CITY
          TX DALLAS
SKIP
ENDDO .NOT. EOF()
? STATE,CITY
          CA SAN DIEGO
SKIP
ENDDO .NOT. EOF()
? STATE,CITY
          TX HOUSTON
SKIP
ENDDO .NOT. EOF()
? STATE,CITY
          FL MIAMI
SKIP
ENDDO .NOT. EOF()
? STATE,CITY
          OH CLEVELAND
```

```
SKIP
ENDDO .NOT. EOF()
? STATE,CITY
            PA PITTSBURGH
SKIP
ENDDO .NOT. EOF()
? STATE,CITY
            CA LOS ANGELES
SKIP
ENDDO .NOT. EOF()
? STATE,CITY
          FL JACKSONVILLE
SKIP
ENDDO .NOT. EOF()
? STATE,CITY
            OH COLUMBUS
SKIP
ENDDO .NOT. EOF()
CLEAR ALL
? 'END OF FILE HAS BEEN REACHED'
            END OF FILE HAS BEEN REACHED
```

FIGURE 6.12 *Studying loop execution with SET ECHO ON (Part 2 of 2).*

Notice how the program continues to branch to the command that follows the DO WHILE .NOT. EOF(), (? STATE,CITY), until the last valid record has been accessed. At this point the program branches to the command following the ENDDO. This branching action is the essence of the DO WHILE/ENDDO.

6.3 OTHER TYPES OF DO WHILE/ENDDO LOOPS

It should be apparent at this point that the DO WHILE/ENDDO is a versatile structure. The first portion of this chapter demonstrated the use of a counter and a test for the end of a file as exit conditions for the loop. This section will present several other types of loops. These examples, combined with those in later chapters, serve to underscore the fact that the effective use of the DO WHILE/ENDDO is an essential skill.

The next example employs the intentions of the program user to determine when the loop will discontinue. More specifically, the user will control every pass of the DO WHILE/ENDDO structure.

The program is based on a variation of an old parable which is often used to illustrate the power of multiplication. In this case, an experienced salesperson managed to close a rather lucrative contract for his company. The sales manager asked him what he would like as a bonus for his outstanding performance. Hoping to take advantage of his supervisor's relative inexperience in business, the salesperson requested that the company grant him a bonus of one penny on the first of the month and double the amount every day for the remainder of the month. Fortunately for the company, the sales manager had recently completed a programming course in dBASE III PLUS. She wrote the following program and quickly discovered the devious nature of the scheme.

```
* RAISE.PRG
SET TALK OFF
STORE 'Y' TO answer
STORE 1 TO day
STORE .01 TO raise
DO WHILE answer = 'Y'
    ? 'RAISE ON DAY NUMBER',day
    ? 'WILL BE',raise
    ACCEPT 'COMPUTE ANOTHER DAY? (Y/N)' TO answer
    STORE day + 1 TO day
    STORE raise * 2 TO raise
ENDDO  answer = 'Y'
```

FIGURE 6.13 *The RAISE.PRG program.*

```
            DO RAISE

BONUS ON DAY NUMBER          1
WILL BE          0.01
COMPUTE ANOTHER DAY? (Y/N)Y
BONUS ON DAY NUMBER          2
WILL BE          0.02
COMPUTE ANOTHER DAY? (Y/N)Y
BONUS ON DAY NUMBER          3
WILL BE          0.04
COMPUTE ANOTHER DAY? (Y/N)Y
BONUS ON DAY NUMBER          4
WILL BE          0.08
COMPUTE ANOTHER DAY? (Y/N)Y
BONUS ON DAY NUMBER          5
WILL BE          0.16
COMPUTE ANOTHER DAY? (Y/N)Y
BONUS ON DAY NUMBER          6
WILL BE          0.32
COMPUTE ANOTHER DAY? (Y/N)Y
BONUS ON DAY NUMBER          7
WILL BE          0.64
```

FIGURE 6.14 *Execution of RAISE.PRG (Part 1 of 2).*

```
COMPUTE ANOTHER DAY? (Y/N)Y
BONUS ON DAY NUMBER            8
WILL BE          1.28
COMPUTE ANOTHER DAY? (Y/N)Y
BONUS ON DAY NUMBER            9
WILL BE          2.56
COMPUTE ANOTHER DAY? (Y/N)Y
BONUS ON DAY NUMBER           10
WILL BE          5.12
COMPUTE ANOTHER DAY? (Y/N)Y
BONUS ON DAY NUMBER           11
WILL BE         10.24
COMPUTE ANOTHER DAY? (Y/N)Y
BONUS ON DAY NUMBER           12
WILL BE         20.48
COMPUTE ANOTHER DAY? (Y/N)Y
BONUS ON DAY NUMBER           13
WILL BE         40.96
COMPUTE ANOTHER DAY? (Y/N)Y
BONUS ON DAY NUMBER           14
WILL BE         81.92
COMPUTE ANOTHER DAY? (Y/N)Y
BONUS ON DAY NUMBER           15
WILL BE        163.84
COMPUTE ANOTHER DAY? (Y/N)Y
BONUS ON DAY NUMBER           16
WILL BE        327.68
```

```
COMPUTE ANOTHER DAY? (Y/N)Y
BONUS ON DAY NUMBER           17
WILL BE        655.36
COMPUTE ANOTHER DAY? (Y/N)Y
BONUS ON DAY NUMBER           18
WILL BE       1310.72
COMPUTE ANOTHER DAY? (Y/N)Y
BONUS ON DAY NUMBER           19
WILL BE       2621.44
COMPUTE ANOTHER DAY? (Y/N)Y
BONUS ON DAY NUMBER           20
WILL BE       5242.88
COMPUTE ANOTHER DAY? (Y/N)Y
BONUS ON DAY NUMBER           21
WILL BE      10485.76
COMPUTE ANOTHER DAY? (Y/N)Y
BONUS ON DAY NUMBER           22
WILL BE      20971.52
COMPUTE ANOTHER DAY? (Y/N)Y
BONUS ON DAY NUMBER           23
WILL BE      41943.04
COMPUTE ANOTHER DAY? (Y/N)Y
BONUS ON DAY NUMBER           24
WILL BE      83886.08
COMPUTE ANOTHER DAY? (Y/N)Y
BONUS ON DAY NUMBER           25
WILL BE     167772.16
```

```
COMPUTE ANOTHER DAY? (Y/N)Y
BONUS ON DAY NUMBER           26
WILL BE     335544.32
COMPUTE ANOTHER DAY? (Y/N)Y
BONUS ON DAY NUMBER           27
WILL BE     671088.64
COMPUTE ANOTHER DAY? (Y/N)Y
BONUS ON DAY NUMBER           28
WILL BE    1342177.28
COMPUTE ANOTHER DAY? (Y/N)Y
BONUS ON DAY NUMBER           29
WILL BE    2684354.56
COMPUTE ANOTHER DAY? (Y/N)Y
BONUS ON DAY NUMBER           30
WILL BE    5368709.12
COMPUTE ANOTHER DAY? (Y/N)Y
BONUS ON DAY NUMBER           31
WILL BE   10737418.24
COMPUTE ANOTHER DAY
       ? (Y/N)N
```

FIGURE 6.14   *Execution of RAISE.PRG (Part 2 of 2).*

After the comment line and SET TALK OFF, STORE statements initialize or preset values for the three memory variables answer, day, and bonus. Since the literal 'Y' is STOREd in the memory variable answer and the DO WHILE is designed to continue as long as the memory variable answer contains a 'Y', it would appear that you have an endless loop. However, the ACCEPT command prompts the program user to store either 'Y' or 'N' in the memory variable. Although another computation will occur as the result of the two STORE commands that follow, the DO WHILE will discontinue the loop if a comparison is made and 'Y' is not found in the memory variable answer. This strategy allows the user to control the number of executions of the DO WHILE/ENDDO. Again, it is the *combination* of the *expression* following the DO WHILE and the *factor within the loop* (the ACCEPT command) which provides the power and flexibility of the structure.

A variation of the DO WHILE loop in Figure 6.2 may be constructed using an accumulator rather than a counter. The principle is the same, since a memory variable will be incremented within the loop, and the expression after the DO WHILE will exit the loop when a certain limit has been reached.

Figure 6.15 illustrates a program that uses an accumulator in a DO WHILE loop. Notice that the pop_total memory variable is initialized to 0. This establishes the variable as numeric and ensures that it contains a base value of 0. The DO WHILE contains an expression that tests the variable and discontinues the loop if the value is equal to or greater than 5 million (=> 5,000,000). Stated another way, the loop should continue as long as the value is less than 5 million (< 5,000,000).

The first command within the loop increases the value of the accumulator by the 1982 population of the current record in the CITIES.DBF file. The ? displays the name and population of the city and the current total. The SKIP, as you have seen before, will move to the next record. After the ENDDO, a ? displays the value contained in the accumulator when the test in the DO WHILE is logically false (pop_total is not < 5,000,000).

```
* TOT_LOOP.PRG
USE CITIES
STORE 0 TO pop_total
SET TALK OFF
DO WHILE pop_total < 5000000
    STORE POP_82 + pop_total TO pop_total
    ? CITY, POP_82, 'CURRENT TOTAL =',pop_total
    SKIP
ENDDO pop_total < 5000000
? 'FINAL TOTAL =', POP_TOTAL
```

FIGURE 6.15   *Using an accumulator.*

The execution of the program, which appears in Figure 6.15, is not completely successful. Although the performance of the accumulator is satisfactory, the test to exit the loop should have been done after San Diego was processed. This illustrates two points concerning the DO WHILE/ENDDO. First, the test to exit the loop should be made before processing, at the top of the loop. Chapter 7 will present some techniques for handling this situation. Second, as shown in Figure 6.12, the test to exit the loop is actually made at the ENDDO.

```
      . DO TOT_LOOP

SAN FRANCISCO          691637 CURRENT TOTAL =       691637
PHILADELPHIA          1665382 CURRENT TOTAL =      2357019
DALLAS                 943848 CURRENT TOTAL =      3300867
SAN DIEGO              915956 CURRENT TOTAL =      4216823
HOUSTON               1725617 CURRENT TOTAL =      5942440
FINAL TOTAL =       5942440
```

FIGURE 6.16   *Execution of TOT_LOOP.PRG.*

It is possible to increase the effectiveness of a DO WHILE/ENDDO by combining two conditions in the DO WHILE. This may be accomplished with the .AND. logical operator. The .OR. is also available for this purpose, although it is less restrictive than the .AND., since either test will end the loop. In Figure 6.17, both tests must be true. The memory variable answer must be equal to 'Y' and raise must be less than 350. This modification to the program would have allowed the manager to limit the executions of the loop to a reasonable amount.

```
* RAISE.PRG
SET TALK OFF
STORE 'Y' TO answer
STORE 1 TO day
STORE .01 TO raise
DO WHILE answer = 'Y' .AND. raise < 350
    ? 'RAISE ON DAY NUMBER',day
    ? 'WILL BE',raise
    ACCEPT 'COMPUTE ANOTHER DAY? (Y/N)' TO answer
    STORE day + 1 TO day
    STORE raise * 2 TO raise
ENDDO answer = 'Y' .AND. raise < 350
```

FIGURE 6.17   *Using a logical operator.*

When you are using this technique with indention, the DO WHILE statement may exceed the right margin. Using the semicolon to break the line, as explained in Chapter 5, will generate an error. Just continue typing; allow word-wrap to bring the final part of the command to the next line; and insert spaces until it lines up with the DO in the line above.

```
DO WHILE ANSWER =   'Y'
.AND. RAISE < 350
```

The concepts presented in this chapter are vital to effective programming. Early mastery of iteration or looping is an excellent basis for the development programs that are flexible and powerful.

CHAPTER SUMMARY

6.1

When a process requires the repeating of an action, the DO WHILE/ENDDO structure provides the repetition. Other commands are repeated in a controlled manner within the DO WHILE/ENDDO envelope. An expression is placed in the DO WHILE which will determine the number of executions of the loop. A command must be included within the loop to affect the expression that follows the DO WHILE to allow an exit. Both the DO WHILE and the ENDDO must be present. Commands inside the loop should be indented for clarity, and a comment should be included in the ENDDO. Comparative or conditional expressions compare two pieces of data, (literals, memory variables, or field names), using a relational operator. The data must be of the same type, and the operator should be selected carefully.

6.2

The combination of a counter within the loop and a test for a specified condition will limit the number of executions. Without them, a DO WHILE/ENDDO can produce an endless loop using a logical .T. The combination of a test for end of file, .NOT. EOF(), and SKIP will access all records in a .DBF file sequentially. The DO WHILE establishes the criterion for ending the loop, and processing will continue as long as the criterion is logically true. The ENDDO will evaluate the test again and will branch either to the first statement within the loop (.T.) or to the statement following the ENDDO (.F.).

6.3

A character type literal such as 'Y' may be used as a criterion in a DO WHILE/ENDDO, allowing the program user to determine when the loop will cease. An accumulator will provide a running total within the loop which can be included in the comparative expression of the DO WHILE to exit the structure at a specified amount. Comparative expressions may also be combined, using logical operators (.AND., .OR.) for certain applications.

KEY TERMS

nesting   accumulator
self-documenting   counter

COMMAND SUMMARY

DO WHILE — The first statement of the DO WHILE/ENDDO structure which includes the condition.

ENDDO — The concluding statement of the DO WHILE/ENDDO structure.

EOF() — A logical function that indicates an end-of-file condition.

SKIP — Move the record pointer to the next record.

dBUG dBASE

- dBASE III PLUS scans each command from left to right and stops if it finds an error. It looks for keywords first, and if the word or phrase that is delimited by blanks is not a keyword, it tries to determine whether it is a valid constant or a literal. It also tests for valid field names.
- SET TALK ON can be annoying when you are displaying data, because it will verify and display the results of commands such as REPLACE, STORE, and SKIP. However, this feature can be very useful if you are debugging and trying to monitor the results of commands.
- Loop problems usually fall into one of the three following catagories:
  1. The loop executes only once.
     There may be only one record in the file. Perhaps the condition controlling the loop exit is being changed at the bottom of the loop.
  2. The loop executes continuously.
     There is no SKIP or change of the exit condition in the loop.
  3. The loop does not execute at all.
     The control factor is not allowing execution. A control variable was not initialized or was changed before the loop executed. There are no records in the file.
- Set up a program template file with CLEAR ALL, SET commands, and identifying documentation as a time saver. The file can be renamed when the code is added.

SELF-CHECK QUESTIONS

1. What is the purpose of the ENDDO?
2. What is the reason for repeating the condition following the ENDDO?
3. Why is the indention of commands within the DO WHILE/ENDDO important?
4. Under what conditions can a Data type mismatch error occur in a DO WHILE/ENDDO?
5. What is an endless loop?
6. What two elements in a DO WHILE/ENDDO determine when the loop will terminate?
7. Is it possible to allow the user to control the number of times a loop will execute? How?
8. What is an accumulator? How does it differ from a counter?
9. Where is the best position to place a test to exit a loop?
10. Which logical operator is more restrictive, .AND. or .OR.?

TRY IT YOURSELF

1. Construct a DO WHILE/ENDDO loop that will count to 12, incrementing by 2. Include a statement after the ENDDO which will display the exit value of the counter variable. Use indention and comments.
2. Write a version of the program in Exercise 1 using no comments or indention. Compare this with a version using structured style, and observe the difference. Do not allow the results of the STORE command to display.
3. Write DO WHILE statements for the following conditions:
   a. BALANCE is less than 1000
   b. CITY is 'GRAND RAPIDS'
   c. CHOICE is not 9
   d. AGE is 16 or more
   e. 1500 or less is in TOTAL and ANSWER is 'Y'
   f. CHOICE is either 2 or 3
4. Assign the value 17 to a variable. Write a STORE command to increase the value by 12 and print the result with the ? command. Include a character literal that identifies the display.
5. Write a DO WHILE/ENDDO loop that will display your name on the screen seven times.
6. Rewrite the program in Exercise 5 using an "endless loop." Execute the program with SET ECHO ON and observe the results.

7. Display the 1980 population of the cities in the CITIES.DBF file using a DO WHILE/ENDDO loop. Remove the SKIP command and observe the results. Place the SKIP command after the DO WHILE and study the display.
8. Use a combination of an accumulator and an ACCEPT within a loop to generate a list of interest rates as shown below. The user has the option to end the loop at any time. The rates begin at 9% (.09) but may not exceed 21%. They are incremented by .0025.

        .0900
        .0925
        .0950
        .0975
        .0100

PROGRAMMING PROJECT

Write a program using structured style which will display all the states in CITIES.DBF, followed by the message 'LIST COMPLETE'. Use SET ECHO ON to study the execution of the commands in the program.

7

DECISION MAKING WITH IF/ENDIF

LEARNING OBJECTIVES

1. To examine the procedures used by dBASE III PLUS to make comparisons of data.
2. To construct IF/ENDIF structures.
3. To use ELSE and IIF().
4. To construct a program that will selectively print records.

Chapter

7

DECISION MAKING WITH IF/ENDIF

One of the most useful tasks that computers perform is the searching and sorting of data. Consider what is occurring in the background when an ATM (Automatic Teller Machine) is used. The customer inserts an ID card that contains an account number. The number is read from the card, and the customer inputs a PIN (Personal Identification Number). Before any transaction can be completed, the computer at the bank must search all the relevant account numbers to find the customer's account. If the account is not found, the card is rejected. Then the PIN that was supplied by the customer must be compared to the PIN in the account. If they match, the customer can perform a transaction. If they do not match, the card is rejected. Despite the existence of thousands of accounts and PIN numbers, all of this searching and comparing occurs almost instantaneously. How does the computer make comparisons? How can it perform two separate tasks on the basis of one piece of data? This chapter focuses on learning to write programs that compare data and execute separate actions on the basis of the results.

7.1 HOW dBASE III PLUS MAKES COMPARISONS

Computers must often compare two sets of data in order to make clear the relationship between the two sources. This process, sometimes called *selection* or *if-then-else*, provides a variety of useful functions to the user, such as searching and sorting data or choosing between two courses of action. One important reason that computers are valuable to business operations is that their ability to compare is combined with both speed and endurance (computers rapidly perform the most boring and repetitive tasks endlessly, without complaint). Comparisons of data, fields, and variables are made by dBASE III PLUS in specific ways for numeric-, character-, and date-type fields.

Here are the relational operators from Chapter 3, since one or more of them will be required for all comparisons.

=	Equal To
<	Less Than
>	Greater Than
<=	Less Than or Equal To
>=	Greater Than or Equal To
# or <>	Not Equal To

FIGURE 7.1 *The relational operators.*

You need only basic arithmetic skills to understand how dBASE III PLUS evaluates a comparison of numeric values. If you use the ? command in front of a comparison, dBASE III PLUS will evaluate the expression as being .T. (true) or .F. (false), and it will display the result. Try the examples in Figure 7.2, and experiment with others. As you can see, the comparisons in Figure 7.2 are all true in dBASE III PLUS.

```
    . ? 6 > 3

.T.

    . ? -5 > -10

.T.

    . ? .01 > .001

.T.
```

FIGURE 7.2 *Numeric comparisons.*

Figure 7.2 demonstrates that dBASE III PLUS evaluates expressions for their actual numeric value, just as you would using algebra.

When comparing character information, dBASE III PLUS uses a different set of rules. The characters that appear on the monitor screen or that are stored on the disk are represented electronically or magnetically and are based on ASCII (American Standard Code for Information Interchange). This is a system of 256 codes that represent all the characters in common use, along with a number of other special characters such as the carriage return. A chart showing these codes may be found in Appendix B. Although it is not necessary to memorize the codes, it is helpful to understand their "pecking order."

ASCII ranks the numerals 0 through 9 low on the scale, with values ranging from 48 for 0 to 57 for 9. Uppercase letters are represented by decimal values from

65 to 90. The higher values, 97 to 122, are reserved for the lowercase letters. Therefore, when any lowercase letter is compared to any uppercase letter, the lowercase letter will always carry the greater value.

48 0	65 A	97 a
49 1	66 B	98 b
50 2	67 C	99 c
51 3	68 D	100 d
52 4	69 E	101 e
53 5	70 F	102 f
54 6	71 G	103 g
55 7	72 H	104 h
56 8	73 I	105 i
57 9	74 J	106 j
	75 K	107 k
	76 L	108 l
	77 M	109 m
	78 N	110 n
	79 O	111 o
	80 P	112 p
	81 Q	113 q
	82 R	114 r
	83 S	115 s
	84 T	116 t
	85 U	117 u
	86 V	118 v
	87 W	119 w
	88 X	120 x
	89 Y	121 y
	90 Z	122 z

FIGURE 7.3   *ASCII codes and values.*

Figure 7.4 illustrates the hierarchy of the ASCII characters in a dialogue that uses the ? command. Try other examples to become familiar with the ways in which the relational operators behave.

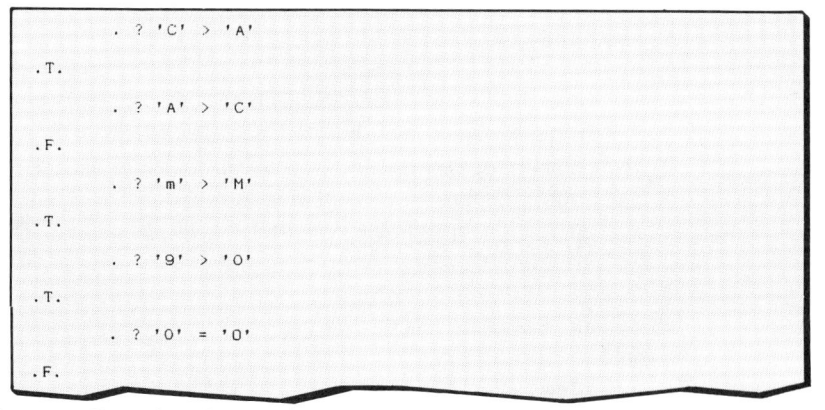

```
    . ? 'C' > 'A'
.T.
    . ? 'A' > 'C'
.F.
    . ? 'm' > 'M'
.T.
    . ? '9' > '0'
.T.
    . ? '0' = '0'
.F.
```

FIGURE 7.4   *Examples of comparisons.*

When characters are compared, the first character on either side which has the highest ASCII value will be considered logically greater than the first character on the other side. In the example below, the first character of the current contents of the field name STATE will be compared to uppercase 'C'. If the condition cannot be determined, IF will then compare the second character on each side. Eventually, either an inequality will be found or no more comparisons will be possible. In the former case the two sides are obviously unequal; in the latter, they are equal *as far as can be determined*. This means that the expression 'AB' has a greater value than 'AAZZZZZZ'.

```
IF STATE = 'CA'

. ? 'CA' = 'C'

.T.
```

It is important to be informed about the way in which dBASE III PLUS compares both character and numeric values, fields, and variables. Chapter 13 contains information about how dates are compared. This will enable you to write clear and accurate conditions for IF/ENDIF, DO WHILE/ENDDO, and other structures. A major source of programming errors is the poor construction of comparative statements. Writing effective comparisons is one way to make programs perform more efficiently, because the power of the computer is better utilized.

7.2 CONSTRUCTING THE IF/ENDIF

In Chapter 3, you used the FOR clause of the LIST command to make decisions about which records should be displayed. This clause can also be used with other dBASE III PLUS commands, such as REPORT or COPY. When used in a command such as LIST FOR STATE = 'CA', the intention is to display records IF the state is California. Since the ability to instruct the computer to make decisions is essential, the IF/ENDIF structure is provided to satisfy this need.

Like the DO WHILE/ENDDO, the IF/ENDIF is a two-command structure, which means that it may be used only in programs. Both the IF and the ENDIF statements must be present. As you will notice in the example below, the IF statement must include a comparative expression, or condition. Also, as with the ENDDO, any text following the ENDIF will be ignored. This provides an excellent means of self-documenting the structure.

```
IF STATE = 'CA'
      ? CITY
ENDIF STATE = 'CA'
```

The field name STATE is being compared to the constant 'CA'. This command could be paraphrased as "if it is true that the contents of the STATE field in the current record are equal to 'CA' . . . ".

If you place the above structure in a DO WHILE/ENDDO loop, you will be able to print the name of only those cities which have 'CA' in the state field.

```
        . TYPE TESTIF1.PRG

* TESTIF1.PRG - Tests how an IF/ENDIF will perform in a
*               DO WHILE/ENDDO loop.

USE CITIES
DO WHILE .NOT. EOF()
    IF STATE = 'CA'
       ? CITY
    ENDIF STATE = 'CA'
SKIP
ENDDO .NOT. EOF

        . DO TESTIF1

SAN FRANCISCO
Record No.        2
Record No.        3
Record No.        4
SAN DIEGO
Record No.        5
Record No.        6
Record No.        7
Record No.        8
Record No.        9
       LOS ANGELES
       Record No.       10
       Record No.       11
       Record No.       12
```

FIGURE 7.5 *Execution of TESTIF1.PRG.*

When the command USE CITIES is executed, the record pointer is positioned at record 1. As you learned in Chapter 6, the DO WHILE statement will evaluate the condition, in this case, .NOT. EOF(). If the condition is not true (in other words, if the end of file has been reached), the program will branch to the statement following the ENDDO. At this point in the program, the record pointer is at record 1, so the command following the DO WHILE statement executes.

The program now enters the IF/ENDIF structure by evaluating the contents of the field STATE to determine whether it contains the characters 'CA'. This is the case in record 1, so the commands within the IF and ENDIF must execute. This is why SAN FRANCISCO is displayed on the screen first (? CITY). After the ENDIF command is passed, the SKIP command will advance the pointer to record 2. The record number is displayed by dBASE III PLUS after each SKIP. The ENDDO command then loops, or passes control back to the DO WHILE. Since the end of file has still not been reached, the IF command will check to see whether there is a 'CA' in the state field. This time there is not, so control is passed to SKIP, the command following ENDIF.

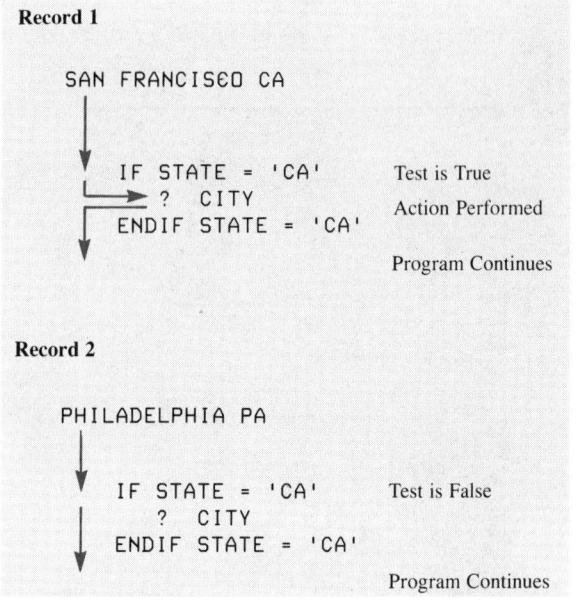

FIGURE 7.6 *Analysis of IF/ENDIF execution.*

Change the IF statement in TESTIF1.PRG to test for 'C' instead of 'CA' and run the program.

```
          . TYPE TESTIF1.PRG

* TESTIF1.PRG - Tests how an IF/ENDIF will perform in a
                DO WHILE/ENDDO loop.

USE CITIES
DO WHILE .NOT. EOF()
    IF STATE = 'C'
        ? CITY
    ENDIF STATE = 'C'
SKIP
ENDDO .NOT. EOF()

          . DO TESTIF1

SAN FRANCISCO
Record No.       2
Record No.       3
Record No.       4
SAN DIEGO
Record No.       5
Record No.       6
Record No.       7
Record No.       8
Record No.       9
```
```
LOS ANGELES
Record No.      10
Record No.      11
Record No.      12
```

FIGURE 7.7 *Modifying the IF statement.*

Notice that the screen display is identical in Figures 7.5 and 7.7. This is because the 'C' in the first position of the state field was compared to the 'C' in the first position of the 'CA' in the IF statement. When dBASE III PLUS could not continue comparing, it evaluated the IF condition as true. The command SET EXACT ON will allow only an exact match to qualify in IF statements. This can be observed in Figure 7.8, where SET EXACT ON has been added.

```
        . TYPE TESTIF1.PRG

* TESTIF1.PRG - Tests how an IF/ENDIF will perform in a
*               DO WHILE/ENDDO loop.

SET EXACT ON
USE CITIES
DO WHILE .NOT. EOF()
    IF STATE = 'C'
        ? CITY
    ENDIF STATE = 'C'
SKIP
ENDDO .NOT. EOF()

        . DO TESTIF1

Record No.      2
Record No.      3
Record No.      4
Record No.      5
Record No.      6
Record No.      7
Record No.      8
Record No.      9
Record No.     10
Record No.     11
Record No.     12
```

FIGURE 7.8 *Effect of SET EXACT ON.*

Imagine that you belong to a student organization that is interested in persuading people to exercise their privilege to vote. You are stationed at an entrance that everyone must use to enter the student center, and you are instructed to ask all persons entering the center whether they are over age 17. Those students who answer yes are given a flyer urging them to vote, while younger students are not. Here is some pseudocode to outline this procedure, along with an idea of how it might be programmed in dBASE III PLUS.

```
Pseudocode
        IF the people are over 17
                Give them a flyer
        That's it
dBASE III PLUS
        IF age > 17
                ? 'PLEASE VOTE ON TUESDAY'
        ENDIF age > 17
```

FIGURE 7.9 *Comparison of pseudocode and IF/ENDIF.*

This series of steps is essentially what dBASE III PLUS does when an IF/ENDIF is executed. The IF/ENDIF structure is placed in the path of records as they loop through the program. The IF statement checks each record to see whether its condition has been met. If it has, the statements after the IF are executed; if not, the record is ignored by the program branching beyond the ENDIF.

7.3 THE ELSE AND IIF()

Returning to the hypothetical case of the civic-minded student organization, what if those students who were 17 years old or younger complained that they were being ignored simply because of their age? The organization might have to adjust the procedure in order to provide something for the younger group. Here is some pseudocode and an example program for addressing this problem.

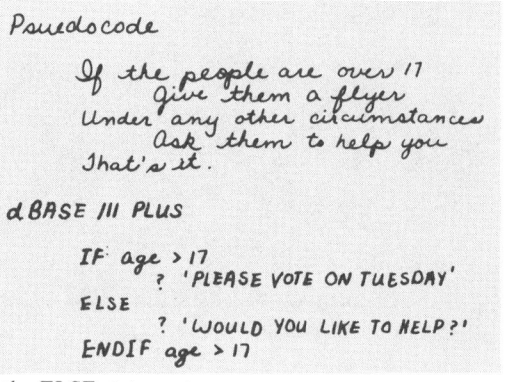

FIGURE 7.10 *Using the ELSE statement.*

As ridiculous as the following may sound, let's consider what might happen if a student walked by with a pet chimp. Would you have to ask the chimp's age? If the chimp were seven years old, would you have to ask it to help? In terms of how a computer program would respond, the answer to both questions is yes. When you include ELSE in an IF/ENDIF structure, it means exactly *anything* else.

When the IF statement is encountered, the comparison will be evaluated as being either true or false. When the condition is true, the statements located between the IF and the ENDIF are executed. If the condition is false, program control will skip to the first statement following the ENDIF. Note that in either case the statements following the ENDIF will execute. This structure will separate records into two groups: those which meet the condition and those which do not. However, only those records which produce a true condition are affected by the contents of the structure, while other records (false) are ignored.

A properly written IF/ENDIF structure uses indention for the statements within the structure and repeats the condition in the ENDIF statement. Any characters after the ENDIF will be ignored by dBASE III PLUS as they are in the ENDDO. As your programs become larger and more complicated, you will find that they will be easier to read and easier to debug if you follow this convention.

In situations where it is useful to provide alternative commands for the false condition, the optional ELSE may be used. The ELSE is placed after the statements provided when the condition is true. The alternate actions appear next before the ENDIF. This arrangement provides two distinct treatments for records. However, this structure is potentially dangerous, since the ELSE means exactly that. *All* records that do not satisfy the IF statement will execute the statements that follow the ELSE, whether or not that was the programmer's intention.

```
* FILTER.PRG
memnum = 9
DO 'HILE memnum < 12
    IF memnum > 10
        ? 'NUMBER IS GREATER THAN 10'
    ELSE
        ? 'NUMBER IS LESS THAN 10'
    ENDIF memnum > 10
memnum = memnum + 1
ENDDO memnum < 12


        . DO FILTER

9
NUMBER IS LESS THAN 10
        10                  <----- Value of memnum
NUMBER IS LESS THAN 10          <-------- Result of ELSE
        11
NUMBER IS GREATER THAN 10
        12
```

FIGURE 7.11   *Execution of FILTER.PRG.*

The program FILTER.PRG works well as long as the value of the variable memnum is either greater than or less than 10, but it produces unintended and incorrect results when the value is exactly 10. The solution to this problem is to provide another test that will test the variable a second time. A good rule of thumb for this sort of situation is to provide one less test than the possible number of options. Chapters 8 and 9 explain ways to program multiple possibilities.

The IIF() or immediate IF command is similar to the IF/ELSE/ENDIF. A condition is placed after the left parenthesis, followed by a comma. Actions to be performed on both true and false conditions are then included, as in Figure 7.12 on the following page.

```
     . USE CUST3

     . ? IIF(PROP_ZIP='55677', 'IN ZIP AREA', 'NOT IN ZIP AREA')
IN ZIP AREA

     . GO 2

     . ? IIF(PROP_ZIP='55677', 'IN ZIP AREA', 'NOT IN ZIP AREA')
NOT IN ZIP AREA
```

FIGURE 7.12   *Using IIF().*

The immediate IF command, IIF() may be used from the dot prompt to perform the same function as an IF/ELSE/ENDIF on one line. This obviously gives the nonprogramming user of dBASE III PLUS the opportunity to perform limited alternative tasks on the basis of a condition. It is also useful to the programmer in that he or she can observe how an IF/ENDIF will perform on certain data before placing it in a program. Another way to test an IF/ENDIF is to write the structure in a brief program and test it against records from the dot prompt.

7.4 WRITING A PROGRAM TO PRINT RECORDS SELECTIVELY

The processing loop used in Figure 7.13 prints all the records in the CUST.DBF file. If the situation required that only certain records should be printed, the program would have to be to include an IF/ENDIF. For example, in order to display the address, city, zip code, and price of all properties costing more than 100,000, the IF/ENDIF structure in Figure 7.13 would be needed.

```
          . TYPE CUST1.PRG

  * CUST1.PRG - Displays all the records in the CUST.DBF file

  SET TALK OFF
  USE CUST3
  DO WHILE .NOT. EOF()
       IF PRICE > 100000              <-- Selects records
          ? NUM, STREET, CITY, ZIP, PRICE  <-- Action performed
       ENDIF PRICE > 100000                 on selected records
  SKIP                            <-- Action performed
  ENDDO .NOT. EOF()                   on all records
  CLEAR ALL

          DO CUST1

  253      BRIAN AVE.        RESSLER       55988   124000
  5052     ALEXIS ST.        MCLAIN        55945   210000
  10       PINCHOT WAY       OVERBROOK     55677   140000
```

FIGURE 7.13   *Execution of CUST1.PRG.*

The program in Figure 7.13 accomplished its purpose. Properties costing 100,000 or less were not included in the display. Of course, if you wanted to provide some action for the unselected records, an ELSE could be used. In the program in Figure 7.14, the unselected properties are displayed with a message.

```
            . TYPE CUST1.PRG

* CUST1.PRG - Displays all the records in the CUST.DBF file

SET TALK OFF
USE CUST3
DO WHILE .NOT. EOF()
    IF PRICE > 100000
        ? PROP_NUM, PROP_ST, PROP_CITY, PROP_ZIP, PRICE
    ELSE
        ? PROP_NUM, PROP_ST, 'Not Selected'
    ENDIF PRICE > 100000
SKIP
ENDDO .NOT. EOF()
CLEAR ALL

. DO CUST1
90        OBERLIN ST.        Not Selected
253       BRIAN AVE.         RESSLER         55988    124000
5052      ALEXIS ST.         MCLAIN          55945    210000
10        PINCHOT WAY        OVERBROOK       55677    140000
```

FIGURE 7.14 *Adding ELSE to CUST1.PRG.*

A common mistake when using the IF/ENDIF is to include the SKIP or some other command that doesn't belong in the structure. Although proper indention, as demonstrated in the program examples above, helps to prevent this error, it can produce results like those in Figure 7.15. The SKIP executes only on records not meeting the condition (after ELSE); the program goes into an endless loop on the first record that satisfies the condition.

```
            . TYPE CUST1.PRG

* CUST1.PRG - Displays all the records in the CUST.DBF file

SET TALK OFF
USE CUST3
DO WHILE .NOT. EOF()
    IF PRICE > 100000
        ? PROP_NUM, PROP_ST, PROP_CITY, PROP_ZIP, PRICE
    ELSE
        ? PROP_NUM, PROP_ST, 'Not Selected'
    ENDIF PRICE > 100000
SKIP
ENDDO .NOT. EOF()
CLEAR ALL

            . DO CUST1

90        OBERLIN ST.        Not Selected
253       BRIAN AVE.         RESSLER         55988    124000
253       BRIAN AVE.         RESSLER         55988    124000
253       BRIAN AVE.         RESSLER         55988    124000
*** INTERRUPTED ***
Called from - C:CUST1.prg
Do cancelled
```

FIGURE 7.15 *Effect of a misplaced SKIP.*

Sometimes records need to be selected on the basis of two criteria, or perhaps more. A logical operator, .AND., may be used to link two conditions so that both must be satisfied in order to enter the IF/ENDIF structure. Figure 7.16 shows the IF statement you would use if you wanted to display properties that were located in zip code area 55677 and that were priced at 100,000. The property on Pinchot Way is the only one that satisfies both tests.

```
          . TYPE CUST1.PRG

* CUST1.PRG - Displays selected records in the CUST.DBF file

SET TALK OFF
USE CUST3
DO WHILE .NOT. EOF()
    IF PRICE > 100000 .AND. PROP_ZIP = '55677'
        ? PROP_NUM, PROP_ST, PROP_CITY, PROP_ZIP, PRICE
    ELSE
        ? PROP_NUM, PROP_ST, 'Not Selected'
    ENDIF PRICE > 100000
SKIP
ENDDO .NOT. EOF()
CLEAR ALL

        . DO CUST1

90         OBERLIN ST.           Not Selected
253        BRIAN AVE.            Not Selected
5052       ALEXIS ST.            Not Selected
10         PINCHOT WAY           OVERBROOK          55677   140000
```

FIGURE 7.16   *Combining conditions with .AND.*

Substituting .OR. for .AND. in the IF statement has an effect on the display. It is obviously much easier for a record to satisfy an .OR. operator than an .AND., as the chart in Figure 7.17 shows.

```
        . DO CUST1

90         OBERLIN ST.           OVERBROOK          55677    78000
253        BRIAN AVE.            RESSLER            55988   124000
5052       ALEXIS ST.            MCLAIN             55945   210000
10         PINCHOT WAY           OVERBROOK          55677   140000
```

RECORD	ZIP	PRICE	.AND.	.OR.
OBERLIN	.T.	.F.	NO	YES
BRIAN	.F.	.T.	NO	YES
ALEXIS	.F.	.T.	NO	YES
PINCHOT	.T.	.T.	YES	YES

FIGURE 7.17   *Comparison of .AND. and .OR.*

A word of caution is appropriate here. Linking two tests with a logical operator can be tricky. Not only do the conditions have to be correctly expressed, but the proper logical operator must also be chosen. Using more than two conditions is ill-advised. Even if you properly state five linked conditions, others will have great difficulty sorting out the possibilities. If such action does become necessary, parentheses should be used to clarify your intentions. The alternatives to this arrangement include *nesting* (Chapter 9). In situations where several options are possible when a condition is tested, it is more convenient to use a DO CASE, which will be discussed in Chapter 8.

A critical decision that all programmers encounter is whether to evaluate a condition with an IF/ENDIF inside a DO WHILE/ENDDO or to make the condition part of the DO WHILE. It is generally advisable to keep the repetitive loop as simple as possible and to do the testing within the loop using IF/ENDIF. The advantages include faster execution and greater flexibility. At first glance, the program in Figure 7.18 may appear to be better than the one in Figure 7.16, but it will not work. At the first opportunity to test PRICE and find it false, the loop will fail.

```
SET TALK OFF
USE CUST
DO WHILE .NOT. EOF() .AND. PRICE >100000
    ? PROP_NUM, PROP_ST, PROP_CITY, PROP_ZIP, PRICE
    SKIP
  ENDDO .NOT. EOF()
CLEAR ALL
```

FIGURE 7.18 *Incorrect use of .AND.*

The ability to write effective IF/ENDIF structures provides power and flexibility in program control. Unfortunately, these commands can be a source of annoying errors. Figure 7.19 contains some guidelines for writing the IF/ENDIF.

1. Is the condition in the IF statement correct?
   — same data type
   — correct relational operator
   — correct logical operator
   — no more than two conditions
2. Is the IF/ENDIF properly structured?
   — indention
   — statements in correct order
   — all required statements present
   — all unwanted statements removed
3. Does it work?
   — test it

FIGURE 7.19 *IF/ENDIF guidelines.*

CHAPTER SUMMARY

7.1

Comparing fields, variables, and expressions in order to determine relationships is critical to computer operations. Alternative actions may be performed as the result of a relationship being true or false. Numeric data is compared on the basis of value, as in algebra. Character data is compared character against character, according to the ASCII value.

7.2

The IF/ENDIF structure consists of the IF statement with a condition, some statements that are to be executed conditionally, and the ENDIF. The condition is repeated after the ENDIF, and interior statements are indented for clarity. The IF statement will evaluate the condition under current circumstances as being true or false. If the condition is true, the interior statements are executed; if it is false, control branches to the statement following the ENDIF. SET EXACT ON will force character comparisons to match exactly, including matches in length.

7.3

The ELSE is an optional statement used in the IF/ENDIF to provide an alternative action if the condition is false. The ELSE should be used with care, since its effect is global. The IIF() function is useful for testing conditions before they are used in programs.

7.4

The placement of an IF/ENDIF within a DO WHILE/ENDDO will permit the selective printing of records. The IF will select certain records that satisfy the condition. The statements within the IF/ENDIF structure that print data are executed, while records that do not meet the criteria are branched around these statements. It is possible to combine two tests with the logical operators (.OR., .AND.). An IF/ENDIF should be written carefully to assure that it performs as expected and generates no errors.

KEY TERMS

selection
if-then-else
ASCII

COMMAND SUMMARY

IF — The first statement in the IF/ENDIF structure which contains the condition.

ENDIF — The concluding statement in the IF/ENDIF structure.

SET EXACT ON — Requires data in conditions to match exactly.

ELSE — Provides an alternative action on a false condition.

IIF() — The immediate IF displays literals after evaluating a condition.

SELF-CHECK QUESTIONS

1. Name some reasons why a comparing operation is useful in programming.
2. Why is it important to be able to compare names or other character fields?
3. What is ASCII? Why is it important to be familiar with it?
4. Why is the ENDIF needed in the IF/ENDIF structure?
5. Why are indention and placing the condition after ENDIF useful?
6. Why must a programmer be cautious when including ELSE in a structure?
7. Could the IIF() be included in a program?
8. Is it possible to write a single IF/ENDIF to handle three possibilities?
9. Is it best to include a selective condition in the DO WHILE or to place an IF/ENDIF within the DO WHILE?
10. Why is the position of the SKIP command important?
11. Describe a situation in which tests could be combined with an .OR. logical operator. Do the same for the .AND.

TRY IT YOURSELF

1. Indicate which relational operator would be used in the following tests:
   a. You must be 18 to vote.
   b. Balances over 500 are charged 15% interest.
   c. Businesses with fewer than five employees are eligible for a special loan.
2. Use the ? to test the following conditions. Indicate whether they are .T. or .F.
   a. 'y' > 'az'
   b. .911 > .910
   c. 'a' > 'A'
   d. 'O Hara' = 'O HARA'
   e. 'ABC' = 'AB'

3. Write an IF/ENDIF structure for each of the following situations. Use your own field names, memory variables, or data where required.
   a. Print the Social Security number of all full-time students who have an F in a field called STATUS.
   b. Print the last name of all part-time students.
   c. Multiply the rate and the hours and print the gross of all employees who worked less than 40 hours.
   d. Print all last names that begin with P.
   e. Print the phone number of clients living in Orlando (exactly as it appears).
4. Write an IIF() statement for each of the following situations:

CONDITION	.T. ACTION	.F. ACTION
a. Over 4 arrests	'Suspended'	'Warning'
b. Age over 17	'Register'	'Under age'
c. Income 5000 or less	'No tax'	'Pay tax'

5. Write a program to test a name input with an ACCEPT. If the name is exactly 'Joe Piscioneri', print 'Valid user'. Any other name input should print 'Unauthorized'.
6. Modify the code in Exercise 5 to also allow the name 'Hank Clay' as a valid user.
7. A credit card company charges 18% on balances under $500. All other balances are charged 21%. Write an IF/ENDIF to test the field, BALANCE, and print an appropriate message stating the correct rate.
8. Write an IF/ENDIF structure to print 'Honors' for any grade point average that is 3.6 or higher. Other averages should print 'Next Semester?'

PROGRAMMING PROJECT

Write a program to print the following data regarding customers with properties priced over 100,000 but under 200,000.

```
Hojak       Joseph      Chicago       IL   180000
```

Print the SAL_NUM and ' – not in price range' for any other customers.

Print the title 'Properties within Quoted Price Range' at the top of the page and 'End of Report' at the bottom.

Write pseudocode and test your comparison with IIF() before coding the program.

```
Structure for database: C:cust3.dbf
Number of data records:      4
Date of last update    : 01/01/88
Field   Field Name   Type         Width   Dec
    1   SAL_NUM      Character      11
    2   LAST         Character      18
    3   FIRST        Character      20
    4   CURR_NUM     Character       8
    5   CURR_ST      Character      20
    6   CURR_CITY    Character      20
    7   CURR_ZIP     Character       5
    8   PROP_NUM     Character       8
    9   PROP_ST      Character      20
   10   PROP_CITY    Character      20
   11   PROP_ZIP     Character       5
   12   CONT_DATE    Date            8
   13   LIST_AGT     Character       4
   14   SELL_AGT     Character       4
   15   PRICE        Numeric         7
   16   ML_NUM       Character       5
** Total **                        184
```

8

MENUS AND
DO CASE/ENDCASE

LEARNING OBJECTIVES

1. To learn the conditions under which DO CASE/ENDCASE should be used in place of a series and nested IF/ENDIF. Also, to learn the use of CASE/ENDCASE and OTHERWISE to set conditions for DO CASE.
2. To learn the use of ACCEPT, WAIT, INPUT, and INKEY() for data entry.
3. To learn the value of menus and how to construct them using DO CASE/ENDCASE and DO WHILE/ENDDO.
4. To learn an efficient way to delete records by batching and PACKing them, using DO CASE/ENDCASE and DO WHILE.

Chapter

8

MENUS AND DO CASE/ENDCASE

Imagine how difficult it would be if you went to a restaurant and the waiter asked you what you would like to eat? You and the waiter would be involved in a lengthy, frustrating conversation because he would know what items are available and you would know your personal preferences. The obvious solution to this problem is the use of a menu. Because the choices are limited and clearly defined, patrons are able to place an order quickly and effectively.

You have learned a great deal about programmming and dBASE III PLUS in the last few chapters. As you develop more sophisticated techniques, you will want to begin to consider the needs of the user. People react best to a program that is convenient to use. Menus are an attractive and useful way of organizing a program.

8.1 CONSTRUCTING THE DO CASE/ENDCASE

Business decisions not always neatly limited to two alternatives. Often a whole range of options and conditions must be evaluated before a single action can be performed. Bracketing is a good example. The Internal Revenue Service typically taxes individuals on the basis of which income range contains their taxable income. You could easily construct an IF/ENDIF to evaluate the first range and return the correct tax. However, Figure 8.1 on the following page shows nine brackets, and that is only a small portion of the actual tax tables.

Income Bracket	Tax
$42,000 — $42,050	$10,106
$42,050 — $42,100	$10,125
$42,100 — $42,150	$10,144
$42,150 — $42,200	$10,163
$42,200 — $42,250	$10,182
$42,250 — $42,300	$10,201
$42,300 — $42,350	$10,220
$42,350 — $42,400	$10,239
$42,400 — $42,450	$10,258

FIGURE 8.1   *Example of multiple options.*

The IF/ENDIF structure is useful, provided that the number of options in a decision situation is no more than two. Sequential IF/ENDIF structures could be used to provide several alternative actions, but they are difficult to write and to understand. Chapter 9 will explore nesting, which can be used to handle several alternatives. However, nested IF/ENDIF structures also tend to be clumsy and unclear. The DO CASE/ENDCASE offers the best means for handling a number of options with ease, clarity, and effectiveness.

The first statement in the structure is the DO CASE, and the last is the END-CASE. Notice that there is a space in the DO CASE and none in the ENDCASE. CASE statements, which express each possible condition and their related commands, are placed between the DO CASE and the ENDCASE. The example in Figure 8.2 tests a memory variable, memstatus, to determine marital status.

```
DO CASE
    CASE memstatus = 'S'
         ? 'Single'
    CASE memstatus = 'M'
         ? 'Married'
    CASE memstatus = 'D'
         ? 'Divorced'
    CASE memstatus = 'W'
         ? 'Widowed'
ENDCASE
```

FIGURE 8.2   *Structure of DO CASE/ENDCASE.*

In effect, dBASE III PLUS is writing a series of IF/ENDIFs for you when you use a DO CASE/ENDCASE. One difference is that the DO CASE/ENDCASE will not evaluate the remaining options after a true condition is found, which makes the DO CASE/ENDCASE more efficient than a series of IF/ENDIFs. Although the DO CASE/ENDCASE places no limit on the number of commands that can be included in a CASE, more than a single screenful of statements makes the program difficult to read. A large number of commands should be placed in another program and called when needed; this will be explained further in Chapter 9.

Study the programs in Figure 8.3. They all perform the same task, but they do vary in their appearance.

```
          . TYPE TEST_IF4.PRG

* TEST_IF4.PRG This program tests an IF/ENDIF series.
STORE ' ' TO memchoice
ACCEPT 'Type a letter ' TO memchoice
        IF memchoice = 'A'
            ? 'You typed the letter A'
        ENDIF
        IF memchoice = 'B'
            ? 'You typed the letter B'
        ENDIF
        IF memchoice = 'C'
            ? 'You typed the letter C'
        ENDIF
        IF memchoice = 'D'
            ? 'You typed the letter D'
        ENDIF
        IF memchoice = 'E'
            ? 'You typed the letter E'
        ENDIF
        IF memchoice = 'F'
            ? 'You typed the letter F'
        ENDIF
        IF memchoice = 'G'
            ? 'You typed the letter G'
        ENDIF
            IF memchoice = 'H'
                ? 'You typed the letter H'
            ENDIF
            IF memchoice = 'I'
                ? 'You typed the letter I'
            ENDIF
            IF memchoice = 'J'
                ? 'You typed the letter J'
            ENDIF

            .DO TEST_IF4

        STORE ' ' TO memchoice

        ACCEPT 'Type a letter' TO memchoice
        Type a letter D
            IF memchoice = 'A'
            IF memchoice = 'B'
            IF memchoice = 'C'
            IF memchoice = 'D'
                ? 'You typed the letter D'
        You typed the letter D
                ENDIF
                IF memchoice = 'E'
                IF memchoice = 'F'
                IF memchoice = 'G'
                IF memchoice = 'H'
                IF memchoice = 'I'
                IF memchoice = 'J'
```

FIGURE 8.3 *Example of sequential IF/ENDIFs (Part 1 of 3).*

```
          . TYPE TESTNEST.PRG
STORE ' ' TO memchoice
ACCEPT 'Type a letter ' TO memchoice
IF memchoice = 'A'
 ? 'You typed the letter A'
ELSE
 IF memchoice = 'B'
  ? 'You typed the letter B'
 ELSE
  IF memchoice = 'C'
   ? 'You typed the letter C'
  ELSE
   IF memchoice = 'D'
    ? 'You typed the letter D'
   ELSE
    IF memchoice = 'E'
     ? 'You typed the letter E'
    ELSE
     IF memchoice = 'F'
      ? 'You typed the letter F'
     ELSE
      IF memchoice = 'G'
       ? 'You typed the letter G'
```

```
        ELSE
         IF memchoice = 'H'
          ? 'You typed the letter H'
         ELSE
          IF memchoice = 'I'
           ? 'You typed the letter I'
          ELSE
           IF memchoice = 'J'
            ? 'You typed the letter J'
           ENDIF
          ENDIF
         ENDIF
        ENDIF
       ENDIF
      ENDIF
     ENDIF
    ENDIF
   ENDIF
  ENDIF
ENDIF

        .DO TESTNEST

STORE ' ' TO memchoice

ACCEPT 'Type a letter ' TO memchoice
```

```
 Type a letter D
 IF memchoice = 'A'
  IF memchoice = 'B'
   IF memchoice = 'C'
    IF memchoice = 'D'
     ? 'You typed the letter D'
 You typed the letter D
    ELSE
    ENDIF
   ENDIF



 ENDIF
```

FIGURE 8.3 *Example of sequential IF/ENDIFs (Part 2 of 3).*

```
         . TYPE TESTCASE.PRG

STORE ' ' TO memchoice
ACCEPT 'Type a letter ' TO memchoice
DO CASE
    CASE memchoice = 'A'
        ? 'You typed the letter A'
    CASE memchoice = 'B'
        ? 'You typed the letter B'
    CASE memchoice = 'C'
        ? 'You typed the letter C'
    CASE memchoice = 'D'
        ? 'You typed the letter D'
    CASE memchoice = 'E'
        ? 'You typed the letter E'
    CASE memchoice = 'F'
        ? 'You typed the letter F'
    CASE memchoice = 'G'
        ? 'You typed the letter G'
    CASE memchoice = 'H'
        ? 'You typed the letter H'
    CASE memchoice = 'I'
        ? 'You typed the letter I'
    CASE memchoice = 'J'
        ? 'You typed the letter J'
    ENDCASE
```

```
          .DO TESTCASE

    STORE ' ' TO memchoice

    ACCEPT 'Type a letter' TO memchoice
    Type a letter D
    DO CASE
        CASE memchoice = 'A'
        CASE memchoice = 'B'
        CASE memchoice = 'C'
        CASE memchoice = 'D'
            ? 'You typed the letter D'
    You typed the letter D
        CASE memchoice = 'E'
```

FIGURE 8.3   *Example of sequential IF/ENDIFs (Part 3 of 3).*

To conserve space only ten options were presented in Figure 8.3. The number of lines required to evaluate 26 options (the whole alphabet) for each of the structures follows:

54 Lines — DO CASE
64 Lines — Nested IF/ENDIF
78 Lines — Series of IF/ENDIF

At the end of each program listing is a sample of the screen output, using SET ECHO ON in order to display the commands as they execute. The series of IF/ENDIF structures continues to evaluate all the remaining IF statements after the letter D was found, which is inefficient. Although the nested IF/ENDIF exits after a true condition is found, it requires dBASE III PLUS to deal with extra lines (ELSE and ENDIF). In comparison, the program clarity is obvious in the DO CASE/ENDCASE example.

There does not appear to be any significant difference in execution time among the above structures, although this is probably only the result of good performance by dBASE III PLUS. All structures tested at one second for the letters A and Z. Although there is no limit on the number of CASE statements, 26 options is an unrealistic number for most applications. Situations that require an unusually high number of options can be handled with the programming strategies presented in Chapter 12. In summary, it would appear that the DO CASE/ENDCASE is the structure of choice in situations where several options must be evaluated.

Make certain that all options are *mutually exclusive*, in other words, that only one option can be true in a given set of circumstances. The reason that this is important becomes clear when you understand how the DO CASE/ENDCASE operates. As the structure executes, each of the CASE statements is evaluated as encountered. The first time a true condition is found, dBASE III PLUS will execute the commands specified between that CASE and the next CASE statement, then it will branch out of the structure. Therefore, if it were possible for two options to be true, the first one encountered would be selected and the other would be ignored.

Figure 8.4 shows how the table in Figure 8.1 might be programmed using the DO CASE.

```
DO CASE
    CASE income > 42000 .AND. income < 42050
        tax = 10106
    CASE income > 42050 .AND. income < 42100
        tax = 10125
    CASE income > 42100 .AND. income < 42150
        tax = 10144
    CASE income > 42150 .AND. income < 42200
        tax = 10163
    CASE income > 42200 .AND. income < 42250
        tax = 10182
    CASE income > 42250 .AND. income < 42300
        tax = 10201
    CASE income > 42300 .AND. income < 42350
        tax = 10220
    CASE income > 42350 .AND. income < 42400
        tax = 10239
    CASE income > 42400 .AND. income < 42450
        tax = 10258
    OTHERWISE
        ? 'Income is not contained in table'
ENDCASE
```

FIGURE 8.4 *Programming with multiple options.*

It is possible to provide an alternative action for all remaining possibilities outside the ones specified in the CASE statements. You have the option of placing an OTHERWISE clause after the final CASE statement for this purpose. This clause is introduced in Figure 8.4 to handle any income less than 42,000 or greater than 42,450. Note that since the conditions in this example test for greater than and less than the bracketed amounts for the sake of clarity, the specified amounts such as 42,000 would be excluded.

Although the DO CASE/ENDCASE is simple to construct, you may on occasion omit or accidentally delete the DO CASE statement. This will prevent any of the statements within the structure from executing, but without the benefit of an error message. If you find that the program ceases execution after one successful pass through the structure, the ENDCASE is probably missing.

8.2 USER INPUT

The five commands available in dBASE III PLUS for user input are as follows:

```
INPUT
ACCEPT
WAIT
INKEY()
@ GET and READ
```

The INPUT statement has little practical programming value, because it requires the user to place quotes around character data and to use special functions for dates. Since it is sometimes unclear what type of data is required by an INPUT, some risk to data integrity is incurred. However, since it provides the only means for storing numeric data without using the @ GET and READ, it is used in the program in Figure 8.10. In the following example, a prompt message, which must be enclosed in quotes, is included to instruct the user. Notice the space after the word PRICE, which will provide a buffer for the user's response. Data entered is stored in the memory variable after the TO.

```
STORE 0 to memprice
INPUT 'ENTER PRICE ' TO memprice
```

ACCEPT will enter a character string of up to 254 characters in a memory variable. It requires a Return key, as opposed to the WAIT. ACCEPT will display a prompt message. Since the programmer has no control over the data that may be entered by the user and stored in the memory variable, the ACCEPT command should be used only for general questions such as the following:

```
ACCEPT 'Would you like to continue? (Y/N) ' TO memanswer
```

The WAIT will allow one character to be entered without the Return key. This is useful for speeding nonrisk operations, such as moving from one menu to another. Users will appreciate the instant response of the program to the touch of one key. Should the wrong key be pressed, the data will not be damaged.

The WAIT is often used in menu programs. Three examples of prompt messages are presented in Figure 8.5 on the following page. A WAIT without a TO clause will simply pause the program until any key is pressed.

```
        . WAIT
Press any key to continue...
        . WAIT ''

        . WAIT 'SELECT OPTION ' TO memchoice
SELECT OPTION 1

        . DISPLAY MEMORY

MEMCHOICE    pub    C    "1"
    1 variables defined,       3 bytes used
  255 variables available,   5997 bytes available
```

FIGURE 8.5   *Using WAIT.*

The first WAIT displays "Press any key to continue..." because no prompt was specified. The second contains a prompt (''), which is a *null string*, meaning that it contains no ASCII characters at all. Finally, the message 'SELECT OPTION' is displayed and, since a memory variable is specified, the response is stored. DISPLAY MEMORY can be used to verify the data stored in memchoice.

The INKEY() function is similar to the WAIT in that it will accept a single keystroke from the user. Unfortunately, it is useful only when placed in a loop, because it does not pause program execution. Also, it returns the ASCII value of the key pressed, which is clumsy to use. However, it could be employed to allow a user to interrupt a procedure with a keystroke by including the INKEY() function in the DO WHILE and a STORE command within the loop, as in Figure 8.6. This could be useful if you wanted to allow a user to stop a printing procedure at any point with a keystroke.

```
memstop = 0
? 'Press any key to interrupt printing.'
DO WHILE .NOT. EOF .AND. memstop = 0
        * (actions performed)
        STORE INKEY() TO memstop
        SKIP
ENDDO .NOT. EOF .AND. memstop = 0
```

FIGURE 8.6   *Using INKEY().*

The @ GET and READ commands, which will be presented in Chapter 11, provide the most useful means for accurate data entry. They allow *full-screen editing*, which means that the user can employ editing keys to enter data in attractive, formatted input blocks. Data can also be validated as it is entered. However, the ACCEPT and the WAIT are both useful on occasion.

8.3 CONSTRUCTING MENUS

Menus are important because users react very well to them and because they present options in a logical way that facilitates programming. Users do not need a knowledge of dBASE III PLUS to work effectively with a menu-driven program. Experienced users and programmers also appreciate the convenience of being able to preprogram lengthy command sequences so that they will execute with the push of a key. The pseudocode for a menu portion of a program might look like this:

Do these commands while the user does not wish to quit.

Display a screen containing instructions and listing options.
Pause the program until the user selects one of the options.
Perform the commands required to complete the option chosen by the user.

A menu program might consist of a DO WHILE containing a screen display and a user input command such as a WAIT. A DO CASE/ENDCASE would provide the appropriate action as a reaction to the user's response.

The DO WHILE loop should be either an endless loop (DO WHILE .T.) or a loop allowing all conditions except the exit option, as in Figure 8.7. This is most safely expressed as testing if the memory variable is not equal to the exit value. This strategy will allow the screen to redisplay until the task is completed. Although the program in Figure 8.7 offers only two choices, the structure is in place to handle many more options by adding more CASE statements. In fact, the only exit for the program is for the user to respond with a '2' in memchoice.

PSEUDOCODE FOR A TYPICAL MENU

```
Set environment
Initialize variables
DO WHILE variable <> exit value
    Clear Screen
    Display choices                CLEAR
    Prompt user for choice         DO WHILE memchoice <> '2'
    DO CASE                            ?
        Menu choices                   ?
        Exit                           ? '1 - Print the report'
    ENDCASE                            ? '2 - Exit'
ENDDO                                  ?
                                       WAIT 'CHOICE - ' TO memchoice
                                       DO CASE
                                          CASE memchoice = '1'
                                              REPORT FORM BUDGET TO PRINT
                                          CASE memchoice = '2'
                                              QUIT
                                          ENDCASE
                                   ENDDO memchoice <> '2'
```

FIGURE 8.7 *Pseudocode and code for a menu program.*

Most studies indicate that users are comfortable with menus that contain between five and nine options. Chapter 9 will explain how in more sophisticated applications a menu often exits to another menu. Since you can create one menu to branch to other menus, you can limit each menu to nine options or less and still create all the options you need by branching. Either letters or numerals can be used to identify the options. Numeric values should be avoided, since they are more error-prone and are difficult to handle. It is important to design the DO CASE and all other structures so that they have only one entrance and one exit. The last option in any menu should always be an exit from the program.

Menu Tips

1. Attempt to develop a consistent style and appearance for all menus.
2. Give each menu a title.
3. Use from five to nine options.
4. Use brief meaningful labels for the options.
5. Include a single exit as the last option.
6. Always enter a menu from a single entry point.

After you have completed Chapter 11, you will be able to construct sophisticated and attractive screen displays that will enhance your menu programs. However, the basic rules presented here will continue to operate in the background to create user-friendly menus.

8.4 WRITING A PROGRAM TO DELETE RECORDS

Usually, a program to delete records should operate in a *batch* mode, because it is more efficient to issue a PACK command once for a group of records than to issue one PACK *per* record. A group of records to be deleted is marked with asterisks, using the DELETE command in a loop, until the user is ready to remove the records from the file. At that point, the program would execute a PACK command to complete the process, assuming that this would be an appropriate program tactic for the user. In certain situations, a user may prefer to have those records which are marked for deletion remain in the database for a period of time. Moreover, records sometimes must be *archived* or placed in a historical file before they are actually removed from the current database. Both of these situations require solutions other than the program outlined below.

The physical removal of records is a drastic action for any organized file but especially for a dBASE III PLUS file, since its relational basis requires that records be numbered sequentially and consecutively. While Chapter 3 explained how this process operates, you must consider the performance aspects of deleting records. Marking a record with the DELETE command, followed by a PACK, can be quite time-consuming, depending on the size of the database. This is because once the unwanted ones are removed, the entire database must be rewritten in order for the records to be in proper order. Batching the deleted records and then issuing one PACK command would obviously save a great deal of time. Figure 8.9 shows that the user would have to sit chin in hand for a period of 13 seconds for each record deleted in a 1000-record database, using the structure presented in Figure 8.8.

```
Structure for database: C:APP.dbf
Number of data records:      0
Date of last update   : 01/01/88
Field  Field Name  Type      Width   Dec
    1  CH_FIELD    Character    25
    2  NUM_FIELD   Numeric       5    2
** Total **                     31
```

FIGURE 8.8 *Structure for APP.DBF.*

```
APPEND  |  3:42 with no data  |  5:05 with REPLACE
DELETE  |  1:54 for all       |
PACK    |   :05 for all       |   :13 for 1 record
```

FIGURE 8.9 *Timing benchmarks.*

The first section of the program establishes an environment. Include SET SAFETY OFF; this will allow files to be overwritten without having to ask the user for permission to do so. SET TALK OFF must be used to prevent the display of system chatter, such as displaying the contents of memory variables during STORE commands. SET STATUS OFF removes the standard three-line display at the bottom of the screen; its removal allows for freedom in screen design. It is also a good idea to use SET DELETED ON. This will exclude any deleted records from any reports or displays.

The user must have a way of indicating which records are to be deleted. This naturally leads to the idea of selecting records by searching through the file. In fact, that is the preferred method of selection. Chapter 10 will show how indexing can make this type of searching possible. The record number will be used in the program below to select records to be deleted. In reality, this method would not be very useful, since the user would have to refer to a list of record numbers and select manually. However, it can be used in the absence of an index.

In Figure 8.10, DEL_REC.PRG combines the INPUT, DO CASE, and menu in a program that automates the deletion process. This program could be called by another menu in addition to being executed with a DO command from the dot prompt.

```
* DEL_REC.PRG A menu program to delete records by record number
STORE ' ' TO memchoice
STORE 0 TO memrec
SET STATUS OFF
SET TALK OFF
USE APP
DO WHILE memchoice <> '2'
   STORE 0 TO memrec
   CLEAR
   ?
   ?
   ?
   ?
   ?
   ? '                    1 - Enter Record # to Delete'
   ? '                    2 - Exit'
   ?
   WAIT '          Enter Choice ' TO memchoice
   DO CASE
        CASE memchoice = '1'
           CLEAR
           ?
           ?
           ?
           ?
           ?
              INPUT '                     Enter Record # to delete ' to memrec
              GO memrec
              DELETE
              GO TOP
           CASE memchoice = '2'
              LOOP
       ENDCASE
ENDDO memchoice <> '2'
CLEAR
? '                     Please Wait While Processing . . . '
PACK
CLEAR ALL
CLEAR
```

FIGURE 8.10 *DEL_REC.PRG.*

After an identifying comment line, the program in Figure 8.10 begins by initializing the two memory variables, memchoice and memrec, to ' ' and 0, respectively.
Since initialization provides good documentation and is required by some commands, it should be included at the start of every program. Next, the environment is
established with the SET commands, and the database file is opened.

The main body of the program is a DO WHILE loop that tests for the exit
option, a '2' in memchoice. This will permit the loop to continue to execute as long
as the user wishes, since the menu inside will be redisplayed after each use. Sometimes a DO WHILE .T. is used for this purpose, but the principles of structured
programming dictate that endless loops are generally to be avoided, if possible.

Because it will be used to temporarily hold record numbers that have been
chosen for deletion, memrec must be reset to 0 at the beginning of the loop. The
screen must also be erased with the CLEAR command in order to display the menu.
The eight ? commands that follow either print a blank line and move the cursor
down the screen, or display the options to the user. Once the options are visible, a
WAIT command stores the user's choice in memchoice.

The DO CASE/ENDCASE provides the means to execute the appropriate commands, depending on the user's response. Either an opportunity will be provided to delete a record or the program will be terminated by LOOPing back to the DO WHILE with '2' stored in memchoice. Since this is the condition programmed to exit the DO WHILE, the program branches to the CLEAR that follows the ENDDO. One advantage of this strategy is that any characters other than '1' or '2' will cause the screen to redisplay.

A '1' in memchoice will require the selection of a record number to delete. Record numbers are numeric, so an INPUT command must be used to store the user's choice in memrec. The GO command positions the record pointer at the desired record before the DELETE command marks it for deletion with an asterisk. The record pointer is repositioned at the top of the file with GO TOP. Since the CASE is finished, the program branches to the statement after the ENDCASE, ENDDO memchoice < > '2'. When the condition is evaluated at the DO WHILE, the body of the loop will execute again. It is this looping that facilitates the batch processing of an unlimited number of records with rapid response.

The final section of the program occurs only once for each execution. The screen is CLEARed and a message is displayed to reassure the user. The PACK command then physically removes the entire batch of records marked for deletion and rewrites the file. The files are closed, and memory variables are released with the CLEAR ALL command. Finally, the screen is CLEARed again.

DEL_REC.PRG is a good example of how useful procedures can be constructed by blending programming structures such as the DO WHILE/ENDDO, DO CASE/ENDCASE, and IF/ENDIF. No magic formula is going to tell you how to write a program! However, having a clear understanding of how the structures will behave in a variety of conditions and examining several examples to observe their effect is an excellent beginning.

CHAPTER SUMMARY

8.1

Compared to the series and the nested IF/ENDIF, the DO CASE/ENDCASE offers the advantages of speed and clarity when several mutually exclusive options must be evaluated. The structure must begin with a DO CASE and must finish with an ENDCASE. CASE statements and associated commands are placed between. The CASE statements each contain a condition that will be evaluated until one is found to be true. The structure is then exited. An optional OTHERWISE can be included for any condition that is not specified in the CASE statements.

8.2

The @ GET/READ is the best method for data entry. However, the ACCEPT and the WAIT are useful. The ACCEPT will store a character string in a variable and will display a prompt. The WAIT will pause the program until a key is pressed and will store as well. The INPUT and INKEY() are not as useful in programming.

8.3

Menus are valuable because they are an attractive and efficient way to direct program activity with user control. A menu displays options on a screen and accepts the user's choice. A DO CASE is used to select and execute the requested action. A DO WHILE/ENDDO is used to redisplay the menu. All menus should have one entry and one exit.

8.4

A program to delete records is more convenient to use if the records are marked for deletion as a batch, then PACKed when the user employs the exit option in the menu. The record number is used to specify deletions. The program uses a menu with a DO CASE/ENDCASE contained within a DO WHILE.

KEY TERMS

mutually exclusive   menu-driven
null string   batch mode
full-screen editing   archive

COMMAND SUMMARY

DO CASE — The initial statement of the CASE structure.

ENDCASE — The final statement of the CASE structure.

CASE — The statement that contains the condition in a CASE structure.

OTHERWISE — A CASE command that identifies actions performed when all cases fail.

INPUT — A command sometimes employed for user input of numeric data.

WAIT — A command that accepts one character of user input.

INKEY() — A function that captures a keystroke from the user.

SET SAFETY OFF — Overwriting of files will be automatic.

SET STATUS OFF — The status display is not displayed.

SET DELETED ON — Deleted records are not displayed.

dBUG dBASE

- SET DEBUG ON sends all the ECHOed commands to the printer rather than the screen for documentation and more thorough study.
- Although it makes no difference in what order menu options are displayed on the screen, you should place the most frequently used option of DO CASE/ ENDCASE as the first option in order to avoid having to scan the unused options frequently.
- Be as skeptical as possible about the new program until constant testing in a variety of circumstances validates the accuracy of the results. Use normal test data, then varied and difficult data.
- When a program is first implemented, always operate in parallel; in other words, use the original program and the new one simultaneously. This is more time-consuming in the short run, but it will protect the business operation from unforeseen disaster.

SELF-CHECK QUESTIONS

1. When is DO CASE/ENDCASE preferable to IF/ENDIF? Indicate whether an IF/ENDIF or a DO CASE/ENDCASE is best for each of the following situations:
    a. Individuals must be 16 years old to obtain a driver's license.
    b. Tennis players must be placed in ten tournament groups on the basis of their ranking.
    c. The dean's list requires a GPA of at least 3.6.
    d. Interest rates on certificates of deposit vary with the six terms (required time).
2. Is a DO CASE/ENDCASE more efficient than several IF/ENDIFs? Why?
3. What are mutually exclusive options?
4. What does OTHERWISE do?
5. What is the difference between ACCEPT and WAIT?
6. What is full-screen editing?
7. Why is a DO WHILE .T. useful in a menu program?
8. What is batch mode? When is it useful?
9. What are the disadvantages of using INPUT and INKEY()?
10. What is archiving?

TRY IT YOURSELF

1. Write an INPUT statement with a prompt to store a salary in the memory variable memsal.

2. Construct a DO CASE/ENDCASE to assign the appropriate tax rate to the variable memtax by evaluating the field STATE for the state code as follows:

PA — 6%

IL — 5%

NE — 4.5%

NM — 4.25%

WY — 3%

3. Write DO CASE/ENDCASE structures for the situations you selected in Self-check Question 1.

4. Write CASE/ENDCASE statements for the following conditions.

a. Only full-time students (FT) may participate in athletics.

b. A tolerance of .0002 must be attained before a part is passed by quality control.

c. A youth club requires that its members be between the ages of 11 and 17.

d. A car is considered an antique if it is more than 25 years old.

5. How could the CASE structures in Figure 8.4 be rewritten to include exactly the specified amounts?

6. Decide whether the INPUT, WAIT, or ACCEPT would be the best choice for each of the following tasks:

a. Allow a user to move quickly through menus by pressing the indicated key.

b. Enter test grades to compute an average.

c. Display this message: 'Press return when printer is ready'.

d. Ask the user's name and store it in a memory variable.

7. Write the appropriate statements for the previous exercise.

8. Write a command to enter the user's choice in Problem 2.

PROGRAMMING PROJECT

Write a DO WHILE and DO CASE/ENDCASE to enclose the following portion of a menu program. (Use the variable memchoice.)

```
?
? '1 - Add a record'
? '2 - Display/Modify a record'
? '3 - Delete a record'
? '4 - Exit'
?
```

9

ORGANIZING A SYSTEM

LEARNING OBJECTIVES

1. To examine the effect of nesting structures.
2. To use the modular concept to construct systems.
3. To compare the behavior of memory variable types in systems.
4. To incorporate data integrity within programs and reexamine structured programming.

Chapter

9

ORGANIZING A SYSTEM

A system may be defined as an interrelated group of elements working together for a common purpose. You have written several freestanding programs. In actual business practice, these programs would be grouped together in a system for ease of use and efficiency. This chapter will present several ways of organizing systems in a structured manner. Sophisticated business problems require this type of approach.

9.1 NESTING

You have studied the three control structures DO WHILE/ENDDO, IF/ENDIF, and DO CASE in the three previous chapters. As you encounter more complex business problems, you will have to combine these structures within programs. Occasionally, some of the program examples in earlier chapters placed an IF/ENDIF within a DO WHILE/ENDDO, using a strategy called *nesting*. A good analogy for nesting is a child's toy: a set of plastic barrels of different colors and sizes, each of which opens into two halves. When the toy is assembled, the barrels are nested one inside the other. Think of structures being nested in this way. As with the toy, the halves must match in order for the program to work. Structures may be nested within one another in any combination as long as the arrangement is logically correct.

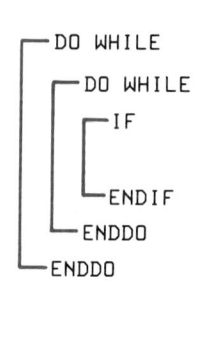

FIGURE 9.1   *Nested toy barrels.*

The nesting arrangements in previous chapters are not complex, since the IF/ ENDIF and the DO CASE are sequential structures, meaning that they do not loop or repeat. For this reason, they are relatively simple to understand when nested in a DO WHILE. In the examples in Figure 9.2, the structures within the loop will execute only once for each pass of the DO WHILE.

```
DO WHILE condition          DO WHILE condition
     IF condition                DO CASE
            action                      CASE condition
     ELSE                                      action
            action                      CASE condition
     ENDIF                                     action
ENDDO                             ENDCASE
                            ENDDO
```

FIGURE 9.2   *Examples of nested structures.*

When one DO WHILE/ENDDO is nested within another DO WHILE/ENDDO it can become difficult to predict or understand how the program will behave, because the status of two loops must be monitored simultaneously. Naturally, the more levels of nesting that are added, the more ambiguous the logic becomes.

```
DO WHILE condition
       DO WHILE condition
              action
       ENDDO
ENDDO
```

FIGURE 9.3   *Nested DO WHILE/ENDDO loops.*

Imagine a ride in an amusement park which would take you to the top of a tower in a car and spin you around three times as you descend. There would be three spins of the car for each trip down the tower. You might take many rides up and down the tower, but for each pass you would spin three times. In other words, three trips up and down the tower would yield nine spins of the car.

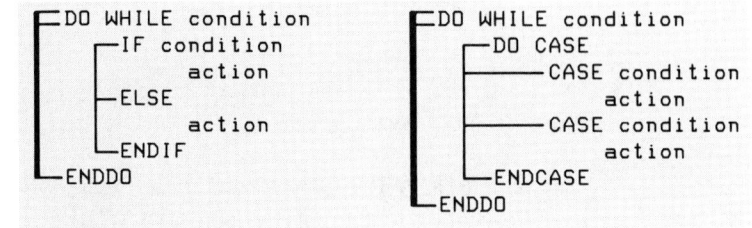

```
DO WHILE stomach <> 'nauseated'
     go up the tower
     start down
     DO WHILE spin < 4
          spin the car
          spin = spin + 1
     ENDDO spin < 4
     spin = 1
ENDDO stomach <> 'nauseated'
```

FIGURE 9.4   *A nested DO WHILE/ENDDO "ride."*

You can see how both DO WHILE conditions must be monitored if you are to understand how the program is operating. If more loops were nested in this way, and perhaps other structures as well, it could be quite difficult to follow the logic. Although the previously explained structured conventions of indention and documentation will help, it is also useful to *bracket* structures for clarification. Figure 9.5 illustrates how the three control structures can be bracketed using *action diagrams*, a technique developed by James Martin.

```
 ┌─DO WHILE condition              ┌─DO WHILE condition
 │   ┌─IF condition                │   ┌─DO CASE
 │   │      action                 │   │      ───CASE condition
 │   ├─ELSE                        │   │             action
 │   │      action                 │   │      ───CASE condition
 │   └─ENDIF                       │   │             action
 └─ENDDO                           │   └─ENDCASE
                                   └─ENDDO
```

FIGURE 9.5   *Diagramming nested structures.*

Figure 9.6 on the following page contains a program to display records on the screen in groups of 15.

```
USE NAMES
memchoice = ' '
DO WHILE memchoice <> '2'
      CLEAR
      ?
      ?
      ? '1 - Print the report'
      ? '2 - Exit'
      ?
      WAIT 'CHOICE - ' TO memchoice
      IF memchoice = '1'
            DO WHILE .NOT. EOF()
               ? NAME
               ROW = ROW + 1
               SKIP
               IF memrow > 15
                  WAIT 'Press Return to Continue'
                  memrow = 1
                  CLEAR
               ENDIF
            ENDDO .NOT. EOF()
      ELSE
         IF memchoice = '2'
            QUIT
         ENDIF
      ENDIF
ENDDO memchoice <> '2'
```

FIGURE 9.6   *A program illustrating nested structures.*

This is a good example of nested DO WHILE/ENDDO loops. One loop will handle the menu, and another will be required to access all the records in the file sequentially. When the necessary IF structures are included, the result is a structure like the one outlined in Figure 9.7.

```
DO WHILE
    IF
        DO WHILE
            IF
            ENDIF
        ENDDO
    ELSE
        IF
        ENDIF
    ENDIF
ENDDO
```

FIGURE 9.7   *Outline of nested structures.*

The nested DO WHILE .NOT. EOF() in Figure 9.6 will execute fifteen times for every execution of the outside loop, DO WHILE memchoice < > '2'. This allows you to browse the names in the file conveniently on the screen as often as you wish. It is rare to exceed two or three levels of nested DO WHILEs, unless you are using more than one .DBF file (as Chapter 12 will explain). Because they are so powerful, DO WHILE structures should be established only when they are clearly required to achieve repetition. You may be tempted to employ the condition testing of the DO WHILE for selection, using a logical operator such as .AND. This practice usually results in overly complicated structures that are difficult to construct and debug. Use IF/ENDIF or DO CASE nested within the DO WHILE instead.

Unfortunately, there are no clear rules that apply to nesting. The problem at hand will dictate how the structures have to be organized in order to produce a solution. However, it can be stated that nested structures must be free from logical errors and that they must perform the intended function efficiently. Although dBASE III PLUS will not allow illogical structures to execute, you must use your knowledge and experience to ensure that the structures perform as expected.

9.2 THE MODULAR CONCEPT

You have become accustomed to writing a program in order to accomplish a single task. While this is a useful, common approach to programming, many business situations require another strategy. When a project has a wide scope, it is often necessary to assign individual tasks to separate programs that are linked together in a system.

Modules are small programs that are sometimes referred to as subroutines, subprograms, and procedures, or called programs. They are designed to perform one function, and they should be written as freestanding sections of code, meaning that they may be run alone or as part of a larger system. The concept of a set of individual modules linked together in a larger structure is an important principle of structured programming.

Modules are generally written as separate .PRG files and are called from a central menu-driven program. The DO and RETURN commands are provided by dBASE III PLUS for this purpose. You have become accustomed to executing .PRG files from the dot prompt, using the DO command. The DO command is also capable of executing or calling other .PRG files from within a program.

```
. TYPE STUB.PRG
* STUB. PRG - Tests the calling of other program with DO and
*              RETURN.
STORE ' '  TO memchoice
SET STATUS OFF
SET TALK OFF
DO WHILE memchoice <> '2'
   CLEAR
      ?
      ?
      ?
```

FIGURE 9.8 *Menu program using stubs (Part 1 of 3).*

```
?
?                       1 - Call Stub Program
?
?                       2 - Exit
?
WAIT                    ENTER CHOICE - TO memchoice
DO CASE
    CASE memchoice = 1
        DO STUB2
    CASE memchoice = 2
        CLEAR
        RETURN
ENDCASE
ENDDO memchoice <> '2'

. TYPE STUB2.PRG
* STUB2.PRG - Called from STUB.PRG
CLEAR
?
?
?
?
?
? '            This is a module called from a menu program '
?
WAIT '            PRESS ANY KEY TO CONTINUE' TO ok
RETURN

. DO STUB
```

```
1 - Call Stub Program

2 - Exit
ENTER CHOICE - 1
```

```
This is a module called from a menu program

PRESS ANY KEY TO CONTINUE
```

FIGURE 9.8   *Menu program using stubs (Part 2 of 3).*

```
1 - Call Stub Program

2 - Exit

ENTER CHOICE - 2
```

FIGURE 9.8   *Menu program using stubs (Part 3 of 3).*

Figure 9.8 contains the listing and execution of a pair of programs that illustrate the use of *stubs*, which are nonfunctional test modules. Notice how STUB2.PRG is called by STUB.PRG with the DO command. Control is passed back to the STUB. PRG program by the RETURN command. This is a convenient way to construct the skeleton of a menu-driven system in order to ensure that the modules are called correctly. The modules can be finished later.

A module should begin by opening any required .DBF or other files and initializing variables. These files are closed, and any memory variables are released at the conclusion of the module's operation. Writing modules in this fashion offers several advantages, as follows.

1. Modules are independent; they do not depend upon each other for data.
2. Each module can be tested and debugged individually.
3. Several programmers may conveniently work on the system.
4. Modules can be modified for use in other applications.

The most obvious examples of functions that modules can perform are appending, modifying, displaying, and deleting records. These functions could be placed together in a menu-driven system in order to allow a user who was unfamiliar with dBASE III PLUS or programming to access them easily. The tasks are performed safely and efficiently because the critical commands are carefully written in .PRG files. Other commonly used functions include displaying individual records, generating summary reports, and performing calculations.

It may be helpful to diagram the system structure in order to verify that the design is correct and effective. Structure diagrams aid in displaying the relationships among program modules. Other persons who become involved with the project will be more comfortable dealing with a structure diagram than with listings of code.

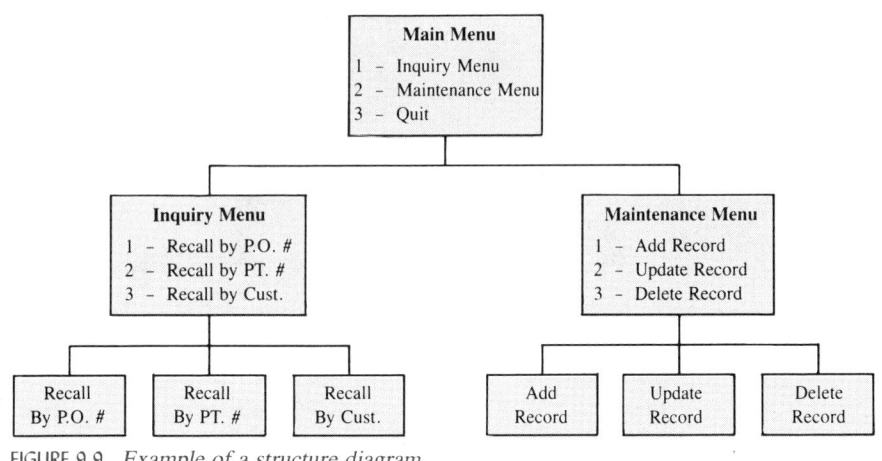

FIGURE 9.9   *Example of a structure diagram.*

The strategy of proceeding from the general goals of a system to more manageable task levels is called *functional decomposition* or *top-down design*. Too many modules on any one level is undesirable. A reasonable number is between two to six. The diagram in Figure 9.10 shows the X level calling nine modules in the Y level. Nine modules are too many. Inserting the Z level solves the problem by subgrouping three modules in each of the Z submenus. The lowest level of the structure should be the individual task modules. Although it is certainly possible, it is unusual for systems to exceed three levels.

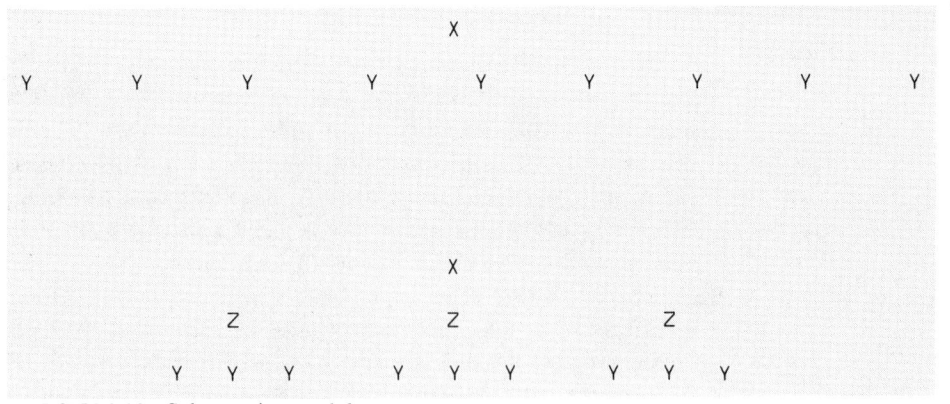

FIGURE 9.10   *Subgrouping modules.*

In the example in Figure 9.10, the X module would allow the user to select any one of the three Z submenus or to leave the system. The Z modules would include three Y options or a return to the X module. The Y options would perform their individual tasks and return to the Z module.

Most business problems you will encounter will be of sufficient scope to require a system of modules rather than several loosely related but separate files. Solving problems in this way is effective, efficient, and responsible.

"The code should be crisp and concise. You should be able to explain any module in one sentence . . . The ideal module should be one page long."

C. Wayne Ratliff
Programmers at Work

9.3 PROGRAMMING WITH MEMORY VARIABLES

As in Pascal or C, two other widely used languages, dBASE III PLUS includes some commands to provide control over memory variables. The PRIVATE ALL command localizes memory variables so that they are not available to any other programs that may be executed. The PUBLIC command, on the other hand, will make specified variables available to any program in the system. It is important to note that if a variable can be accessed, it can be changed. The programmer has control over PUBLIC variables. Variables are automatically declared PUBLIC when they are established at the dot prompt and declared PRIVATE when they are created within a program (unless they are declared PUBLIC by the programmer).

Variables that are created in a higher level program, the *calling* program, are available in any lower level programs, the *called* programs. For example, in the bottom of Figure 9.10, a variable created in level Z would be available in level Y but not in level X. Variables can be passed down the structure diagram but cannot move up, because dBASE III PLUS will RELEASE all PRIVATE variables when a RETURN command executes.

If a variable is declared PUBLIC before it is assigned a value with a STORE command, it will be available to programs at any level, even after the system has returned control to dBASE III PLUS. It might be useful to declare a memory variable to hold the state sales tax PUBLIC in a program for retail merchants. The value would then be universally available for calculations throughout the system. Should the tax rate change, only one line of code, the STORE command, would need to be modified. Be cautious when declaring variables PUBLIC; you should always have a specific reason for doing so.

The two programs in Figure 9.11 on the following page demonstrate how memory variables behave under a variety of conditions. The variable "upper" was declared PUBLIC and appears consistently in all LIST MEMORY displays. Since "first" was created in MEMTRACK, it remains available in that program and in all programs below it in the system structure. It also remains the same in all LIST MEMORY displays. However, "second" had its value changed in LOWER and brought that value back to MEMTRACK after the RETURN.

```
   TYPE MEMTRACK.PRG
* MEMTRACK.PRG Tracks public and private memory variables and
             their behavior.
SET TALK OFF
SET STATUS OFF
PUBLIC upper
STORE ' Created in MEMTRACK as PUBLIC ' TO upper
STORE 100 TO first
STORE 200 TO second
STORE 300 TO third
STORE 400 TO fourth
LIST MEMORY
WAIT 'Press Return'
DO LOWER WITH third
? 'Let us check the memory now that we have RETURNed to MEMTRACK
WAIT 'Press Return'
LIST MEMORY
?
?
? 'Notice that first, second & third could be used by lower, but since'
? 'LOWER also created a fourth, the fourth in MEMTRACK is masked'
?
WAIT 'Press Return'
? 'The PARAMETER in LOWER allowed the value of third from MEMTRACK to'
? 'be shared by fifth'
? 'LOWER also created sixth for local use'
```

```
WAIT 'Press Return'
?
? 'STATUS REPORT'
? first, ' - first could be accessed by LOWER'
? second, ' - second was redefined by LOWER'
? third, ' - third was changed as PARAMETER fifth in LOWER'
? fourth, ' - fourth not affected since LOWER had a fourth also'
? fifth, ' - fifth is only available in LOWER'
? sixth, ' - sixth was created by LOWER and RELEASEd by RETURN'
RETURN


. TYPE LOWER.PRG
* LOWER.PRG Called by MEMTEST.PRG to illustrate memory variable behavior.
PARAMETER fifth
PRIVATE fourth
STORE 900 TO fourth
CLEAR
? ' This is LOWER.PRG which was called from MEMTRACK.PRG. Here is
a look at memory.
LIST MEMORY
? fourth, ' - fourth was redefined here and becomes another variable
          with the same name'
? fifth, ' - fifth is really third because of the PARAMETER '
WAIT 'Press Return'
STORE 75 TO fifth
STORE 89 TO fifth
```

```
STORE 67 TO second
STORE 98 TO sixth
RETURN

. DO MEMTRACK
UPPER      pub  C " Created in MEMTRACK as PUBLIC "
FIRST      priv N     100  (     100.00000000)     C:MEMTRACK.prg
SECOND     priv N     200  (     200.00000000)     C:MEMTRACK.prg
THIRD      priv N     300  (     300.00000000)     C:MEMTRACK.prg
FOURTH     priv N     400  (     400.00000000)     C:MEMTRACK.prg
     6 variables defined,      86 bytes used
    250 variables available,  5914 bytes available
```

FIGURE 9.11   *Illustration of PUBLIC and PRIVATE (Part 1 of 2).*

```
Press Return
 This is LOWER.PRG which was called from MEMTRACK.PRG. Here is a look at
memory.
MEMTEST      pub   C " PUBLIC VARIABLE "
UPPER        pub   C " Created in MEMTRACK as PUBLIC "
FIRST        priv  N       100  (        100.00000000)        C:MEMTRACK.prg
SECOND       priv  N       200  (        200.00000000)        C:MEMTRACK.prg
THIRD        priv  (hidden) N       300  (        300.00000000)C:MEMTRACK.prg
FOURTH       priv  (hidden) N       400  (        400.00000000)C:MEMTRACK.prg
FIFTH        priv  @  THIRD
FOURTH       priv  N       900  (        900.00000000)        C:LOWER.prg
     8 variables defined,      95 bytes used
   248 variables available,  5905 bytes available

        900  - fourth was redefined here and becomes another
               variable with the same name
        300  - fifth is really third
               because of the PARAMETER

Press Return
Let us check the memory now that we have RETURNed to MEMTRACK
Press Return
MEMTEST      pub   C " PUBLIC VARIABLE "
UPPER        pub   C " Created in MEMTRACK as PUBLIC "
FIRST        priv  N       100  (        100.00000000)        C:MEMTRACK.prg
SECOND       priv  N        67  (         67.00000000)        C:MEMTRACK.prg
```

```
THIRD         priv  N       75  (         75.00000000)        C:MEMTRACK.prg
FOURTH        priv  N      400  (        400.00000000)        C:MEMTRACK.prg
     6 variables defined,      86 bytes used
   250 variables available,  5914 bytes available


Notice that first, second, & third could be used by lower, but
since LOWER also created a fourth, the fourth in MEMTRACK is
masked

Press Return
The PARAMETER in LOWER allowed the value of third from MEMTRACK to
be shared by fifth. LOWER also created sixth for local use
Press Return

STATUS REPORT
        100  - first could be accessed by LOWER
         67  - second was redefined by LOWER
         75  - third was changed as PARAMETER fifth in LOWER
        400  - fourth not affected since LOWER had a fourth also
Variable not found.
        ?
? fifth, ' - fifth is only available in LOWER'
Called from - C:MEMTRACK.prg
Cancel, Ignore, or Suspend? (C, I, or S) Ignore
Variable not found.
```

```
          ?
? sixth, ' - sixth was created by LOWER and RELEASEd by RETURN
Called from - C:MEMTRACK.prg
Cancel, Ignore, or Suspend? (C, I, or S) Ignore

. LIST MEMORY
UPPER         pub    C ' Created in MEMTRACK as PUBLIC '
     1 variables defined,      33 bytes used
   255 variables available,  5967 bytes available

. RELEASE ALL
. LIST MEMORY
     0 variables defined,       0 bytes used
   256 variables available,  6000 bytes available
```

FIGURE 9.11   *Illustration of PUBLIC and PRIVATE (Part 2 of 2).*

The DO WITH and PARAMETER commands allow variables to be passed to other programs. PARAMETER must be the first executable command in the program. "Third" was passed to "fifth" in LOWER as a parameter and is hidden. Notice that "fifth" does not show a value in the "second" LIST MEMORY. Assigning the value 75 to "fifth" actually assigned it to "third," as you can see in the last LIST MEMORY. When the RETURN command executed, "fifth" was destroyed because it was created in LOWER and could not move to a higher program.

The variable "fourth" was hidden and retained its value in LOWER, because another "fourth" was created and then RELEASEd at the RETURN, as was "sixth." By examining the results of each of the LIST MEMORY commands, you can follow the status of each of the variables in Figure 9.11 as control passes between the two programs. RELEASE ALL will eliminate all PRIVATE memory variables, while CLEAR MEMORY eliminates both PUBLIC and PRIVATE, as the last three commands in Figure 9.11 illustrate.

It is important to understand the ways in which the two types of memory variables behave, because you are likely to encounter them in advanced systems. In general, it is best not to declare variables PUBLIC unless it is absolutely necessary.

9.4 DATA INTEGRITY

Data integrity refers to the practice of controlling all access to the database through programming in order to ensure that the data is reliable and can be used with confidence. Of course, little can be done to prevent a well-meaning novice from tinkering with the data outside the system. However, the programmer can carefully prompt and monitor the user's activity. This will help provide a safe environment for appending, modifying, deleting, and displaying records efficiently within the system.

.DBF files are fragile when they are open because any unexpected exit from dBASE III PLUS, such as turning off the computer, will seriously damage the *header*, the portion of the file that contains the structure, the record count, and other information. Systems constantly pass control back and forth among individual programs. Since .DBF files must be properly closed with the CLEAR ALL, CLOSE ALL/DATABASES, or QUIT command in order to ensure proper updating, you should always open the files that are required for the operation and be sure to close them at the end of the module. This is especially true for maintenance functions.

Whenever possible, include a *key field* in each record which contains some *unique identifier* such as a Social Security number, an account number, an employee number, or a part number. Names are usually a poor choice (Jim Smith?). Chapter 10 describes programming strategies for retrieving records quickly through the use of a unique identifier. Programs must insist on valid data in the key field before altering the file in any way. This is important when appending because of the danger of blank or duplicate records. Figure 9.12 on the opposite page lists points you should consider when writing modular programs.

1. Make certain that .DBF files are opened and closed *within* the module.
2. Extra precautions must be taken during maintenance operations such as append, modify, and delete. Avoid duplicate or blank records.
3. Force the user to provide a vital piece of data as a unique identifier before performing any maintenance function.
4. Data should be checked for *reasonableness* and proper form.
5. Ask users to verify their intentions with a Y or a Return key, or both.
6. Present users with verifying data to confirm their selection.

FIGURE 9.12 *Guidelines for data integrity.*

When programming was introduced in Chapter 5, you were encouraged to apply structured principles to your work. Since many of the critical programming concepts have now been presented, it is appropriate to take a closer look at structured programming.

The inclusion of the three control structures DO WHILE/ENDDO, IF/ENDIF, and DO CASE/ENDCASE in dBASE III PLUS relates to the ideas of Edsger W. Dijkstra. The concept that all programming can be accomplished by means of sequencing and nesting basic structures is central to the concept of structured programming. These fundamental control structures (if-then-else, while loop, and do case) must all be closed structures with a single entrance and exit. Further, the decision to enter or execute a structure should occur at the top. Programs are forced in dBASE III PLUS to conform to structured principles through the restriction of branching to the limits of the control structures.

DIJKSTRA STRUCTURES	dBASE III PLUS
Basic Actions (printing, etc.)	? NAME
If-Then-Else	IF/ENDIF, DO CASE
Iteration	DO WHILE/ENDDO

FIGURE 9.13 *Dijkstra structures in dBASE III PLUS.*

The structures in Figure 9.13 are sequenced in cascaded sections or nested, as section 9.1 illustrated.

As your programs become more complex, the need for documentation will increase. The points in Figure 9.14 on the following page can help to make this process painless. Make them part of your programming style.

Self-documentation Tips

1. Spell out all dBASE III PLUS commands fully in uppercase.
2. Memory variables should be in lowercase and should be preceded with mem or m.
3. Use enough comments to explain the purpose of all sections of code.
4. Place blank lines before and after sections of code.
5. Provide indention for internal commands of DO WHILE/ENDDO, IF/ENDIF, and DO CASE/ENDCASE.
6. Repeat the condition as a comment following ENDDO, ENDIF, and ENDCASE.

FIGURE 9.14   *Features of self-documentation.*

A valuable piece of documentation can be generated with the STRUCTURE EXTENDED. A database containing all the field names, types, and widths is produced with the COPY command. The structure will contain the generic specifications, as shown in Figure 9.15. The LIST command will display all the fields and their characteristics. IF you use MODIFY STRUCTURE to add a description field, the data becomes more useful. Since dBASE III PLUS will permit a maximum of 128 fields per .DBF file, a printed listing such as the one in Figure 9.16 becomes the *data dictionary* in larger applications.

```
. USE CITIES
. COPY TO stru-doc STRUCTURE EXTENDED
. USE stru-doc
. LIST STRUCTURE
Structure for database: C:stru-doc.dbf
Number of data records:        4
Date of last update   : 01/01/88
Field  Field Name  Type       Width     Dec
    1  FIELD_NAME  Character     10
    2  FIELD_TYPE  Character      1
    3  FIELD_LEN   Numeric        3
    4  FIELD_DEC   Numeric        3
** Total **                     18

. LIST
Record#  FIELD_NAME  FIELD_TYPE  FIELD_LEN  FIELD_DEC
       1  CITY       C               20          0
       2  STATE      C                2          0
       3  POP_70     N                7          0
       4  POP_82     N                7          0
```

FIGURE 9.15   *Using STRUCTURE EXTENDED.*

```
. MODIFY STRUCTURE
       4 records added
. LIST STRUCTURE
Structure for database: C:stru-doc.dbf
Number of data records:       4
Date of last update   : 01/01/88
Field  Field Name  Type      Width    Dec
    1  FIELD_NAME  Character    10
    2  FIELD_TYPE  Character     1
    3  FIELD_LEN   Numeric       3
    4  FIELD_DEC   Numeric       3
    5  DESC        Character    25
** Total **                    43

. LIST
Record#  FIELD_NAME FIELD_TYPE FIELD_LEN FIELD_DEC DESC
       1  CITY        C                  20         0 NAME OF THE CITY
       2  STATE       C                   2         0 NAME OF THE STATE
       3  POP_70      N                   7         0 POPULATION IN 1970
```

FIGURE 9.16   *Creating a data dictionary.*

Chapters 5 through 9 have presented the basics of programming. You should now be capable of writing many useful programs and organizing them into systems. The remaining chapters of this text will address ways in which you can make your programs more powerful and useful and have them produce more attractive output.

CHAPTER SUMMARY

9.1

Nesting is placing one or more structures within one another. Structures can be nested in any pattern if they are logically correct. Bracketing can help show how nested DO WHILE loops will behave, since they can produce complex programs.

9.2

Arranging programs as modules in a system is a flexible and effective way of programming larger projects. Modules are called with the DO command from menu-driven main programs. The RETURN command reexecutes the calling program. Top-down design divides a project into manageable modules that can be called from submenus. Structure diagrams clarify the relationships in a system.

9.3

Memory variables are either PUBLIC (available to all programs) or PRIVATE (restricted to the source and all called programs). PARAMETER can be used to pass a variable to another program. Variables are usually PRIVATE, unless the situation requires a PUBLIC variable. Both types have specific behavior characteristics when used in systems.

9.4

Data integrity requires that programs that maintain data be carefully written in order to eliminate the possibility of blank, duplicate, or invalid fields. .DBF files must be opened and closed within the module. All data should be verified. In accordance with the principles of structured programming, dBASE III PLUS nests and sequences control structures and basic actions. Self-documentation is another important concept that has several aspects. STRUCTURE EXTENDED is useful as a data dictionary.

KEY TERMS

nesting
bracket
action diagrams
modules
subroutine
subprograms
structure diagram
functional decomposition
top-down design

calling program
called program
data integrity
header
unique identifier
reasonableness
Dijkstra Structures
iteration

COMMAND SUMMARY

PRIVATE ALL — Declare all memory variables private.
PUBLIC — Declare memory variables public.
RETURN — Pass program control to the next higher level.
PARAMETER — Specify variables to be passed.
DO WITH — Execute a program with passed variables.
STRUCTURE EXTENDED — Create a documentary .DBF file.

dBUG dBASE

- SET STEP ON produces a pause after each command executes. You then have the option of executing the next command by pressing the space bar, S to suspend, or Esc to cancel. The Suspend option will return you to the dot prompt, where you can check the status of memory variables or record pointers. The program can be restarted at the next command with RESUME. By using SET STEP ON with SET ECHO ON, you can observe the execution of your program in precise detail. This is especially useful in diagnosing nesting problems.

- Declare all memory variables PUBLIC when you are debugging so that they will be available for inspection at any level, including the dot prompt. Of course, you must remember to reverse the action when debugging has been completed.

SELF-CHECK QUESTIONS

1. Would it be useful to include a direct branching statement, such as a GOTO, in dBASE III PLUS? Why?
2. What is nesting? Why is it useful?
3. What is a module? How are modules used?
4. Describe how the DO and RETURN function with modules.
5. What is a stub?
6. What are some advantages of modularization?
7. Why is top-down design important?
8. What happens when a variable is declared PUBLIC?
9. How is a PARAMETER used?
10. What is data integrity? Why is it important?
11. What is self-documentation?
12. What is a data dictionary? How can it be documented?

TRY IT YOURSELF

1. Using Figure 9.2 as an example, write the bare commands for the following structures. Bracket the structures.
   a. IF/ENDIF nested within a DO WHILE.
   b. DO WHILE containing a DO CASE.
   c. IF/ENDIF within a DO WHILE within another DO WHILE.
2. As in Exercise 1, write a structure for the following problem: Go through a student file. If the student is full-time, print five name labels.
3. Draw a structure diagram for a system with a main menu and two submenus. One submenu calls modules to append, modify, and delete records; the other has functions for displaying a single record and printing a summary report.
4. Write a set of stub programs that are similar to those in Figure 9.8, which calls two modules. Run the set with SET ECHO ON, and study the order of execution.
5. Place several STORE commands in the programs in Exercise 4. Declare at least one variable PUBLIC and include LIST MEMORY commands, as in Figure 9.11. Study the status of each variable.
6. Construct a STRUCTURE EXTENDED as in Figure 9.16 for any .DBF file on your disk.

7. Predict the output of this program and then test it.

```
x = 1
DO WHILE x <= 5
        Y = 1
        DO WHILE y <= 3
                ? x, '     ',y
        ENDDO WHILE y <= 3
        x = x + 1
ENDDO WHILE x <= 5
```

PROGRAMMING PROJECT

Construct a menu-driven system with the following options. Use stubs and test the movement through the submenus.

```
MAIN MENU

1. Maintenance
2. Query
3. Exit
```

```
MAINTENANCE MENU               QUERY MENU

1. Add a record                1. Search by PO#
2. Edit a record               2. Search by Dept.
3. Delete a record             3. Search by Part
4. Return to Main Menu         4. Return to Main Menu
```

PART III

ADVANCED TECHNIQUES

10

INDEXING

LEARNING OBJECTIVES

1. To compare and use SORT and INDEX.
2. To apply INDEX in a variety of situations.
3. To use FIND and SEEK.
4. To become familiar with the functions used with INDEX.

Chapter

INDEXING

When you request a piece of information from a computer system, you expect an instantaneous response. When a report is prepared from the contents of a database, you expect the data to be in a useful order. Names should be in alphabetical order, and account balances should be either in ascending or descending order. Unfortunately, data that is stored in a database is very rarely arranged in any specific order. This makes it difficult to locate individual items. The commands and techniques presented in this chapter will help you to solve these problems.

10.1 SORT AS AN ORDERING TOOL

Two methods are provided in dBASE III PLUS for putting data in order: INDEXing and SORTing. INDEXing is far superior to SORTing in almost all situations, as will become apparent in the following discussion.

The SORT command produces a copy of the original .DBF file reordered on a selected field, which becomes the key field. This method is initially satisfactory, but maintaining it is awkward for the following reasons:

1. You will have to re-SORT after each APPEND, PACK, or modification to the data.
2. Only one key may be used for each SORT.
3. The powerful SEEK and FIND commands are not available when you use SORT.

Other more subtle reasons for choosing INDEX will become apparent as you gain the skills necessary to use them effectively.

If a .DBF file is static (the data rarely changes), then SORT will be a more convenient ordering tool. New users of dBASE III PLUS may find that SORT is simpler to use; it involves less responsibility. Try understanding and using SORT. A good use for SORT might be a diary or file that required that the entries, or records, always appeared in chronological order. Set up a .DBF file with the following structure:

```
.  USE DIARY

.  LIST STRUCTURE

Structure for database: A:DIARY.dbf
Number of data records:       3
Date of last update    : 01/01/88
Field  Field Name  Type       Width  Dec
    1  EVENT       Character    25
    2  DATE        Date          8
** Total **                     34
```

FIGURE 10.1 *Structure of DIARY.DBF.*

```
.  LIST

Record#  EVENT                    DATE
     1   IBM-PC INTRODUCED        01/01/81
     2   MOON LANDING             07/20/69
     3   BICENTENNIAL - USA       07/04/76
```

FIGURE 10.2 *DIARY.DBF records.*

Note that these three records were APPENDed to the DIARY.DBF file out of chronological order. Use the following command to SORT the records into the new .DBF file, DIARY_ST.DBF, then LIST its contents.

```
.  SORT ON DATE TO DIARY_ST

.  USE DIARY_ST

.  LIST

Record#  EVENT                    DATE
     1   MOON LANDING             07/20/69
     2   BICENTENNIAL - USA       07/04/76
     3   IBM-PC INTRODUCED        01/01/81
```

FIGURE 10.3 *DIARY_ST.DBF records.*

What will happen if this record is APPENDed to DIARY_ST.DBF?

```
    4   FIRST MICROCOMPUTER       01/10/75
```

What is needed in order to present these records in alphabetical order by EVENT? Records that are added to the file will probably be out of order, which means that you will have to re-SORT. At this point, you can see that SORTing is of limited value for ordering data.

10.2 HOW TO USE INDEX

In dBASE III PLUS, INDEXing is accomplished by creating an .NDX file that is separate from, but related to, the .DBF file. This file contains only the selected key field or fields from each record and the related record number. You are unable to LIST or examine the .NDX file because it is designed specifically for use by the dBASE III PLUS program.

INDEX is simple to use. The command INDEX ON is followed by the field name(s) (which becomes the key), the word TO, and the name that you will assign to the .NDX file.

```
. INDEX ON CITY TO CITY
```

There is no redundancy in this example, because the first CITY is the name of the key field from the .DBF file; the second CITY will become the file name (CITY.NDX). This helps you to remember how the .NDX file relates to the .DBF file.

Use the following example to study the effect of INDEXing. Use the CITIES.DBF file from Chapter 3 and try the commands.

```
       . USE CITIES

       . LIST STRUCTURE
  Structure for database: A:CITIES.DBF
  Number of data records:      11
  Date of last update   : 01/01/88
  Field  Field Name  Type      Width    Dec
      1  CITY        Character    20
      2  STATE       Character     2
      3  POP_70      Numeric       7
      4  POP_82      Numeric       7
  ** Total **                     37
```

FIGURE 10.4 *Structure of CITIES.DBF.*

```
 . LIST

Record#   CITY                STATE   POP_70    POP_82
      1   SAN FRANCISCO        CA      715674    691637
      2   PHILADELPHIA         PA     1949996   1665382
      3   DALLAS               TX      844401    943848
      4   SAN DIEGO            CA      697471    915956
      5   HOUSTON              TX     1233535   1725617
      6   MIAMI                FL      334859    382726
      7   CLEVELAND            OH      750879    558869
      8   PITTSBURGH           PA      520089    414936
      9   LOS ANGELES          CA     2811801   3022247
     10   JACKSONVILLE         FL      504265    556370
     11   COLUMBUS             OH      540025    564871
```

FIGURE 10.5 *CITIES.DBF records.*

When maintaining index files, you must be sure that the file is active, or attached, to the .DBF file every time the data is changed. This means that you must be alert each time you use APPEND, DELETE/PACK, EDIT, BROWSE, or REPLACE.

An index file is normally created only once. After this is done, however, it must be attached to the .DBF file when it is needed, as in the example below.

```
 . USE CITIES INDEX CITY
```

If the .DBF file is already open and you must attach the index file, use the SET INDEX TO command.

```
 . USE CITIES

 . SET INDEX TO CITY
```

The first method is generally preferable because it is more compact and easier to remember. It would be wise to get in the habit of attaching all .NDX files at each USE when a modification to the .DBF file is anticipated. If it becomes necessary to turn off the index files, you can use the SET INDEX TO command. Notice that no files are mentioned in the command and that this will be the equivalent of USEing the database without having attached any indexes. Also, you can close all open index files by using the CLOSE ALL INDEX command.

```
 . USE CITIES INDEX CITY

 . SET INDEX TO
```

If we now establish the CITY.NDX file with the following command:

```
 . INDEX ON CITY TO CITY
```

then activate the index with a SET command:

```
. SET INDEX TO CITY
```

and finally LIST the records, the result is:

```
. LIST

Record#  CITY               STATE   POP_70   POP_82
      7  CLEVELAND          OH      750879   558869
     11  COLUMBUS           OH      540025   564871
      3  DALLAS             TX      844401   943848
      5  HOUSTON            TX     1233535  1725617
     10  JACKSONVILLE       FL      504265   556370
      9  LOS ANGELES        CA     2811801  3022247
      6  MIAMI              FL      334859   382726
      2  PHILADELPHIA       PA     1949996  1665382
      8  PITTSBURGH         PA      520089   414936
      4  SAN DIEGO          CA      697471   915956
      1  SAN FRANCISCO      CA      715674   691637
```

FIGURE 10.6 *Indexed CITIES.DBF records.*

The cities appear in alphabetical order, and the record numbers are scrambled because the CITY.NDX file is displaying the records ordered on the CITY field. The actual physical order of the records remains, as the record numbers show. Compare this LIST to the first one.

Another advantage of INDEXing is that you can attach up to seven indexes for each .DBF file. These indexes can use any field or combination of fields from the .DBF file as a key. You can open all index files with the USE or the SET INDEX TO commands, and all indexes will be automatically updated or changed with any change to the .DBF file. However, the first index file mentioned in the command will be in effect.

Example: USE CITIES INDEX CITY, STATE_CIT,STATE_POP

In this example, CITY.NDX, STATE_CIT.NDX, and STATE_POP.NDX will all be updated, but the records will appear in order by CITY.

Although it is possible to establish and store as many .NDX files as you wish, only seven may be attached or active at once. Additionally, you will have to maintain or update all indexes any time the .DBF file is changed. For these reasons an index is valuable and worth the responsibility involved in its maintenance.

Index files present records from the .DBF file in either ascending or descending order. Think of the index as a lens or filter that allows the user to see the data organized in a useful fashion.

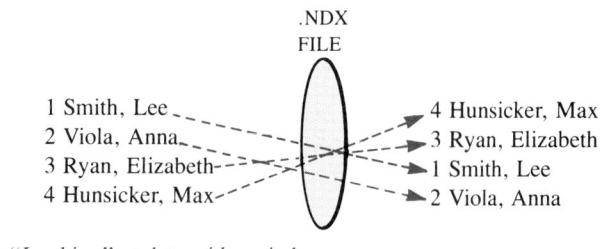

FIGURE 10.7   *"Looking" at data with an index.*

Although indexing is fast, three factors (other than hardware considerations) have an impact on indexing speeds. They are the following:

1. The number of indexes that are attached to the file.
2. The number of records in the .DBF file.
3. The length of the key field.

Create index files only if they are actually going to be used, because having them open during an APPEND, for example, will slow processing and occupy disk space. Remember that each index is an additional responsibility, because you must have it open during changes to the .DBF file.

10.3 SPECIAL USES FOR INDEX

Character-, numeric-, or date-type fields can be key fields for index files. In the example below, the numeric field POP_82 is used to create an index that shows cities in order of population from smallest to largest.

```
.  USE CITIES

.  INDEX ON POP_82 TO POP_82

   100% indexed            11 Records indexed

.  SET INDEX TO POP_82

.  LIST

Record#  CITY                 STATE   POP_70    POP_82
      6  MIAMI                FL       334859    382726
      8  PITTSBURGH           PA       520089    414936
     10  JACKSONVILLE         FL       504265    556370
      7  CLEVELAND            OH       750879    558869
     11  COLUMBUS             OH       540025    570588
      1  SAN FRANCISCO        CA       715674    691637
      4  SAN DIEGO            CA       697471    915956
      3  DALLAS               TX       844401    943848
      2  PHILADELPHIA         PA      1949996   1665382
      5  HOUSTON              TX      1233535   1725617
      9  LOS ANGELES          CA      2811801   3022247
```

FIGURE 10.8 *Indexing on a numeric field.*

If it becomes necessary to display the records in descending order on a numeric field, create an index on minus (–) the numeric field name.

```
.  INDEX ON -POP_82 TO POP_82_D

.  SET INDEX TO POP_82_D

.  LIST

Record#   CITY                    STATE   POP_70    POP_82
      9   LOS ANGELES             CA      2811801   3022247
      5   HOUSTON                 TX      1233535   1725617
      2   PHILADELPHIA            PA      1949996   1665382
      3   DALLAS                  TX       844401    943848
      4   SAN DIEGO               CA       697471    915956
      1   SAN FRANCISCO           CA       715674    691637
     11   COLUMBUS                OH       540025    570588
      7   CLEVELAND               OH       750879    558869
     10   JACKSONVILLE            FL       504265    556370
      8   PITTSBURGH              PA       520089    414936
      6   MIAMI                   FL       334859    382726
```

FIGURE 10.9   *Indexing in descending numeric order.*

The same effect can be achieved for character fields through the use of ASC, a dBASE III PLUS function. ASC operates on the numeric ASCII value of the characters involved rather than on the characters themselves. In this case, you should INDEX on the –ASC of the character field name.

```
.  INDEX ON -ASC(CITY) TO CITY_DESC
```

This will display the records in descending (Z to A) order by CITY.

```
.  SET INDEX TO CITY_DESC

.  LIST

Record#   CITY                    STATE   POP_70    POP_82
      1   SAN FRANCISCO           CA       715674    691637
      4   SAN DIEGO               CA       697471    915956
      2   PHILADELPHIA            PA      1949996   1665382
      8   PITTSBURGH              PA       520089    414936
      6   MIAMI                   FL       334859    382726
      9   LOS ANGELES             CA      2811801   3022247
     10   JACKSONVILLE            FL       504265    556370
      5   HOUSTON                 TX      1233535   1725617
      3   DALLAS                  TX       844401    943848
      7   CLEVELAND               OH       750879    558869
     11   COLUMBUS                OH       540025    564871
```

FIGURE 10.10   *Indexing in descending character order.*

Sometimes it is helpful to display records indexed on two keys instead of one. This is similar to subtotaling numbers. For example, you may wish to see states in the database displayed in order, and cities within each state in alphabetical order. This can be done through *concatentation*, which is the process of combining two character fields so that they will appear or operate as one. The field appearing first after concatenation is called the primary key, and the next field to appear is the secondary key.

```
     . INDEX ON STATE+CITY TO ST_CITY

     . SET INDEX TO ST_CITY

     . LIST

Record#  CITY               STATE  POP_70   POP_82
      9  LOS ANGELES        CA     2811801  3022247
      4  SAN DIEGO          CA      697471   915956
      1  SAN FRANCISCO      CA      715674   691637
     10  JACKSONVILLE       FL      504265   556370
      6  MIAMI              FL      334859   558869
      7  CLEVELAND          OH      750879   558869
     11  COLUMBUS           OH      540025   564871
      2  PHILADELPHIA       PA     1949996  1665382
      8  PITTSBURGH         PA      520089   414936
      3  DALLAS             TX      844401   943848
      5  HOUSTON            TX     1233535  1725617
```

FIGURE 10.11   *Indexing on two character fields.*

This technique can be used with character fields and numeric fields if you first convert the numeric field to character by means of the STR() function. Functions will be discussed in Chapter 13. However, you should know that the 7 and the 0 in the parentheses represent seven digits and no decimal places in the field POP_82.

```
     . INDEX ON STATE+STR(POP_82,7,0) TO ST_POP

     . SET INDEX TO ST_POP

     . LIST

Record#  CITY               STATE  POP_70   POP_82
      1  SAN FRANCISCO      CA      715674   691637
      4  SAN DIEGO          CA      697471   915956
      9  LOS ANGELES        CA     2811801  3022247
      6  MIAMI              FL      334859   382726
     10  JACKSONVILLE       FL      504265   556370
      7  CLEVELAND          OH      750879   558869
     11  COLUMBUS           OH      540025   570588
      8  PITTSBURGH         PA      520089   414936
      2  PHILADELPHIA       PA     1949996  1665382
      3  DALLAS             TX      844401   943848
      5  HOUSTON            TX     1233535  1725617
```

FIGURE 10.12   *Indexing on a character and a numeric field.*

Be careful when attempting to concatenate two numeric fields, because the plus sign (+) will be understood by dBASE III PLUS to mean addition, not concatenation, and you will end up with an index on the sum of the two numeric fields. The solution is to convert both numeric fields with the STR() function while concatenating. In this particular case, the result is probably not of practical use.

In our example, it might be more useful to INDEX on the total population for both years by naming both numeric fields separated by the + .

```
    . INDEX ON POP_82+POP_70 TO POP_TOT

    . SET INDEX TO POP_TOT

    . LIST

Record#   CITY                    STATE   POP_70   POP_82
      6   MIAMI                   FL      334859   382726
      8   PITTSBURGH              PA      520089   414936
     10   JACKSONVILLE            FL      504265   556370
     11   COLUMBUS                OH      540025   570588
      7   CLEVELAND               OH      750879   558869
      1   SAN FRANCISCO           CA      715674   691637
      4   SAN DIEGO               CA      697471   915956
      3   DALLAS                  TX      844401   943848
      5   HOUSTON                 TX     1233535  1725617
      2   PHILADELPHIA            PA     1949996  1665382
      9   LOS ANGELES             CA     2811801  3022247
```

FIGURE 10.13 *Indexing on a numeric total.*

You can determine the population growth of the cities between 1970 and 1982 by INDEXing on the difference between the two numeric fields (Figure 10.14) and using LIST (Figure 10.15).

```
    . INDEX ON -(POP_82-POP_70) TO GROWTH

100% indexed            10 Records indexed

    . SET INDEX TO GROWTH

    . LIST

Record#   CITY                    STATE   POP_70   POP_82
      5   HOUSTON                 TX     1233535  1725617
      4   SAN DIEGO               CA      697471   915956
      9   LOS ANGELES             CA     2811801  3022247
      3   DALLAS                  TX      844401   943848
     10   JACKSONVILLE            FL      504265   556370
      6   MIAMI                   FL      334859   382726
     11   COLUMBUS                OH      540025   570588
      1   SAN FRANCISCO           CA      715674   691637
      8   PITTSBURGH              PA      520089   414936
      7   CLEVELAND               OH      750879   558869
      2   PHILADELPHIA            PA     1949996  1665382
```

FIGURE 10.14 *Indexing on a numeric difference.*

```
. LIST CITY, POP_82-POP_70

Record#    CITY                POP_82-POP_70
      5    HOUSTON                    492082
      4    SAN DIEGO                  218485
      9    LOS ANGELES                210446
      3    DALLAS                      99447
     10    JACKSONVILLE                52105
      6    MIAMI                       47867
     11    COLUMBUS                    30563
      1    SAN FRANCISCO              -24037
      8    PITTSBURGH                -105153
      7    CLEVELAND                 -192010
      2    PHILADELPHIA              -284614
```

FIGURE 10.15 *Displaying a numeric difference.*

10.4 FIND AND SEEK

The FIND and the SEEK commands are critical to the programmer because they allow rapid access to specific records in the .DBF file on the basis of criteria that the user specifies. Users type in some information (such as a name or an account number) in order to retrieve additional relevant information. This is what most people envision when they think of a database, or, for that matter, a computer. To produce such power and ease of use requires much effort on the part of the programmer. In general, you may conclude that the easier a program is to use, the more difficult it will be to write, and vice versa.

The FIND and SEEK commands reference .NDX files that must be active at the time. The principal advantage of the FIND and SEEK commands is that they provide the fastest access to specific records that are available to the programmer. They work by taking a piece of information, such as a name, and through the use of a rapid search algorithm, matching the piece of data with an identical or nearly identical field in the .NDX file. The .NDX file contains the key field and the associated record number from the .DBF file. If a match is made, the record pointer is positioned at the proper record number in the .DBF file. It is then up to the programmer to present the other data contained in the record to the user or to perform some other function with the record. Two potential problems with this technique are the following:

1. The matching field may not be found.
2. Other fields in the .NDX file may also match the criteria provided.

These possibilities are addressed in Chapter 11.

The FIND command works only with string or character data. Because you will almost always use memory variables for searches, you must be able to properly program with the FIND command, employing correctly user input and stored data.

This requires the use of the macro expansion function, &, which must be placed immediately in front of the memory variable name.

Try to FIND a specific piece of data, using an INDEX.

```
. SET INDEX TO CITY

. FIND 'MIAMI'

. DISPLAY

Record#  CITY                  STATE       POP_70  POP_82
      6  MIAMI                 FL          334859  382726
```

FIGURE 10.16 *Using FIND.*

Now try to FIND a city STOREd in a memory variable, using &.

```
. SET INDEX TO CITY

. STORE 'PHILADELPHIA' TO MEMCITY

PHILADELPHIA

. FIND &MEMCITY

. DISPLAY

Record#  CITY                  STATE       POP_70    POP_82
      2  PHILADELPHIA          PA          1949996   1665382
```

FIGURE 10.17 *Using FIND with a memory variable.*

If & is not used, the FIND command will search for MEMCITY as a field in the .NDX file, will fail to find it, and will display a No Find error message.

```
. FIND MEMCITY

No Find.
```

The SEEK command is useful because both numeric expressions and character data may be accessed.

```
. SET INDEX TO POP_82

. SEEK 558869

. DISPLAY

Record#  CITY                  STATE       POP_70  POP_82
      7  CLEVELAND             OH          750879  558869
```

FIGURE 10.18 *Using SEEK with a numeric key.*

Also, the macro expansion function, &, is not required when SEEK is used with memory variables.

```
        . STORE 558869 TO MEMPOP

558869

        . SEEK MEMPOP

        . DISPLAY

Record#   CITY                   STATE        POP_70   POP_82
      7   CLEVELAND              OH           750879   558869
```

FIGURE 10.19   *Using SEEK with a memory variable.*

Other functions are useful when working with index files. One of these is FOUND(), which will be true (.T.) if FIND or SEEK commands are successful, and false (.F.) if they are unsuccessful.

```
        . USE CITIES

        . SET INDEX TO CITY

        . ? FOUND()

.F.

        . FIND 'WASHINGTON'

No find.

        . ? FOUND()

.F.

        . FIND 'HOUSTON'

        . ? FOUND()

.T.
```

FIGURE 10.20   *Using FOUND().*

NDX() displays the name of the open .NDX file specified by a number within the parentheses.

```
      . SET INDEX TO CITY, GROWTH, CITY_DESC, POP_82, POP_82_D

      . ? NDX(2)

A:GROWTH.ndx

      . ? NDX(4)

A:POP_82.ndx

      . ? NDX(1)

A:CITY.ndx

      . ? NDX()

Invalid function argument.

      . ? NDX(7)
```

FIGURE 10.21   *Using NDX().*

The REINDEX command automatically issues the necessary commands to recreate all index files that are currently open. This is convenient, since it means that you will not have to type each INDEX command.

```
      . SET INDEX TO CITY, GROWTH, CITY_DESC, POP_82, POP_82_D

      . REINDEX
Rebuilding index - A:CITY.ndx
      100% indexed              11 Records indexed
Rebuilding index - A:GROWTH.ndx
      100% indexed              11 Records indexed
Rebuilding index - A:CITY_DESC.ndx
      100% indexed              11 Records indexed
Rebuilding index - A:POP_82.ndx
      100% indexed              11 Records indexed
Rebuilding index - A:POP_82_D.ndx
      100% indexed              11 Records indexed
```

FIGURE 10.22   *Using REINDEX.*

SET ORDER TO is used to allow any open or active index file to be the controlling file without wasting time to open or close files.

```
. SET INDEX TO POP_82,GROWTH,CITY

. SET ORDER TO 3
```

All three indexes remain open, but the records will be presented by CITY rather than POP_82 after the SET ORDER TO command.

If duplicate entries must not be allowed into the index file during the APPEND operation, the UNIQUE option can be added to the INDEX command or the SET UNIQUE ON command. This will allow only unique additions to the file in the case of Social Security numbers, for example.

```
. INDEX ON SOC_SEC TO SOC_SEC UNIQUE
or
. SET INDEX TO SOC_SEC
. SET UNIQUE ON
```

It should be apparent at this point that a programmer must be competent in the effective use of indexes. They have value not only as the best means of displaying data in a desired order, but as a tool for the rapid access of records. Many of the more advanced techniques that will be explored in later chapters will require a sound working knowledge of this concept.

CHAPTER SUMMARY

10.1

SORT produces a copy of the .DBF file sorted on a specified field, but is of little use since it requires too much maintenance, allows only one key field, and provides slow access to records.

10.2

INDEX writes an .NDX file that allows data to be viewed in a variety of orders, is easy to maintain, and allows rapid access through the FIND and SEEK commands. Index files must be active during any process that will alter the file, such as APPEND, EDIT, or DELETE.

10.3

Records can be displayed in many ways by establishing .NDX files creatively. By using combinations of fields, functions, and arithmetic operations, relationships among the records can be examined.

10.4

FIND positions the record pointer on a record that matches the expression after the command. Criteria that are stored in memory variables must use the macro-expansion function, &. The SEEK will operate with numeric fields and does not require the &.

10.5

Several other functions, such as FOUND(), NDX(), SET ORDER TO, and UNIQUE, are useful in working with index files.

COMMAND SUMMARY

SORT — Sort records on a key field and write to a new file.

INDEX — Create an .NDX file that contain sorted key fields.

.NDX — An index file containing key fields and record numbers.

SET INDEX TO — Activate index files.

CLOSE ALL INDEX — Close index files.

STR() — Convert a numeric value to a character string.

FIND — Point to a record using an indexed search.

SEEK — Point to a record using an indexed search.

& — The macro expansion function.

FOUND() — Indicates success or failure of an indexed search.

NDX() — Display names of open .NDX files.

REINDEX — Rebuild all open .NDX files.

SET ORDER TO — Specify an open .NDX file as master.

SET UNIQUE ON — Ignore duplicate records.

dBUG dBASE

- The status of indexes is a constant concern in programs. Records may appear to be missing, or a "Record out of range" error may occur as the result of an .NDX file that is not synchronized with the .DBF file. The solution to this problem is to regenerate the index.
- Avoid using dBASE III PLUS commands as memory variable names. For example, if you use COUNT = 9 in a program, dBASE III PLUS will assume a COUNT command and issue a "No database in use" error.

SELF-CHECK QUESTIONS

1. Name three disadvantages of using SORT as opposed to INDEX.
2. What happens when you issue an INDEX ON . . TO command?
3. When is it important to activate index files?
4. Are .NDX files created every time they must be used?
5. Will an index file change the physical order of the records in the .DBF file?
6. How many .NDX files can be attached to a .DBF file?

7. Is it possible to index on numeric- or date-type fields?
8. What is concatenation?
9. Why is the STR() function sometimes useful during indexing?
10. What does the SEEK command do?
11. What are some disadvantages of the FIND command?
12. What does the FOUND() command do?

TRY IT YOURSELF

1. Using the structure from the DIARY.DBF in Chapter 10, APPEND at least ten events and dates from your own life. SORT by date and LIST the new file. APPEND your date of birth, and LIST.
2. CREATE and APPEND a copy of CITIES.DBF. INDEX on the name of the city, and LIST the file.
3. APPEND DENVER, CO with a 1982 population of 505,563, and a 1970 population of 514,678 to the file. LIST and note the position of the record.
4. INDEX on the 1982 population and LIST the file. Making certain that both this index and the index from Exercise 2 are active, EDIT the JACKSONVILLE record. Change the the 1982 population to 4 million, and LIST the file.
5. INDEX and LIST the file by state and city in descending alphabetical order. The first three records should be HOUSTON, DALLAS, and PITTSBURGH.
6. Activate the index by city name. STORE 'DALLAS' to a memory variable, and use FIND to position the record pointer. Place the following message on the screen by combining the city field name with a literal. (Hint: Use the ? and the &.)

   DALLAS is close to FT. WORTH

7. Activate the index by 1982 population. Use SEEK to position the record pointer at the record containing a 1982 population of 915,956. DISPLAY the record and check the status of the FOUND() function.

PROGRAMMING PROJECT

Write a program that will perform the following functions:

Open CITIES.DBF with CITY index attached.
Clear the screen.
Accept a city name from the user.
Find the name.
If the name is not found, display 'CITY NOT FOUND' and return to the dot prompt.
If the name is found, display the name, state, and 1982 population and return to the dot prompt.

11

CONSTRUCTING SCREENS

LEARNING OBJECTIVES

1. To design and code input screen modules.
2. To use the screen painter to create both general and specific designs.
3. To validate input data.
4. To write a program to append records.

Chapter

11

CONSTRUCTING SCREENS

Most people agree that first impressions are important. An attractive cover and title page, for instance, are likely to place the reader of a report in a positive state of mind. On the other hand, material that is disorganized and unattractive in appearance may be dismissed regardless of its content. The same is true of programs. Satisfied users are the best measure of a program's success, and attractive screens that are a pleasure to use are a critical factor in user satisfaction. Many dBASE III PLUS features have been designed to create screens that will greatly contribute to the success of your programs.

11.1 INPUT SCREENS

As a programmer, you are naturally concerned with the internal operation of your programs. Tasks such as opening and closing files, repeating procedures, and using indexes demand a great deal of your attention and energy. Yet, unlike the internal operation of your programs, the elegance and efficiency of your work—or the absence thereof—will be *transparent* to the user. Although speed of operation and reliability of performance are unquestionably desirable, users will be affected to a much greater degree by the physical appearance of your program.

Users are going to spend most of their time viewing the screens and reports that are produced by your system. Therefore, user satisfaction will always depend, to some degree, upon the appearance and convenience of these aspects. This chapter focuses on designing custom input screens. A program to append records through the use of a custom screen will also be discussed.

FIGURE 11.1   *Custom screens increase user satisfaction.*

When you APPEND or EDIT from the dot prompt, dBASE III PLUS automatically provides an input screen that contains positions for all of the fields in the .DBF file. dBASE III PLUS adjusts for the proper length and type of each field and displays the field names. This method is convenient if you are the person who is entering the data, but it may present some problems for an inexperienced or uninformed user.

Further confusion may attend to indexes that are to be attached to the file. The user may not know how (or may forget) to activate them. Moreover, although data may not be required in all fields, the fields will all be displayed. Your field names may be ambiguous to the user. NAME, for example, could have many meanings. Also, there will be no opportunity for the programmer to check the validity of the data as it is entered in order to preserve data integrity.

Rather than APPEND or EDIT from the dot prompt, it is more useful to generate custom data entry screens and use the APPEND BLANK command. The BLANK option will not present the dBASE III PLUS input screen. The BLANK option requires the programmer to provide the input format for the user. With the data that is presented, dBASE III PLUS will merely position the record pointer and add the new record to the file. Modules whose purposes are to update or modify records employ a similar strategy, as you will see in Chapter 12. This process provides maximum flexibility, but it demands additional responsibility on the part of the programmer. An example of an APPEND program can be found in section 11.4, but first you need to learn how to design and code a custom input screen.

FIGURE 11.2   *A custom screen.*

So many options are available for screen design in dBASE III PLUS that they can become a source of confusion. Ten programmers could design ten screens that varied widely in their appearance and operation, yet accomplished the same task. Consequently, you need to have a clear idea of what will best serve the interests of the user. To do this, you may have to observe office operations or interview those persons who will be using the programs you design, or both. It is the needs of users that drive the design specifications. Especially when you are designing input screens—but really at all times—you *must* think first of the user. The following is a list of things to consider when you are designing screens.

Screen Design Considerations

1. Determine the level of computer experience.
2. Find out whether the screen is replacing a paper form.
3. Ascertain whether the speed of data entry is a consideration.
4. Find out how much help or "hand-holding" will be required.
5. Use a consistent screen design throughout the system.
6. Make screens attractive and easy to understand and to change.
7. Display titles and borders in a uniform way from screen to screen.
8. Use color, boxes, and lines to produce a pleasant design.

FIGURE 11.3   *Things to consider when designing screens.*

Custom screens are produced with a series of commands that display data or that allow data entry at specific locations on the screen. A system of coordinates enables the commands @ SAY and @ GET to use the entire screen more conveniently and more accurately than the ?, WAIT, or ACCEPT commands. Screen coordinates range between 0 and 24 vertically (rows) and between 0 and 79 horizontally (columns). The number of the row is always expressed first. Row 6, column 10 would be coded 6,10. The maximum number which can be used in printing for either coordinate is 255 but exceeding 24 or 79 will generate an error message in a screen display. Line 22 usually contains the scoreboard display, and line 0 usually contains the status line. These can be removed with SET SCOREBOARD OFF and SET STATUS OFF to make the entire screen available for displays.

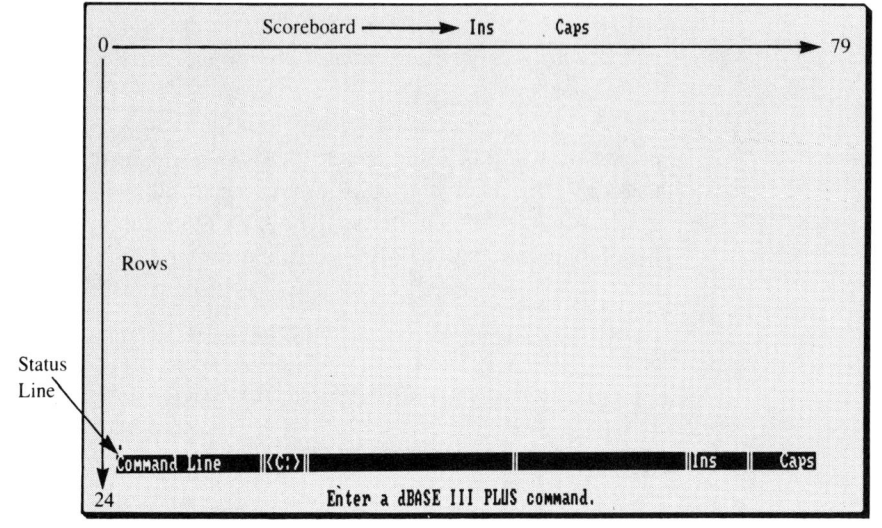

FIGURE 11.4   *Screen coordinates.*

Screen coordinates are addressed with the @ command. A row number and column number must be included for the cursor to be positioned. The command is usually combined with SAY to display data or with GET to allow data entry by the user. SAY will display variables, constants, or the contents of fields in the current record. Typing @ 2,10 will clear the line from that point. Figure 11.5 shows the syntax for @ SAY.

```
@ 10,20 SAY memname          && Memory Variable
@ 10,20 SAY 'Enter Name'     && Constant
@ 10,20 SAY ACCT_NO          && Fieldname
```

FIGURE 11.5   *Uses of @ SAY.*

Placement of data on the screen should be planned first on a coding form (Figure 11.6 opposite) or on a piece of graph paper, since the position of the coordinates can be difficult to visualize. Although it is usually placed in .PRG files, @ SAY can be used from the dot prompt to examine the result on the screen.

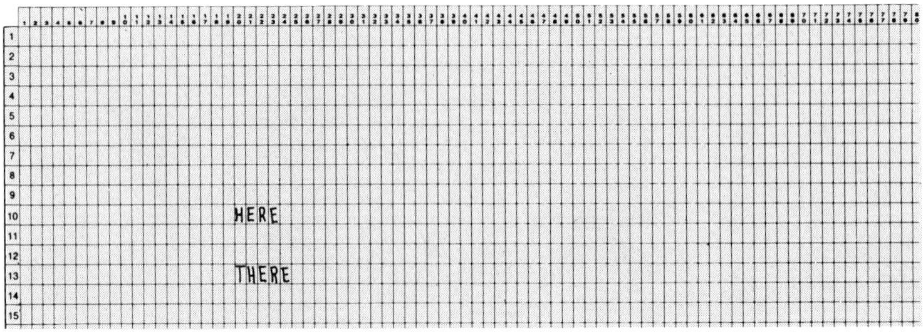

FIGURE 11.6   *Using a coding form.*

If the distance between two rows or columns must remain static, you can use relative addressing to specify a location a certain distance away from the present position of the cursor. The ROW() and COL() functions will return the current numeric value of that position, and they can be used in arithmetic expressions.

```
@ 10, 20 SAY 'HERE'
@ ROW() + 3, 20 SAY 'THERE'
```

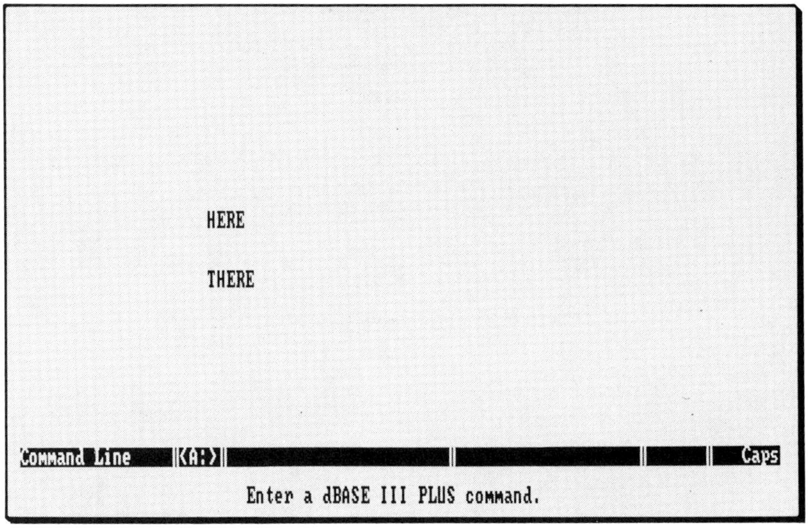

FIGURE 11.7   *Using ROW().*

You can use memory variables to act as tab functions by initializing them at the start of the program, then including them in @ SAY/GET commands.

```
T1 = 5
T2 = 15
T3 = 25
CLEAR
@ 10, T1 SAY 'Here is the first tab'
@ 12, T2 SAY 'Here is the second tab'
@ 14, T3 SAY 'Here is the third tab'
```

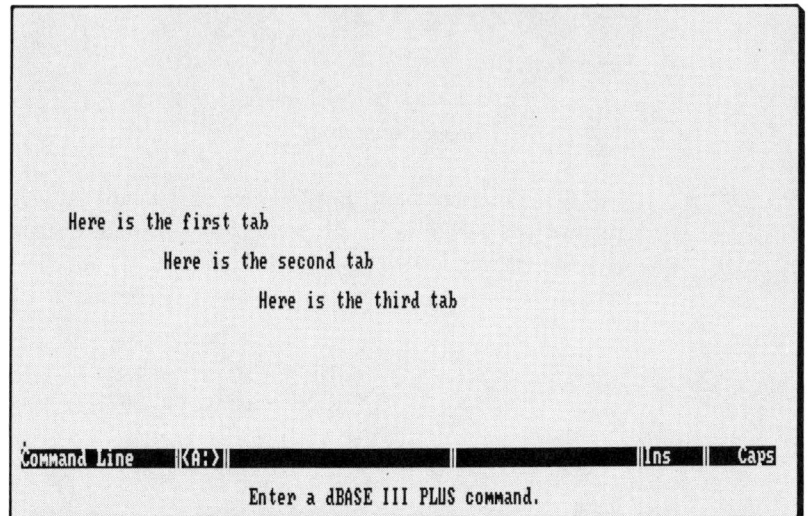

FIGURE 11.8   *Setting tabs with @ SAY.*

Store frequently used titles or prompts to variables in order to reduce coding in programs.

```
STORE 'ACME SHIPPING CORPORATION' TO memtitle
@ 10,20 SAY memtitle
```

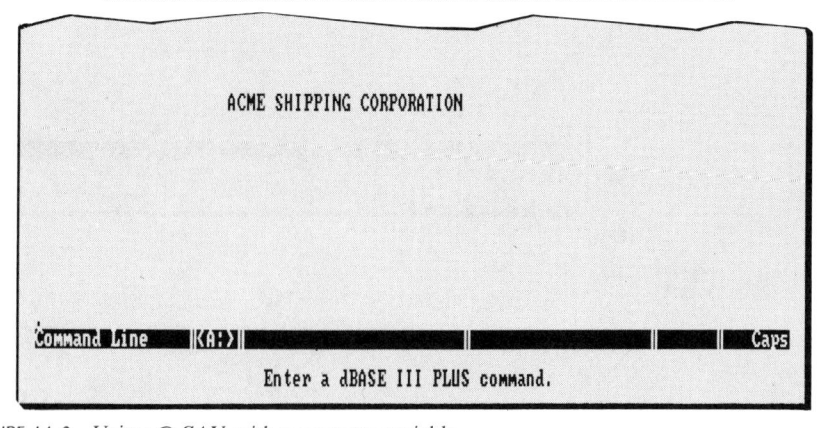

FIGURE 11.9   *Using @ SAY with a memory variable.*

Individual rows are cleared simply by specifying the row and column with the @ sign. For instance, @ 15,0 will clear row 15. Another effective way is to fill a row, or part of a row, with spaces, as in @ 15,10 SAY SPACE(35).

A useful option in screen design is the capability to draw lines and boxes. This feature can be used to frame entry areas and to replicate paper forms. All that is required to draw a line or a box is an @ symbol and the proper coordinates. The option DOUBLE placed after the last coordinate will produce a double line or box.

```
@ 5,1 TO 5,79             && Draw a line across the fifth row.

@ 5,1 CLEAR TO 5,79       && Erase it.

@ 5,5 TO 15,60            && Draw a box.

@ 5,5 CLEAR TO 15,60      && Erase the box and its contents.

@ 10,10 to 20,70 DOUBLE   && Draw a box with double lines.

@ 11,11 CLEAR TO 19,69    && Erase the contents, leave the box.
```

All the commands can be easily tested from the dot prompt if an occasional CLEAR is issued. The program in Figure 11.11 on the following page illustrates the scope of the boxes that can be specified.

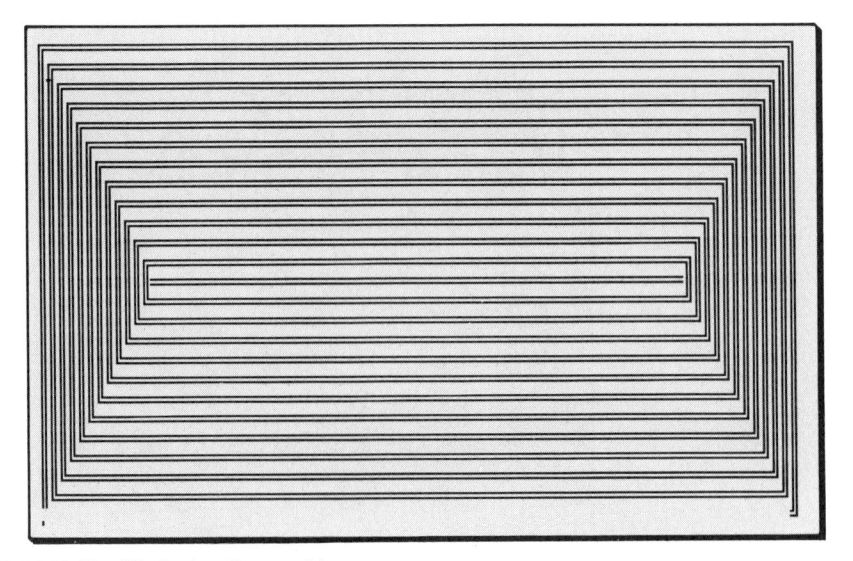

FIGURE 11.10 *Displaying lines and boxes.*

```
CLEAR
A  =  0
B  =  0
C  =  24
D  =  79
DO WHILE A < 12
      @ A,B TO C,D DOUBLE
      A  =  A+1
      B  =  B+1
      C  =  C-1
      D  =  D-1
ENDDO A < 12
```

FIGURE 11.11   *A box drawing program.*

On occasion, it may be useful to display large blocks of text on the screen. The TEXT/ENDTEXT is available when many @ SAY commands would be inconvenient, as in Figure 11.12.

```
CLEAR
TEXT

Large blocks of pure text such as descriptions or instructions
like this are easily displayed using TEXT/ENDTEXT. This is
similar to displaying with a word processing program, since
"what you see is what you get" (WYSIWYG).

ENDTEXT
```

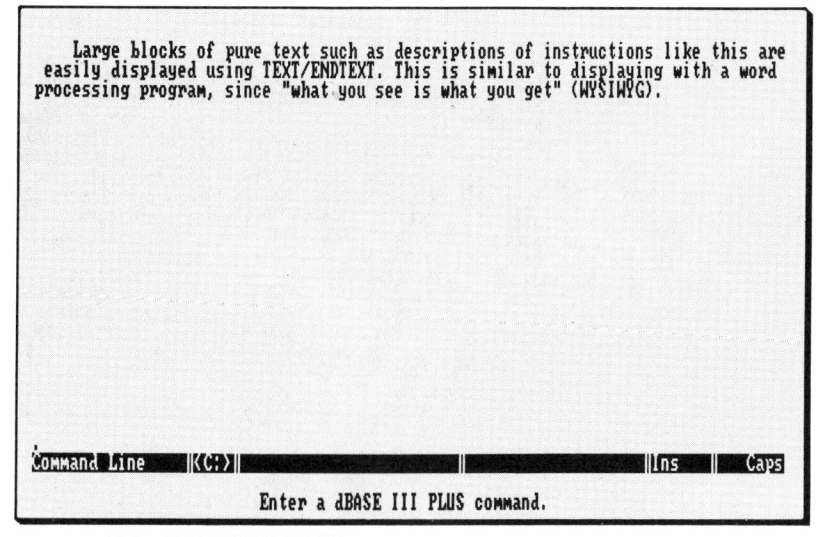

FIGURE 11.12   *Using TEXT/ENDTEXT.*

The @ SAY command is frequently used as a prompt for @ GET commands to produce custom data entry screens. Using @ SAY/GET is called *full-screen editing*, because the user can roam over the screen at will, making changes as if a paper form were being completed. This is preferable to single-command responses at the dot prompt, such as responding to ACCEPT commands.

When you use a GET, dBASE III PLUS will provide an enhanced video block that displays the current value of the specified variable or field. The cursor will be placed at the first position of the GET block. As in the full-screen editing of APPEND, the cursor will leave enhanced blocks produced by GETs when the last position is filled or the Return key is pressed. The user will be able to move freely around the GET blocks on the screen, using the editing keys until the last GET is filled or the Return key is pressed before a READ command is issued. The READ command actually retrieves the data from the GET blocks and stores it in the specified variables or field names.

If you have too many characters for the available space, truncation will occur. It is worse in the case of numeric fields. Numbers that are too large to display cause a numeric overflow. They are then displayed in exponential format. If you use REPLACE to place that data in a database field, the value cannot be edited and retained. Make certain that numeric fields are large enough to hold the greatest value expected. Also, whenever possible, do *not* include fields that ask the user to do calculations, because this slows down data entry and increases the chance of error. It is better to do the calculation with a STORE command in the program.

A GET can be combined with a SAY on the same line or can be specified separately. Since the block for memacc will be placed immediately after the prompt in the first statement in Figure 11.13, a space must be provided as the last character in the prompt to separate it from the user's response.

```
memacc = '

@ 15,25 SAY 'Enter Account Number ' GET memacc
or
@ 15,25 SAY 'Enter Account Number '
@ 15,46 GET memacc
```

FIGURE 11.13 *Combining GET and SAY.*

The @ SAY will be used to generate screen reports in Chapter 13 and printed reports in Chapter 14. The @ GET is also used in modules to update or modify records. Since a large portion of a programmer's effort is involved with input and output, the effective use of these commands is essential.

11.2 USING THE SCREEN PAINTER

The screen painter feature can be useful when you are designing screens because it allows you to see the screen as it develops. The alternative, for instance, would be to try to imagine exactly where 17,38 was located. The commands CREATE/MODIFY SCREEN will operate on a file with an .SCR extension following the file name of your choice. Then dBASE III PLUS will convert the .SCR file to an .FMT file, which you can call from your program or edit and include as *in-line* code. The .SCR file cannot be modified except through MODIFY SCREEN. CREATE SCREEN expects you to use the actual field names from the relevant .DBF file for the GETs. It will allow you to load them to the screen. This is convenient, but as you have seen, it is preferable to use variables for input and REPLACE commands to write to the file. Titles, lines, and boxes can easily be arranged on the screen.

CREATE SCREEN is used initially to establish the .SCR file. You must provide a file name that is acceptable to DOS. MODIFY SCREEN must then be used to access the file in the future. MODIFY SCREEN uses four pull-down menus that are similar to those of the assistant feature.

SETUP
    Select database file
    Create database file
    Load fields — place selected fields on screen

MODIFY
    Action — Choose SAY or GET
    Source — .DBF file
    Content — Select field name
    Type — Display data type
    Width — Display width
    Decimals — Display decimal places
    Picture — Format data
    Range — Restrict values to a range

OPTIONS
    Create text file image — Display screen documentation
    Single/double bar — Draw boxes or lines

EXIT
    Save — Save .SCR and .FMT file and exit
    Abandon — No save and exit

FIGURE 11.14 *CREATE SCREEN menus (Part 1 of 2).*

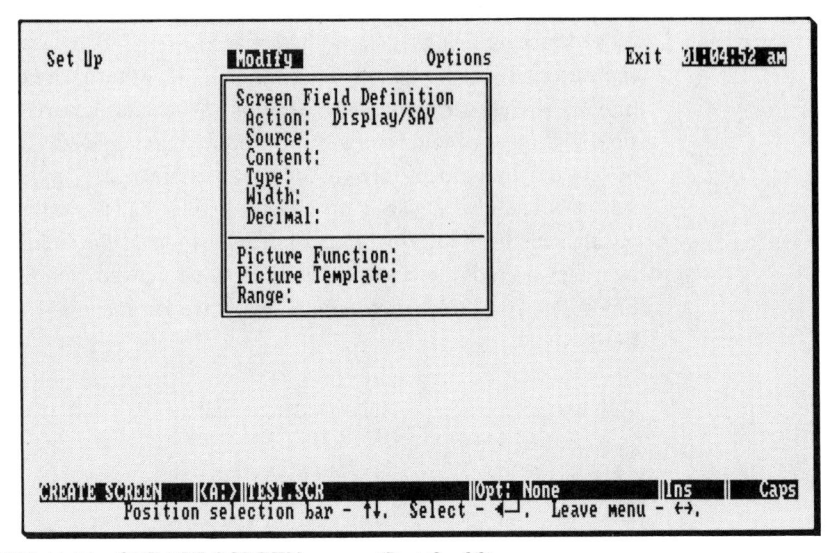

FIGURE 11.14   *CREATE SCREEN menus (Part 2 of 2).*

When you enter the screen painter, the first menu will require you to select a
.DBF file if one is not currently active. You can then load all the fields from the
database onto a blank screen work area called the blackboard, which is activated
with the F10 key. Fields can also be placed or modified on the screen with the
second menu.

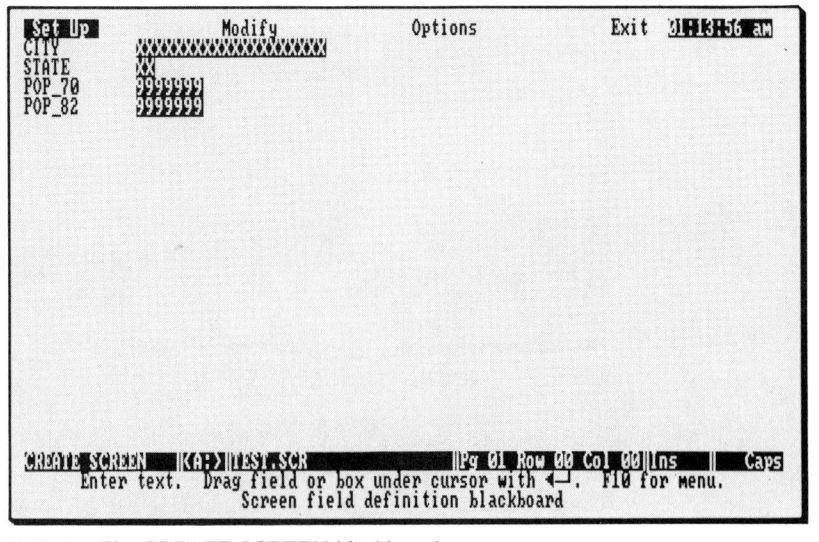

FIGURE 11.15   *The CREATE SCREEN blackboard.*

The most useful functions are found on the blackboard. Fields and text can be moved around using the space bar in the insert mode or the Del key. Fields can be repositioned on the screen by pressing the Return key in the first position and moving the cursor to the new location. When the Return key is pressed again, the field will move. Fields can also be modified and deleted. The third menu will permit boxes and lines to be drawn, using the Return key and the cursor. The text file image is useful because it provides a listing that is similar to LIST STRUCTURE but that includes the row and column location of the fields on the screen, followed by a facsimile of the screen. The file can be viewed with the TYPE command, as in Figure 11.16. The screen painter will save or abandon the file, then exit with the fourth menu.

```
     . TYPE SARA1.TXT

Field definitions for Screen : SARA1.scr

Page   Row   Col   Data Base   Field          Type             Width   Dec
  1     3     9    SARA        LOC            Character         15
  1     3    30    SARA        LOC_CODE       Character          2
  1     1    10    SARA        SUBSTANCE      Character         50
  1     1    64    SARA        PN             Character         10
  1     3    36    SARA        NAME           Character         15
  1     3    57    SARA        CITY           Character         15
  1     3    76    SARA        STATE          Character          2
  1     1    78    SARA        MP             Character          1
. . .

Content of page :  1

SUBSTANCE XXXXXXXXXXXXXXXXXXXXXXXXXXXXXXXXXXXXXXXXXXXXXXXXXX PN XXXXXXXXXX MP X

LOCATION XXXXXXXXXXXXXXX CODE XX CO XXXXXXXXXXXXXXX CITY XXXXXXXXXXXXXXX ST XX

COMP1 XXXXXXXXXXXXXXXXXXXXXXXXXXX  CAS1 XXXXXXXXXX    % X XXXXX        FORM XX
COMP2 XXXXXXXXXXXXXXXXXXXXXXXXXXX  CAS2 XXXXXXXXXX    % X XXXXX
COMP3 XXXXXXXXXXXXXXXXXXXXXXXXXXX  CAS3 XXXXXXXXXX    % X XXXXX   CONTAINER XX
COMP4 XXXXXXXXXXXXXXXXXXXXXXXXXXX  CAS4 XXXXXXXXXX    % X XXXXX
COMP5 XXXXXXXXXXXXXXXXXXXXXXXXXXX  CAS5 XXXXXXXXXX    % X XXXXX        NUMBER XXX

  SIZE XXXXX   UNIT XX  MAX-AMT XXX  MAX-UNIT XX   AV DAILY AMT   XXXX AV UNIT XX

 1 COMBUST LIQUID X 6 ORGANIC H2O2       X  1 CARCINOGEN   X 8 KIDNEY TOXIN X
 2 COMBUST GAS     X 7 OXIDIZER          X  2 HIGHLY TOXIC X 9 LIVER TOXIN  X
 3 CORROSIVE       X 8 PYROPHORIC        X  3 IRRITANT     X 10 LUNG TOXIN  X
 4 EXPLOSIVE       X 9 UNSTABLE/REACTIVE X  4 SENSITIZER   X 11 CNS TOXIN   X
 5 FLAMMABLE       X 10 H2O REACTIVE     X  5 TOXIC        X 12 REPRODUCT TOXIN X
                                           6 BLOOD TOXIN  X 13 SKIN HAZARD X
 ADD DATE XXXXXXXX                         7 EYE HAZARD   X
 SDS DATE XXXXXXXX  A/D X  DOT XX
```

FIGURE 11.16   *The CREATE SCREEN text file.*

The screen painter is intended to generate an .FMT or format file that can be called from a program to replace the screen. The .FMT file is easily tested by executing the file with a DO command. This can be convenient, but the disadvantages have to be considered. The .FMT file is an additional open file that counts

against the limit in the CONFIG.SYS file (Chapter 2). In advanced applications, the
.FMT file can rarely be used without modifications such as arranging the GETs or
READS. Also, the screen painter is insistent about the use of field names rather than
memory variables. Since inputting data to variables is preferable, you will have to
convert each field name to a memory variable by means of MODIFY COMMAND
or a word processing program.

Use the procedure in Figure 11.17 to create custom data entry screens.

How to Create Custom Data Entry Screens

1. Use the screen painter to arrange the boxes, lines, titles, and field names as needed.
2. Use MODIFY COMMAND to edit the .FMT file.
3. Arrange the GETs in another order if necessary and place READs where needed.
4. Change all the field names to memory variables and add PICTURE clauses.
5. Using a word processing program or ˆKR in MODIFY COMMAND, move the
   altered .FMT file into the .PRG file.

FIGURE 11.17   *Creating custom data entry screens.*

If a more subtle screen is preferred, SET INTENSITY OFF will prevent the
enhanced blocks from displaying when a GET is issued. You will then have to provide
some delimiter so that the user will know what the limits of the field are. This can be
accomplished with SET DELIMITERS TO and SET DELIMITERS ON.

```
memamt = 0
SET INTENSITY OFF
SET DELIMITERS TO '¦¦'
SET DELIMITERS ON
@ 10,20 GET memamt
```

```
memamt = 0
SET INTENSITY OFF
SET DELIMITERS TO '¦¦'
SET DELIMITERS ON
@ 10,20 GET memamt


    ¦                 ¦
```

FIGURE 11.18   *Changing the GET block.*

Underlining can also be substituted for the enhanced video blocks for GETs,
although some monitors may not support underlining. Issue a SET COLOR TO W/,
U/W, W command for this effect.

Under normal circumstances, all @ SAY or GET commands should be placed
in chronological order by row and column so that they are filled exactly as you

would read. This is a good habit to form, because the printer will insist upon it, as you will see in Chapter 14. If data must be entered as columns, you will have to arrange the GETs carefully so that they execute in the required order. For this purpose, a word processing program that will move blocks of text is more useful than MODIFY COMMAND.

The position of the READ command is important. Usually it is placed at the end of a number of GETs. This allows a whole screen of fields to be input before you move on to another screen or operation. Occasionally you may wish to place a READ after each GET to validate each field as it is filled or to provide special features such as help screens. Screens can also be split, or "windowed," through the use of this concept.

The READ statement will clear all GETs. This provides opportunities to manipulate the screen. By using more than one READ, you can split the screen. The CLEAR command will remove GETs from the screen. READ checks the status of SET FORMAT TO before operating on the GETs in the program in case an .FMT file is in effect. The SET FORMAT will also clear the screen if called by the program. READ will reset COL() to 0 and ROW() to 23. READ SAVE can be used to prevent the READ from clearing the GETs; you can then issue a CLEAR GETS to remove them at the appropriate time.

11.3 VALIDATING USER INPUT

The importance of data integrity in a system was discussed in Chapter 9. The most important aspect of data integrity is the validation of the data that is entered by the user. Several tools are provided by dBASE III PLUS to protect the contents of the .DBF file during append or update operations. Among these are the PICTURE and RANGE options of the GET and character string searches.

The PICTURE clause of the GET is useful for preventing errors during a GET by screening out unwanted characters or converting characters to a more desirable form, as in the conversion from lowercase to uppercase. The PICTURE clause will function as a template for any character position in the memory variable field. This is accomplished by placing functions and symbols within quotation marks, as in Figure 11.19.

```
mname = '            '
@ 10,20 GET mname PICTURE '!!!!!!!!!!!'
```

FIGURE 11.19   *Using the PICTURE clause.*

After initializing mname to a length of ten characters, the GET in Figure 11.19 will display a highlighted block of the same length. The PICTURE clause will convert lowercase alphabetic characters entered by the user to uppercase as a result of the ! in each position. Character fields are frequently validated with PICTURE clauses, because they will normally accept any character; in contrast, date or numeric fields have built-in verification capabilities.

The PICTURE clause is a character string that contains some combination of functions and template symbols. It does not change the raw data, but it does change its appearance on the screen. A function is a specific character preceded by an @ sign that will control the appearance of the contents of a GET or a SAY. Template functions appear first in the PICTURE clause. They can be combined to achieve a variety of effects. One template symbol is placed in the PICTURE clause for each expected character of data.

If you elect to use a PICTURE clause, you must include enough symbols in the template to satisfy the length of the expected data; '999' specifies the number of columns to be displayed, whereas the interactive commands such as ACCEPT will display ten positions for a numeric field. The @ function is a convenient way to fill a template with a specified symbol if the length has already been established. For example, the following PICTURE clause produces the same result as that shown in Figure 11.19.

```
                    @ 10,20 GET mname PICTURE @!'
```

CHARACTER DATA

Functions

	GET	SAY
A	Only alpha characters	N/A
!	Accept as uppercase only	Display in uppercase
R	Do not save template charcters	N/A
S	Scrollable input	N/A

Template Symbols

	GET	SAY
A	Accept alpha only	No effect
X	Accept all characters	No effect
!	Change to uppercase	Display in uppercase
L	Accept logical symbols	No effect
9	Accept only digit character	No effect
,	Place , in field	Place , every 3 digits
Others	Accept character in data	Mask data with character

FIGURE 11.20 *PICTURE functions and symbols (Part 1 of 2).*

NUMERIC DATA

Functions

	GET	SAY
C	N/A	Place CR after + value
D	N/A	Place DB after −value
(	N/A	Place () around −value
B	Left-justify display	Left justify display
Z	Replace zeros with blanks	Replace zeros with blanks
X	N/A	Allow all characters

Template Symbols

	GET	SAY
9	Accept — or digit	No effect
#	Accept digit — or blank	No effect
$	No effect	Replace zeros with $
*	No effect	Replace zeros with *
,	Plase , in data	Plase , every 3 digits
.	Place . in data	Place . in data
Others	N/A	Insert character in data

DATE

D	Accept in American format	Display in American format
E	Accept in European format	Display in European format

LOGICAL

Y	Accept Y, y, N, n	Convert to uppercase Y or N

FIGURE 11.20 *PICTURE functions and symbols (Part 2 of 2).*

Functions can be nested in PICTURE clauses; '@(999.99' will display negative values in parentheses and establish the length and decimal positions. Some functions can be combined for useful effects. For example, '@XC999.99' will print DB after negative numbers but CR after positive values. However, '@A!', '@DE', and '@X(' are all invalid combinations. The comma, decimal point, and slash are insertion characters that are placed at the desired location in the template. The 9 and # will be replaced by data, so they are substitution characters.

```
* PIC.PRG - TESTS THE EFFECT OF THE PICTURE CLAUSE
SET TALK OFF
mname = SPACE(10)
msoc_sec = '          '
mdob = CTOD('01/01/88')
mpay = 0
```

FIGURE 11.21 *PIC.PRG (Part 1 of 2).*

```
CLEAR
@ 5,5 SAY 'NAME'
@ 5,10 GET mname PICTURE '@!'
READ
@ 5,25 SAY 'RESULT -'
@ 5,35 SAY mname

@ 7,5 SAY 'SS#'
@ 7,10 GET msoc_sec PICTURE '999-99-9999'
READ
@ 7,25 SAY 'RESULT -'
@ 7,35 SAY msoc_sec

@ 9,5 SAY 'BORN'
@ 9,10 GET mdob RANGE CTOD('01/01/45'),CTOD('01/01/55')
READ
@ 9,25 SAY 'RESULT -'
@ 9,35 SAY mdob

@ 11,5 SAY 'PAY'
@ 11,10 GET mpay RANGE 150,1000
READ
@ 11,25 SAY 'RESULT -'
@ 11,45 SAY mpay PICTURE '9,999.99'
```

FIGURE 11.21   *PIC.PRG (Part 2 of 2).*

The program PIC.PRG demonstrates how several uses of the PICTURE clause will behave. The first GET, mname, will permit only alphabetic characters and will automatically convert them to uppercase in the highlighted block. The variable msoc_sec displays hyphens in the correct positions and will accept only numerals. The RANGE option will filter any numeric response that is not within the specified limits.

If a date that falls outside the specified RANGE is entered in mdob, a message 'RANGE IS 01/01/45 TO 12/31/55' is displayed at the bottom of the screen, and the user must press the space bar to correct the entry. The same action will occur in the last GET if the figure that is entered is not between 150 and 1000. In the case of the birth date no '(PRESS SPACE)' message will appear, although it will appear in the numeric mpay field. Also, the user can press Return and the initialized value will be accepted. The RANGE will be tested only if characters are typed in the GET block.

When the '@R' function is present, template literals will not be stored. Insertion characters will be removed before storing. However, in screen displays, the literals will display.

The European format for dates will be used with '@E' as a PICTURE clause. The date will appear as DD/MM/YY, not as MM/DD/YY.

The $ and * are used to protect higher decimal positions not in use with the symbol. This is often used to protect monetary checks. For example, '@$999.99' will display $$1.98 on the screen for the value 1.98.

A scrollable character field that allows you to "put ten pounds of sand in a five-pound sack" is produced by '@S'. Further, '@S10' will allow entries that are larger than 10 to be placed in a block of that length. Use the control characters ˆF and ˆA to scroll and view data in the block.

The PICTURE clause will be used often in the program examples in the remaining chapters. Observe the variety of uses, and experiment with them in the exercises. In some situations, additional validation is required. For example, RANGE is useful for checking to see whether numeric or date fields fall within a *continuous* range. This idea can be applied to character fields to ensure that data is included in a given set of characters. A DO WHILE loop and the $ are required for this type of validation.

```
memstat = ' '
CLEAR
@ 10,35 SAY 'Student Status'
@ 10,50 GET memstat
READ
DO WHILE .NOT. UPPER(memstat) $ 'PF'
        memstat = ' '
        @ 10,35 SAY 'Enter P or F'
        @ 10,50 GET memstat
        READ
ENDDO
```

FIGURE 11.22   *Validating data with $.*

The variable memstat is initialized to a length of one blank, which will provide an empty input block. The next four commands permit the user to input the student status as full-time or part-time (F or P). The $ function will search a character field to determine whether it contains only those characters which are listed in the set 'PF'. Since the DO WHILE loop will execute only when memstat does not contain P or F, the user will be forced to continue entering data until the condition has been satisfied. Although this technique will ensure data integrity in selected fields, it should be employed cautiously. It would obviously be inappropriate for a name field, for example.

Validation of User Input

1. Are the data type and length correct?
2. Is the range correct (numeric and date)?
3. Is the data part of an acceptable set (character)?
4. Is the data correct when compared to other data?
5. Have you checked the status of the data? (Is an order being accepted for an item that is no longer carried in inventory?)

FIGURE 11.23   *Factors in validating user input.*

11.4 WRITING A PROGRAM TO ADD RECORDS

There are two strategies for an append module. You can use either GETs alone or a combination of GET and REPLACE to load the data into the fields for the new record. The use of the GET alone will require that the actual field names be used, which is how the screen painter feature works. The actual .DBF field names are loaded to the screen, which defines their type and length. Any additional validation will have to be coded later. However, the preferred method is to use a set of memory variables, which must first be initialized, and then to use the REPLACE command to transfer the data from the memory variables to the actual field names. This allows the user to change the data before it is written to the file and, more importantly, allows the data to be validated by the program.

Append Module Program Steps

1. Define all memory variables.
2. Use @ GET to input data to variables.
3. Validate the contents of the variables.
4. Have the user decide whether or not to append.
5. APPEND BLANK and REPLACE to add record.
6. Loop.

FIGURE 11.24 *Strategy for an append module.*

Memory variables should be carefully initialized with a STORE command at the start of the program. Attempts to reference an uninitialized variable will generate a syntax error, which will interrupt the program. Figure 11.25 provides some guidance for this process.

Initialization of Memory Variables

`mstate = ' '`	Initialization of character fields will establish the length of the field.
`mprice = 0.00`	Numeric fields should be initialized to a value that contains the expected number of decimal places. Only valid numeric characters are permitted in the field by dBASE III PLUS.
`mdob = CTOD('01/01/88')`	Dates must be converted with the CTOD function. Only allowable date values will be accepted as input. The month must be a number between 1 and 12; the day must be within the range for that month. Even leap years are taken into account for February. Years are assumed to be in the twentieth century, but they can be adjusted with the SET CENTURY command. (Chapter 13 will explain date arithmetic and the use of the SET CENTURY command.)
`ok = .T.`	Logical variables will accept only T,F,Y,N in uppercase or lowercase.

FIGURE 11.25 *How to initialize memory variables.*

A helpful strategy is to provide the user with the ability to edit entries before the data is actually written to the file in an APPEND or a modification. All the data entry operations must be nested within a DO WHILE that will execute as long as the user wants to continue editing. The user will respond to a prompt at the bottom of the loop, indicating the intention to edit or to move on to the next activity.

Steps to Accept a User's Response

1. Initialize a logical variable to 'Y'.
2. Include a DO WHILE with the logical variable.
3. Place a GET/READ before the ENDDO to accept the user's intentions.

```
memname = SPACE(25)
ok = .Y.
DO WHILE ok
    CLEAR
    @ 10,35 SAY 'Name'
    @ 10,50 GET memname
    READ
    @ 15,50 SAY 'Any Changes? (Y/N)' GET ok
    READ
ENDDO ok
```

FIGURE 11.26   *User termination of a loop.*

The program section in Figure 11.26 will allow the user to input and edit until the information is correct. Although only a name field is requested here, a whole screenful of fields could be nested in the DO WHILE loop. When the user types n (or any character other than y or t), control will pass to the command after the ENDDO ok. Once the user has indicated that the data is correct, REPLACE commands can be used to begin the critical operations of appending or modifying.

Figure 11.29 contains a complete program to append records to the CLIENT.DBF file. The structure is listed in Figure 11.27 on the opposite page for your reference. You will find that most of the ideas presented in this chapter are included in the pseudocode in Figure 11.28, also on the opposite page.

```
Structure for database: C:client.dbf
Number of data records:        11
Date of last update   : 01/01/88
Field  Field Name  Type      Width    Dec
    1  LIST_NUM    Character    11
    2  LAST        Character    18
    3  FIRST       Character    20
    4  NUM         Character     6
    5  ST          Character    15
    6  CITY        Character    20
    7  ZIP         Character     5
    8  AGT         Character     4
    9  PRICE       Numeric       7
   10  LIST_DATE   Date          8
   11  CONT_DATE   Date          8
** Total **                    124
```

FIGURE 11.27   *Structure for CLIENT.DBF.*

Pseudocode for an Append Module

```
Set environment
Initialize memory variables and open files
Display screen
Input Listing Number
Exit if number is blank
Loop if number exists
GET to memory variables
Append blank when user is done
Replace
```

FIGURE 11.28   *Pseudocode for ADD_CLIE.PRG.*

```
* ADD_CLIE.PRG -  Add records to the CLIENT.DBF file

* Set Environment
PRIVATE ALL
SET HEADING OFF
SET TALK OFF
SET BELL OFF
SET STATUS OFF
SET SCOREBOARD OFF
SET SAFETY OFF
CLEAR ALL

* Initialization
USE CLIENT INDEX LIST_NUM
```

FIGURE 11.29   *Program to append records (Part 1 of 3).*

```
DO WHILE .T.
   CLEAR
   mlist_num = SPACE(11)
   mlast = SPACE(18)
   mfirst = SPACE(20)
   mnum =SPACE(6)
   mst =SPACE(15)
   mcity =SPACE(20)
   mzip =SPACE(5)
   mprice = 0
   magt =SPACE(4)
   mlist_date = CTOD('  /  /  ')
   mcont_date = CTOD('  /  /  ')

   * GET Listing Number and display screen
   @  2, 29   SAY "CLIENT ENTRY"
   @  4, 29   SAY "LIST #"
   @  4, 36   GET  mlist_num PICTURE 'AA-99999-99'
   @  6, 12   SAY "LAST"
   @  6, 38   SAY "FIRST"
   @  8, 19   SAY "NUMBER"
   @  8, 34   SAY "STREET"
   @ 10, 19   SAY "CITY"
   @ 10, 47   SAY "ZIP"
```

```
   @ 12, 15   SAY "PRICE"
   @ 12, 50   SAY "AGENT"
   @ 14,  9   SAY "LIST DATE"
   @ 16, 16   SAY "CONTRACT DATE"
   @  1,  5   TO 17, 72    DOUBLE
   READ

   * Check for blank Listing Number
   IF mlist_num = '           '
       CLEAR
       CLEAR ALL
       RETURN
   ENDIF mlist_num = '           '

   * Check if record already exists
   SEEK mlist_num
   IF FOUND()
       @ 5,30 SAY 'Listing Number on File'
       mpause = 0
       DO WHILE mpause < 25
          mpause = mpause + 1
       ENDDO mpause < 100
       @ 5,30 SAY SPACE(25)
       LOOP
   ENDIF FOUND()
```

```
   * GET remaining fields
   ok = .Y.
   DO WHILE ok
      @  6, 17   GET   mlast PICTURE '@!'
      @  6, 44   GET   mfirst PICTURE '@!'
      @  8, 26   GET   mnum PICTURE '@9'
      @  8, 41   GET   mst PICTURE '@!'
      @ 10, 25   GET   mcity PICTURE '@!'
      @ 10, 51   GET   mzip PICTURE '@9'
      @ 12, 21   GET   mprice PICTURE '9,999,999' RANGE 1000,2000000
      @ 12, 56   GET   magt
      @ 14, 20   GET   mlist_date
      @ 16, 30   GET   mcont_date
      READ
      @ 16,40 SAY 'Any Changes? (Y/N) ' GET ok
      READ
   ENDDO ok
```

FIGURE 11.29   *Program to append records (Part 2 of 3).*

```
APPEND BLANK
REPLACE LIST_NUM WITH mlist_num, LAST WITH mlast,;
   FIRST WITH mfirst, NUM WITH mnum, ST WITH mst,;
   CITY WITH mcity, ZIP WITH mzip,;
   AGT WITH magt, PRICE WITH mprice,;
   LIST_DATE WITH mlist_date, CONT_DATE WITH mcont_date .
ENDDO .T.
```

FIGURE 11.29 *Program to append records (Part 3 of 3).*

The first section of the program establishes settings to provide a good working environment. The database is opened with an index for the listing number, which is a unique identifier. Eleven memory variables are initialized to match the database fields. This is done within a DO WHILE .T. to clear the fields at the conclusion of an entry cycle. Title and prompt lines for each field are displayed on the screen with @ SAY commands framed by a double-line box. A GET with a PICTURE clause to match the expected form for the listing number is placed at the appropriate location. The READ will store the user's response in mlist_num.

The value stored in mlist_num must be carefully validated. The PICTURE clause will ensure the proper form, which includes two letters and seven numbers separated by two hyphens. If the user simply presses the Return key, the field will be filled with blanks because of the initialization. An IF/ENDIF is used to avoid unusable blanks in the unique identifier. It provides a convenient exit from the module. In addition, there cannot be two records with the same listing number in the database. The fastest means for this validation is to use a SEEK with the index and test to determine whether the record can be found. Success, in this case, is undesirable, so an error message is issued, and, after a delay to view the message, the DO WHILE is reexecuted with the LOOP command.

A nested DO WHILE is used to GET the remaining data fields, which are validated with PICTURE and RANGE clauses. The DO WHILE ok command will allow the user to return to the blocks to edit by responding with a Y in the GET ok command after the READ. Eventually the user will respond with N, and the APPEND BLANK will position the record pointer at a new record number. The REPLACE command then places the data that is in the memory variables into the field names. The CLEAR GETS will empty the GET blocks after the user enters a new listing number in the next pass of the loop.

Circumstances may dictate a modification of the strategy in ADD_CLIE.PRG. For example, there may be no unique identifier. More stringent data validation may be required in some cases. However, the basis of this program is a good one to emulate. Studying examples and writing modules yourself are excellent ways to develop your ability to construct effective programs.

Chapter Summary

11.1

Custom screens can be produced by plotting the specific locations of titles, prompts, data entry blocks, lines, and boxes on a grid of coordinates. Literals, variables, and field names are displayed by @ SAY commands in any desired arrangement, using tabbing, ROW(), and COL(). Areas can be cleared, and single or double lines and boxes can be drawn with the @ and CLEAR commands. Large blocks of text are displayed with TEXT/ENDTEXT. The @ GET displays an enhanced block to accept input data to variables or field names with the READ.

11.2

The screen painter is a menu-driven feature that produces an .FMT file containing @ SAY and @ GET commands that may be edited and used in a .PRG file. It enables you to add, delete, and move fields, titles, and boxes on a work screen easily. GET blocks can be replaced by delimiters or underlining if you so desire. Rearranging the order of GETs and READs in a file will produce a variety of useful effects, such as split screens or column-wise input.

11.3

The validation of user-entered data is critical to data integrity. The initialization of variables, by means of PICTURE and RANGE clauses and programming checks, is used for this purpose. The PICTURE clause is an option of GET, which uses templates consisting of functions and symbols to restrict the user's response to acceptable characters. The RANGE option will permit only values that fall between two limits in a numeric or date field. The $ function can be used to ensure that a character response is part of a specific set.

11.4

An effective strategy for an APPEND module is to accept data to initialized variables through a custom screen, validate the data, and use APPEND BLANK to write the record when the user is finished editing. Nested DO WHILE and IF/ENDIF structures will be required as well as an indexed search using SEEK to check for blank or duplicate records.

Key Terms

transparent	template functions
in-line code	WYSIWYG
template symbols	

COMMAND SUMMARY

@ SAY — Display data at a screen location.

@ GET — Input data at a screen location.

SET SCOREBOARD OFF — Suppress scoreboard display.

ROW() — Returns the row position.

COL() — Returns the column position.

SPACE() — Display a number of spaces.

DOUBLE — Draw a double line or box.

CLEAR TO — Remove a line or box.

TEXT — Display a block of text.

ENDTEXT — End of TEXT/ENDTEXT structure.

CREATE SCREEN — Use the screen painter to create a screen.

MODIFY SCREEN — Use the screen painter to modify a screen.

.SCR — An internal file used by CREATE SCREEN.

.FMT — A file containing @ SAY and @ GET commands.

SET INTENSITY OFF — Suppress block highlighting.

SET DELIMITERS TO — Specify symbols to delimit GET blocks.

SET FORMAT TO — Direct @ SAY to screen or printer.

PICTURE — Control data input with GET.

RANGE — Set limits for numeric data input with GET.

SELF-CHECK QUESTIONS

1. Why is designing custom screens preferable to using those which are provided automatically by dBASE III PLUS?
2. What does the APPEND BLANK command do?
3. What are some important considerations to bear in mind when designing screens?
4. Why is @ SAY/GET more desirable than other input commands for custom screens?
5. How can one row of a screen display be cleared?
6. What does TEXT/ENDTEXT do?
7. Why is it important to be concerned with the size of GET blocks?
8. What is the end product of the proper use of the screen painter?
9. Why is it important to place @ SAY commands in chronological order?
10. What does the READ command do?
11. Why is it advantageous to use memory variables as opposed to field names in custom screens?
12. Name three potential uses for a PICTURE clause.
13. What does a RANGE clause do?

14. What is the importance of data validation?

15. How are date-type fields initialized?

TRY IT YOURSELF

1. Working from the dot prompt, STORE your name and address to variables, CLEAR the screen, and place the data with titles at any preselected location on the screen.

2. Do Exercise 1 again, using variable tab settings as coordinates and storing a title to a variable before displaying it.

3. Produce a facsimile of an organization chart, using literals, boxes, and lines. Use TEXT/ENDTEXT for the description. Erase the top box and its contents.

4. Write a module that uses GETs to input the data in Exercise 1. Test the results with ? from the dot prompt.

5. Use the screen painter to design an input screen for the CITIES database. Include a box and titles. Test the screen with a DO command.

6. Modify the .FMT file in Exercise 5 to include PICTURE clauses on all fields. Convert the field names to memory variables, and specify RANGEs for the populations in order to reject values that are less than 50,000 or greater than 10,000,000.

PROGRAMMING PROJECT

Write a program to append records, using the file in Exercise 6. Exit the procedure if a blank is placed in the CITY field.

12

SYSTEM DESIGN USING MULTIPLE FILES

LEARNING OBJECTIVES

1. To organize a system and its data.
2. To manipulate files with SELECT and ALIAS.
3. To chain multiple files using SET RELATION TO.
4. To write a program to display records.

SYSTEM DESIGN
USING MULTIPLE FILES

When applications are developed in mainframe installations, the work is traditionally shared by system analysts and programmers. The system analysts study needs and requirements, and develop specifications for the proposed system. The programmers then write the code to produce the final product. In a microcomputer environment, all these tasks are often performed by one person. You will need additional tools besides the ones you have already acquired if you are to work with complicated sets of data. Chapter 12 presents some advanced methods and commands that will assist you greatly in designing a system that utilizes more than one database.

12.1 SYSTEM PLANNING

The previous chapters have prepared you to approach business problems with a set of tools for managing, retrieving, and reporting data. All of the examples in these chapters have involved a single database, which is often sufficient to meet a user's needs. However, there are many instances in which the complexity of the data and the tasks to be performed require the use of more than one database. This chapter will present ways to plan systems effectively for more complicated business problems.

It may seem obvious that a system should be planned, but it is surprising how often a dBASE III PLUS system grows "organically," without plans. This is the result when problems are addressed as they come up. Planning then may be short-term and directed toward solving one immediate crisis after another. The end result of such haphazard development is that the system eventually becomes unable to perform necessary functions and contains so many errors that it is no longer usable.

Besides the inevitable downfall of a haphazard design, there are other reasons to plan a database system. Planning uncovers opportunities to utilize the features and power of dBASE III PLUS. It allows programming to be directed toward accurate modeling, which means that the objective or purpose of the program can be achieved and the needs of the user can be met. Moreover, planning often uncovers error-generating or inefficient procedures before they are implemented.

One tool that is useful for system planning is the I-P-O chart. The acronym stands for input, processing, and output. The input consists of all the stored-data fields, but they might also include some data input by the user for calculations. The functions and procedures to be performed upon the data are listed under processing. Finally, any reports or query screens are listed under output. The advantage of this approach is that you can get a concise image of the essential parts of the system. Each area can be expanded in further detail as necessary. The I-P-O chart is an implementation of top-down design. For example, the processing section can become the basis for the pseudocode, and the output section can evolve into screen or report designs. Figure 12.1 is an I-P-O chart for a proposed system to track employee training activity.

Input	Processing	Output
Org. Code	Add Records	Display Record
Emp. #	Modify Records	Print Yearly Report
Supervisor	Delete Records	Print Rosters
Mail Stop	Calculate Attendance	
Job Code	Calculate Frequency using Course Date	
Job Title		
Date of Hire		
Course #		
Course Date		
Emp. Name		

FIGURE 12.1   *I-P-O chart to track employee training.*

The goal of planning is to develop a system in which data is easy to maintain and access. The key to achieving the goal is the data itself. You will need to examine data in terms of its interrelationships in order to make certain that it is limited to essential dependencies. This may involve assigning data fields to multiple .DBF files according to their function. Fortunately, established methods are available to achieve integrity of purpose among the data fields.

The processing and output aspects of the system have been examined in previous chapters. They are both dependent on the *data dictionary*, meaning the system's characteristics and the complete set of all data used by the system. The data dictionary that will be included in the system will eventually become the field names in whatever the databases are established. Attempt to identify as many data items as possible at first, since they can be organized and reduced later if necessary. Eventually you will maintain or include only the data that is needed to satisfy user needs.

Often, you will be gathering the data items from an existing manual system. Specify type and length for the fields to prepare for establishing the structure of the databases. The fields must then be examined to determine the relationships that may exist.

Before establishing a field, be sure that it is unique in the set. Two fields should not contain the same information under different names. For example, including the fields NAME and EMP_NAME is redundant. Although dBASE III PLUS does not allow duplicate field names, you should also avoid names that are too similar, such as NUMBER_PH and NUMBER_PO; PHONE and PURCH_ORD might be better.

Another common problem is handling mutually exclusive fields. This term was used to describe the options of a menu in Chapter 8. When mutually exclusive fields occur among data, they should be handled by one category field. Since it is impossible to be both a full-time and a part-time student, for instance, placing an F or a P in one field called STATUS is preferable to maintaining two logical fields, PART_TIME and FULL_TIME.

It is often better to calculate a field than to store it. Dates frequently provide a good example of this. You might store the first date of registration for a student and subtract it from the system date (the current date stored in the computer) in order to yield the number of days the student has been enrolled. This is more efficient than attempting to maintain a second date field in the database for this purpose. Chapter 13 will explain how to calculate dates. Figure 12.2 lists the steps to be taken in the initial phase of system design.

1. Design the input from the manual system.
2. Place the data elements in a data dictionary.
3. Design the output with paper and pencil.
4. Define the functions that are to be performed.
5. Design the files so as to avoid redundancy.
6. Revise as needed.

FIGURE 12.2 *Initial system design.*

Structured data design uses *normalization* to lower the incidence of redundancy in the data dictionary. The benefits of normalization include clarity, optimum grouping for performance, and reduced need for future maintenance. E. F. Codd is responsible for the mathematical basis for normalization, which he proposed in the early 1970s, using relational algebra and calculus. A list of all the fields or data entities in an individual .DBF file is called a *flat file*. It is much like a sequential file, but unlike a table. Normalization of the flat file establishes the necessary relationships among the data entities. The five forms of normalization, first through fifth, gradually eliminate redundancy. In practice, however, the fourth and fifth forms are rarely used. The forms define the relationships, according to function, among the data fields.

First normal form names a data organization in which every field in the record is linked to the *key field*, which is a unique value that is used to identify other attached fields. For example, a Social Security number is a unique identifier for an individual's name, city, and other data. The set of data must then be searched for repeating fields. Using the same example, if the Social Security number is part of a payroll record, the various check amounts issued to that person are obviously repeating fields. These fields should be grouped in another record and file, along with a copy of the key.

Figure 12.3 shows how a record containing repeating fields can be normalized. The example used is an employee training record. The key is a combination of an organization code and an employee number. The organization code refers to the department in which the employee works. If the structure were left in the state shown in the column on the left, the first seven fields would have to be included every time the employee completed a training course. This would be a highly redundant data situation. The solution is to create a second file that contains the key fields and the repeating fields. When all repeating fields and a copy of the key are removed and placed in a new record, the data is in first normal form.

BEFORE		AFTER
First Normal Form		
Org. Code	Org. Code	Org. Code
Emp. #	Emp. #	Emp. #
Supervisor	Supervisor	Course #
Mail Stop	Mail Stop	Course Date
Job Code	Job Code	
Job Title	Job Title	
Date of Hire	Date of Hire	
Course #	Emp. Name	
Course Date		
Emp. Name		
Second Normal Form		
Org. Code	Org. Code	Org. Code
Emp. #	Emp. #	Supervisor
Supervisor	Job Code	Mail Stop
Mail Stop	Job Title	
Job Code	Date of Hire	
Job Title	Emp. Name	
Date of Hire		
Emp. Name		

FIGURE 12.3 *The normalization process (Part 1 of 2).*

BEFORE   **AFTER**

Third Normal Form

Org. Code   Org. Code   Job Code
Emp. #   Emp. #   Job Title
Job Code   Job Code
Job Title   Date of Hire
Date of Hire   Emp. Name
Emp. Name

FIGURE 12.3   *The normalization process (Part 2 of 2).*

The supervisor's name and the mail stop present another type of problem. It would not be necessary to store the two fields in the record if the data could be retrieved by keying on the organization code. Since there is one supervisor and one mail stop per organization code, the solution is to remove these two fields and place them in another record and file, using part of the key. The supervisor and mail stop fields use only part of the key, because the employee number is not referenced. Therefore, a *functional dependency* (one that references only part of a key) exists. When data is in first normal form (with no repeating fields) and fields that are dependent on part of the key have been removed, the data is said to be in second normal form.

Sometimes fields in a record are redundant but do not have a relationship with the key. This situation is called a *transitive dependency*. An example is the job title, which is directly related to the job code, a nonkey field. Data is in third normal form when it is in second normal form, and all transitive dependencies are removed. In Figure 12.3, the job title can be retrieved from another record keyed on the job code that both records contain.

Systems in dBASE III PLUS systems are based on third normal form (3NF) or the *Boyce-Codd Normal Form (BCNF)*. This means, in addition to the concepts presented above, that the data is arranged in strict columns that share a dependence on each other. Data arranged in this way can be referenced from two directions, row and column. Because dBASE III PLUS includes both procedural and nonprocedural modes, it is considered a fourth generation language (4GL). In the nonprocedural mode, you simply state the action to be performed (from the dot prompt); while in procedural mode, you list each action to be performed later (.PRG file).

Larger systems require a careful analysis of the data dictionary to remove repeating fields, functional dependencies, and transitive dependencies. Each time such elements are removed, they are moved to another file. Obviously, this will produce several databases that will have to work together to provide the user with necessary data. The benefits of multiple files are considerable. Storage requirements are dramatically reduced, since redundancy is all but eliminated. (However, the key fields will still be redundant among the databases.) Data entry and maintenance, and the associated errors, are kept to a minimum. Also, major changes are made much more easily than in a single database. In the example in Figure 12.3 on the previous page, only one record has to be updated in order to change a job title for *all* employees when the data is in third normal form. In the previous structures, every employee bearing a given title would require a record modification.

```
Org. Code
Emp. #
Supervisor
Mail Stop
Job Code            Original File
Job Title
Date of Hire
Course #
Course Date
Emp. Name
```

Normalization Produces

```
Org. Code
Emp. #
Job Code            Employee File
Date of Hire
Emp. Name
```

```
Org. Code
Emp. #               Course Transaction
Course #             File
Course Date
```

```
Org. Code
Supervisor           Organization File
Mail Stop
```

```
Job Code             Job Code File
Job Title
```

FIGURE 12.4   *The result of normalization.*

---

1. Identify the fields.
2. Identify how each field will be used for access, interactive query, reports, or archiving.
3. Identify the keys (unique identifiers).
4. Identify the relationships among the fields and files (indexes, common fields in each database).
5. Arrange the data in Third Normal Form.

FIGURE 12.5   *Procedure for analyzing data.*

12.2 SELECT, ALIAS, AND MULTIPLE FILES

The process of normalization will usually define two or more separate database files from the data dictionary. You will need the commands and programming strategies used with multiple files to perform typical functions such as appending or reporting in these situations.

With dBASE III PLUS, you can assign each .DBF file to a separate *work area*. Ten work areas are available for storing individual database files, and the data that is contained in these areas can be accessed simultaneously. However, only the active work area will accept changes to the data. The SELECT command assigns a particular .DBF file and any associated indexes to a specific work area, which may be labeled either one of the sets A through J or one of the sets 1 through 10. The SELECT statements should be placed at the start of the program to initialize it.

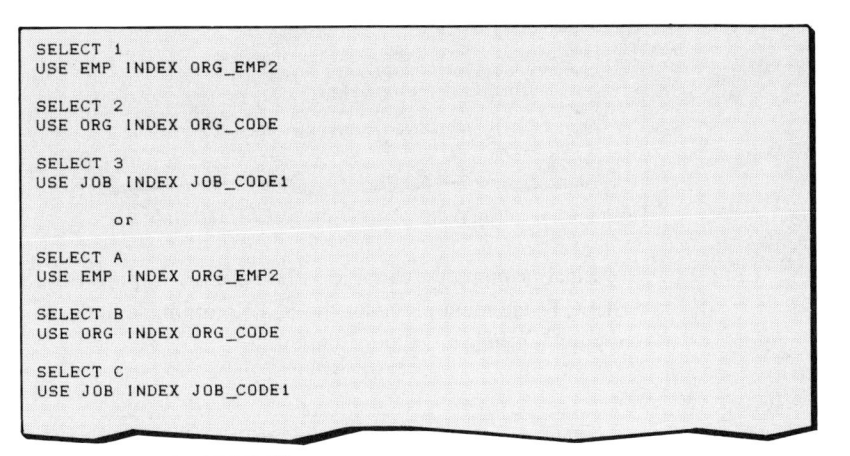

```
SELECT 1
USE EMP INDEX ORG_EMP2

SELECT 2
USE ORG INDEX ORG_CODE

SELECT 3
USE JOB INDEX JOB_CODE1

            or

SELECT A
USE EMP INDEX ORG_EMP2

SELECT B
USE ORG INDEX ORG_CODE

SELECT C
USE JOB INDEX JOB_CODE1
```

FIGURE 12.6 *Using the SELECT statement.*

After these commands have been issued, the data in any database can be accessed through the appropriate work area. This is accomplished by using the work area name with a – and > symbol to form an "arrow" as a prefix to a field name. For example, A – > EMP_NAME identifies the field name EMP_NAME as part of the .DBF file and indexes that are specified in the SELECT statement. The major benefit is that all field names in all SELECTed work areas can be referenced for display simply by including the prefix.

As a convenience, an ALIAS can be used in place of another identifier. However, the proper file name can no longer be used after an ALIAS has been specified. An ALIAS may make it more evident what database is being used. The program example at the end of this chapter uses both conventions for comparison. In Figure 12.7, the prefix EMPLOYEE-> would replace EMP->.

```
SELECT 1
USE EMP INDEX ORG_EMP2 ALIAS EMPLOYEE
```

FIGURE 12.7   *Using ALIAS.*

Figure 12.8 shows how you can read and display fields from any SELECTed file. However, if the ALIAS is included in the field name, the data can be written to the file. Figure 12.9 demonstrates that when any operation other than displaying the data must be performed using a certain file without an ALIAS or prefix, you will have to include a SELECT statement first.

```
* Display remaining fields
@  6, 21  SAY  EMPLOYEE->EMP_NAME
@  6, 64  SAY  EMPLOYEE->HIRE_DATE
@  8, 16  SAY  EMPLOYEE->JOB_CODE
@ 10, 17  SAY  TWO->MAIL
@ 10, 34  SAY  TWO->SUPERVISOR
```

FIGURE 12.8   *Displaying fields from SELECTed files.*

Since a memory variable is being used to perform a search in Figure 12.9, a SELECT statement precedes the SEEK command here so that dBASE III PLUS will know which indexed file to search.

```
SELECT 3
SEEK memjob
IF .NOT. FOUND()
    @ 8,33 SAY 'Record Not Found'
ENDIF .NOT. FOUND()
@  8, 33 SAY THIRD->JOB_TITLE
```

FIGURE 12.9   *Using SEEK with a SELECTed file.*

Study the use of SELECT, ALIAS, and the -> prefix in the program to display records in Figure 12.15. The four .DBF files that are used there simultaneously in a variety of operations demonstrate the power of this feature.

12.3 CHAINING FILES WITH SET RELATION TO

The SET RELATION TO command is used to link database files on a common indexed field. It is a convenient replacement for the SEEK command in a programming strategy with two .DBF files. Both methods perform equally well, but SET

RELATION TO is more concise. When you need to retrieve only one matching record from another file on the basis of a single key, you are establishing a *one-to-one* relationship. A common static field exists in both files, and it is accessible through a matching index.

```
SELECT 1
USE EMP INDEX ORG_EMP2 ALIAS EMPLOYEE

SELECT 2
USE ORG INDEX ORG_CODE ALIAS TWO
SET RELATION TO ORG_CODE INTO EMPLOYEE
```

FIGURE 12.10   *Using SET RELATION TO.*

SET RELATION TO positions files in a one-to-one relationship, meaning that the files track each other so that the record pointer in one file tracks the record pointer in another file. The record pointers will then be positioned on records with the same value for a keyed field. The database specified after INTO will probably be the larger in order to reduce search time. In Figure 12.10, each time the record pointer is moved to a new record in the EMP file, the record pointer in the ORG file will be set to the first record that bears a matching indexed value. Note that SET RELATION TO will position the record pointer at the *first* matching record. Other matching records will not be accessed.

Although each work area will be permitted only one SET RELATION TO, the procedure can be repeated for a number of files. The logical connection of files in this manner is called *chaining*. When using the SET RELATION TO, make certain that the TO phrase precedes the INTO phrase; otherwise, it will not perform. Notice the example in Figure 12.10.

When the possibility exists of several matching records in the related file, SET RELATION TO will no longer be effective, because it will position the record pointer at the first occurrence only. This type of relationship is referred to as *one-to-many*. You will have to program the solution in a one-to-many situation by passing the key value, which has been found in the first .DBF file, to a DO WHILE loop, which will perform an indexed search on the second .DBF file to retrieve all instances of matching records.

The code in Figure 12.11 on the following page uses a value in memkey, which was retrieved from another file, to search for multiple occurrences of the key value in the .DBF file specified in SELECT 4. The SET RELATION TO would not be useful in this case.

Many-to-many relationships require a third linking table with common elements from both files. This is a very complex arrangement that does not occur frequently.

```
* Display Courses for Employee
SELECT 4
SEEK memkey
        .
        .
DO WHILE .NOT. EOF()
    IF FOUR->ORG_CODE + FOUR->EMP_NO = memkey
        @ row, 25   SAY FOUR->COURSE
        @ row, 44   SAY FOUR->CRSE_DATE
        row = row + 1
        IF row > 22
            @ row, 35 SAY 'Press Return '
            @ 14, 25 CLEAR
            row = 14
        ENDIF row > 22
    ELSE
    GO BOTTOM
    ENDIF FOUR->ORG_CODE + FOUR->EMP_NO = memkey
    SKIP
ENDDO .NOT. EOF()
```

FIGURE 12.11   *A one-to-many relationship.*

12.4 WRITING A PROGRAM TO DISPLAY RECORDS

The rapid retrieval and display of data is an essential function of a system. Users expect accurate and informative responses to their inquiries. The program that is presented in this section is an example of how you can use planning to achieve effective results.

The four databases that resulted from the normalization in section 12.1 are listed in Figure 12.12, followed by the .DBF structures in Figure 12.13. The purpose of the program is to retrieve all the relevant data about an employee. The data will be based on the organization code and employee number, which will be supplied by the user. Clearly, this will involve working with all the databases simultaneously.

```
Org. Code
Emp. #
Job Code          }  Employee File
Date of Hire
Emp. Name


Org. Code
Supervisor        }  Organization File
Mail Stop

Job Code          }  Job Code File
Job Title

Org. Code
Emp. #            }  Course Transaction
Course #             File
Course Date
```

FIGURE 12.12   *Four related database files.*

Sample data are included in Figure 12.13 in order to show how the program is working.

```
    . USE EMP

    . LIST STRUCTURE

Structure for database: C:EMP.dbf
Number of data records:      6
Date of last update   : 01/01/88
Field  Field Name  Type        Width   Dec
    1  ORG_CODE    Character       4
    2  EMP_NO      Character       5
    3  EMP_NAME    Character      25
    4  JOB_CODE    Character       2
    5  HIRE_DATE   Date            8
** Total **                      45

    . USE ORG

    . LIST STRUCTURE

Structure for database: C:ORG.dbf
Number of data records:      4
Date of last update   : 01/01/88
Field  Field Name  Type        Width   Dec
    1  ORG_CODE    Character       4
    2  SUPERVISOR  Character      20
```

```
    3  MAIL         Character      5
** Total **                      30

    . LIST

Record#  ORG_CODE SUPERVISOR        MAIL
      1  0194     HAWKINS, J.       03-55
      2  0354     PARRISH, D.       83-44
      3  0544     POLLARD, D.       92-33
      4  0365     HU, W.            77-11

    . LIST STRUCTURE

Structure for database: C:JOB.dbf
Number of data records:      6
Date of last update   : 01/01/88
Field  Field Name  Type        Width   Dec
    1  JOB_CODE    Character       2
    2  JOB_TITLE   Character      20
** Total **                      23

    . USE JOB

    . LIST
```

```
Record#  JOB_CODE JOB_TITLE
      1  19       Micro Support Spec.
      2  11       Manager
      3  45       Secretary
      4  28       Programmer/Analyst
      5  73       Data Entry/Reception
      6  62       Executive

    . USE COURSE
```

FIGURE 12.13   .DBF structures for EMP_LIST.PRG (Part 1 of 2).

```
. LIST STRUCTURE

Structure for database: C:COURSE.dbf
Number of data records:        9
Date of last update   : 01/01/88
Field  Field Name  Type       Width    Dec
    1  ORG_CODE    Character      4
    2  EMP_NO      Character      5
    3  COURSE      Character      4
    4  CRSE_DATE   Date           8
** Total **                     22
```

FIGURE 12.13   *.DBF structures for EMP_LIST.PRG (Part 2 of 2).*

Examine the pseudocode in Figure 12.14 in terms of the structure. There is a nested DO WHILE/ENDDO to deal with the one-to-many access of the course data. Several nested IF/ENDIFs will also be required for error checking and for responding to user requests.

```
Pseudocode for EMP_DISP.PRG


Open files and set relations
Do while user does not want to exit
        Get a key from user
        If key is blank - exit
        Find matching record in Employee file
        If key is not found - try again
        Use key to access Organization file
        Use key to access Job Code file
        Display employee data
        Use key to access Course Transaction File
        Do while key matches
                Retrieve transactions
                Display course data
                Adjust screen rows
        End of transaction routine
End of user does not want to exit routine
Close files
```

FIGURE 12.14   *Pseudocode for EMP_LIST.PRG.*

The EMP_DISP.PRG file in Figure 12.15 on pages 264 and 265 begins typically by setting an environment and initializing some variables that will be used to accept the user's request. Each of the four databases is assigned to a work area with a SELECT statement. The EMP file, indexed on a combination of the ORG_CODE and EMP_NO, is placed in work area 1 using the ALIAS EMPLOYEE. Work area 2 contains the ORG.DBF file indexed on the ORG_CODE as ALIAS TWO. The SET RELATION TO command will establish a chaining relationship with the EMP.DBF file, which will automatically position the record pointer. The JOB database and its index on JOB_CODE occupies work area 3, and the repeating fields concerning the course transactions are in work area 4.

The DO WHILE .T. loop will permit any number of inquiries until blank fields are found in the first IF/ENDIF. The SELECT 1 command is included in preparation for a SEEK on the data placed in the memory variables morg_code and memp_no. A custom screen displays all the titles and the GET blocks to accept the user's request. After the READ executes, storing the values found in the GET blocks to the variables, the two variables are concatenated into memkey for the sake of convenience. A SEEK is issued against the index in the first work area and a check is made in case the user provides data that does not exist. The IF/ENDIF structure that follows allows another chance by LOOPing back to the command following the DO WHILE .T.

When a valid record is found, @ SAYs using the ALIAS prefix will display the data from both the EMP database and the ORG database as a result of the SET RELATION TO. Note that this routine depends on the data integrity of the JOB.DBF file and its index. Next, the value in JOB_CODE is stored in memjob; the JOB work area is SELECTED; and a SEEK locates the appropriate record. This search was necessary, since no relation was set to work area 1. Should the EMPLOYEE->JOB_CODE field contain an error, the screen will simply print an error message and the program will continue.

The next section of the program contains a one-to-many search of the COURSE database placed in work area 4. A SEEK will use the memkey variable and a check will be made for the possibility that the employee has not had any training activity. A DO WHILE .NOT. EOF() will be required to access the remaining records if at least one valid record is found. An IF/ENDIF is nested in the DO WHILE to display any consequent valid records. Since the top portion of the screen contains the previously displayed data, the course data must be scrolled underneath between rows 14 and 22 if needed. This is accomplished by using the variable row in the @ SAY and incrementing it each time a new record must be displayed. Should the list of courses approach the bottom of the screen, an IF/ENDIF will pause, reset the row counter, and CLEAR the bottom half of the screen when the user presses a key. When a record that does not satisfy the matching condition or the end of file is eventually encountered, the entire screen will clear. The user will then have another opportunity to display an employee record.

This chapter combined some elements of system planning and dBASE III PLUS multiple-file handling features that are essential for addressing more complex business needs. These concepts can be applied to other system functions besides the screen display program you have just studied. Consider what strategy would be required to append records, for example. It would be necessary to append to both the EMP and the COURSE files after checking the validity of the data in the JOB_CODE and ORG_CODE fields, among other things. If the system is thoughtfully designed, including the data dictionary, these tasks will much more manageable, and the user will eventually be well served.

```
* EMP_DISP.PRG -   Display records from four databases.

* Set Environment
PRIVATE ALL
SET HEADING OFF
SET TALK OFF
SET BELL OFF
SET STATUS OFF
SET SCOREBOARD OFF
SET SAFETY OFF
CLEAR ALL

* Initialization
morg_code = '    '
memp_no = '       '
memkey = SPACE(9)

SELECT 1
USE EMP INDEX ORG_EMP2 ALIAS EMPLOYEE

SELECT 2
USE ORG INDEX ORG_CODE ALIAS TWO
SET RELATION TO ORG_CODE INTO EMPLOYEE

SELECT 3
USE JOB INDEX JOB_CODE1 ALIAS THIRD
```

```
SELECT 4
USE COURSE INDEX ORG_EMP ALIAS FOUR

* Processing Loop
DO WHILE .T.
   SELECT 1
   morg_code = '    '
   memp_no = '    '
   * GET Org. Code and Emp. # and display screen
   @  2, 29  SAY "DISPLAY TRAINING RECORD"
   @  4, 17  SAY "ORGANIZATION CODE"
   @  4, 35  GET  morg_code
   @  4, 42  SAY "EMPLOYEE NUMBER"
   @  4, 58  GET  memp_no
   @  6,  7  SAY "EMPLOYEE NAME"
   @  6, 51  SAY "DATE OF HIRE"
   @  8,  7  SAY "JOB CODE"
   @  8, 23  SAY "JOB TITLE"
   @ 10,  7  SAY "MAIL STOP        SUPERVISOR"
   @ 12, 21  SAY "COURSE NUMBER        COURSE DATE"
   @  0,  2  TO 11, 77    DOUBLE
   READ
```

```
   * Check for blank Org. Code or Emp. #
   IF morg_code = '    ' .OR. memp_no = '       '
        CLEAR
        CLEAR ALL
        RETURN
   ENDIF morg_code

   * Check if record exists
   memkey = morg_code + memp_no
```

FIGURE 12.15 *Listing for EMP_LIST.PRG (Part 1 of 2).*

```
 SEEK memkey
IF .NOT. FOUND()
     @ 5,40 SAY 'Record Not Found'
     mpause = 0
     DO WHILE mpause < 25
        mpause = mpause + 1
     ENDDO mpause < 100
     @ 5,40 SAY SPACE(25)
     LOOP
ENDIF .NOT. FOUND()

* Display remaining fields
@  6, 21  SAY  EMPLOYEE->EMP_NAME
@  6, 64  SAY  EMPLOYEE->HIRE_DATE
@  8, 16  SAY  EMPLOYEE->JOB_CODE
@ 10, 17  SAY  TWO->MAIL
@ 10, 34  SAY  TWO->SUPERVISOR

* Find job title and display
memjob = EMPLOYEE->JOB_CODE
SELECT 3
SEEK memjob
IF .NOT. FOUND()
     @ 8,33 SAY 'Record Not Found'
ENDIF .NOT. FOUND()
@  8, 33 SAY THIRD->JOB_TITLE
```

```
    * Display Courses for Employee
    SELECT 4
    SEEK memkey
    row = 14
    IF .NOT. FOUND()
       @ row, 33 SAY 'No Courses on File'
       @ row+1 , 33 SAY 'Press Return to Continue'
       WAIT ''
    ENDIF .NOT. FOUND()
    DO WHILE .NOT. EOF()
       IF FOUR->ORG_CODE + FOUR->EMP_NO = memkey
            @ row, 25  SAY FOUR->COURSE
            @ row, 44  SAY FOUR->CRSE_DATE
            row = row + 1
            IF row > 22
                @ row, 35 SAY 'Press Return '
                @ 14, 25 CLEAR
                row = 14
            ENDIF row > 22
       ELSE
       GO BOTTOM
       ENDIF FOUR->ORG_CODE + FOUR->EMP_NO = memkey
       SKIP
    ENDDO .NOT. EOF()
```

```
    @ row, 35 SAY 'Press Return'
    WAIT ''
    CLEAR
ENDDO .T.
CLEAR ALL
RETURN
```

FIGURE 12.15   *Listing for EMP_LIST.PRG (Part 2 of 2).*

CHAPTER SUMMARY

12.1

System planning is essential in larger applications because design errors and inefficiency will be magnified in them. I-P-O charts help the programmer assemble the elements of the system and develop them further. The data dictionary is a collection of all the fields used within the system. Redundant and mutually exclusive fields should be eliminated. Normalization is a process whereby data is organized on the basis of function and relationship in order to reduce redundancy. A unique identifier, the key, must be identified, and all fields that are not totally dependent on it should be removed with the key to another file. Data that has been effectively normalized is said to be in third normal form.

12.2

The SELECT statement is used to assign multiple files to any of ten work areas. All fields in the work areas are available for display, using either a prefix containing the file name or ALIAS with the $->$ symbols. Other operations, such as an indexed search, require a SELECT statement.

12.3

The SET RELATION TO is a convenient way to synchronize the record pointers in two files that are indexed on the same key. It is a substitute for programming a search with SEEK and a DO WHILE/ENDDO. SET RELATION TO is used for chaining files that have a one-to-one relationship. A one-to-many relationship requires the SEEK and DO WHILE/ENDDO to retrieve the desired fields.

12.4

A program to display records using multiple files will include several nested control structures. SELECT statements must be issued for each .DBF file and for indexes. Files having a one-to-one relationship on the same key can use SET RELATION TO. When the record pointer is positioned at the queried record, all related fields can be displayed using prefixes with @ SAY. Scrolling can be used to display repeating fields that have been retrieved with a one-to-many indexed search.

KEY TERMS

I-P-O chart	transitive dependency	$->$
normalization	third normal form	chaining
flat file	Boyce-Codd Normal Form	one-to-one
key field	fourth generation language (4GL)	one-to-many
functional dependency	work area	many-to-many

COMMAND SUMMARY

SELECT — Open a work area for a .DBF file.
ALIAS — Specify an alias name for a .DBF file.
SET RELATION TO — Link two .DBF files through an index.

dBUG dBASE

- Using the same column number and PICTURE clause will cause numeric values to display in an aligned column.
- When names of memory variables and field names are similar, dBASE III PLUS assumes that a name refers to a memory variable first in a STORE, but a field name first in a GET. The M–> feature can be used with memory variables and the GET command.

SELF-CHECK QUESTIONS

1. List three reasons that system planning is important.
2. Define the following terms.

> I-P-O chart
> Data dictionary
> Normalization
> Flat file
> Key field
> Functional dependency
> Transitive dependency
> Third normal form
> Work area
> ALIAS
> Chaining
> One-to-one
> One-to-many
> Scrolling

3. Why is redundancy undesirable?
4. Name three criteria for determining whether a field should be placed in a separate .DBF file.
5. What does the SELECT command do?
6. What is the function of the –> prefix?
7. What is the advantage of using the SET RELATION TO command?

8. Under what circumstances would an ALIAS be useful?
9. Is the normalization of data always appropriate? Why?

TRY IT YOURSELF

1. Develop an I-P-O chart and a data dictionary for any application presented in Chapter 6 through Chapter 11.
2. Place the following data dictionary in third normal form. (The key field is the Social Security number.)

   Payroll System
   Social Security Number
   Name
   Address
   City
   Zip
   Department
   Supervisor
   Local Tax Code
   Local Municipality Name
   Gross Pay

3. Write SELECT statements for the following files. Include an ALIAS for each.

   TAXMSTR.DBF   TAXNO.NDX
   TAXTRANS.DBF   TAXNUM.NDX

4. Chain the TAXRANS file to the TAXMSTR file with a SET RELATION TO statement.

PROGRAMMING PROJECT

Using the data dictionary in Exercise 2, write a program to display records keyed on the Social Security number. CREATE three databases: one for the basic employee fields; one for the gross pay keyed on the Social Security number; and one containing the local municipality name keyed on the local tax code. Design a screen to input the employee's Social Security number and to exit if the field is blank or the number is not found. Display the employee's data, including the local municipality name and all gross pay entries, on an attractive screen.

13

FUNCTIONS — THE PROGRAMMER'S TOOLKIT

LEARNING OBJECTIVES

1. To use functions to manipulate strings.
2. To perform arithmetic operations with functions.
3. To calculate and display dates with functions.
4. To use utility functions.
5. To write a program to update files.

Chapter

FUNCTIONS — THE PROGRAMMER'S TOOLKIT

There is much more to dBASE III PLUS than the programming and the interactive commands you have learned. Every good programming language also contains a so-called programmer's toolkit. The tools, called functions, are small internal programs that are always available to perform very useful and interesting tasks.

Would you like to know on what day of the week you were born or how many days you have been alive? Perhaps you need to find the square root or logarithm of a number. If a user had entered names in a file with the first name followed by the last name, and you wanted to index by last name, what could you do about it? In this chapter, you will learn the functions that exist to deal with all of these tasks and many more. In addition, you will learn how dBASE III PLUS performs arithmetic operations in order to take a manual math process and replicate it in code. This is critical, since business deals largely with numbers. The user's needs can best be served by using functions that help expand the form and usage of existing data.

13.1 HANDLING STRINGS

Functions are preset routines that are available in dBASE III PLUS to solve a wide variety of programming problems. They are most often used to look at data in different and useful ways. The UPPER() function mentioned in Chapter 11 is a good example. It will *display* any alphabetic character in uppercase without actually converting the data. This means that the characters in the database remain in lowercase but display in uppercase. However, a STORE command can be used to replace the original value with the converted value if the effect of the function must be retained. Functions are often cosmetic in effect, as is the case with UPPER(), but sometimes they are the only means available to accomplish a task. For example, the DOW() function will return the day of the week for any date a user might enter. For your convenience, the authors of dBASE III PLUS included a very sophisticated *algorithm*, which is a prescribed set of processes to solve a problem. Replicating this algorithm yourself would be extremely difficult and, obviously, a waste of your time and effort.

All functions include a keyword and a set of parentheses that may or may not require specifications. Functions can be sensitive to improper syntax, especially within the parentheses, where *arguments*—the values that the function will operate—are placed. It is best to experiment first with the function in the interactive mode to be sure it will perform as expected.

Also, functions may be nested if the data type of the expressions is consistent. Type the given examples or others of your choosing at the dot prompt as you study the behavior and usage of the functions presented in the rest of this chapter.

```
      . mtest = 'lower'
lower

      . ? UPPER(mtest)        <---- Displaying with a function
LOWER

      . mcaps = UPPER(mtest) <---- Storing the result
LOWER

      . ? mcaps
LOWER
```

FIGURE 13.1   *Testing functions with ?*

The rich collection of functions that are available in dBASE III PLUS for manipulating strings makes it difficult to imagine a task that cannot be performed. Through the use of functions, you can cut and paste strings and change their appearance in many ways, as the examples in this section demonstrate. For example, LOWER(), the inverse of UPPER(), will convert all characters in the argument to lowercase.

```
      . ? LOWER('CAPS')
caps

      . ? UPPER('caps')
CAPS
```

FIGURE 13.2   *Using UPPER() and LOWER().*

The dollar sign ($) function was used earlier to search a set of characters and determine whether a user's response was valid. It will return a logical .T. or .F., depending on the presence or absence of the object of the search in the specified string. The function will operate on string expressions that are delimited with quotation marks or brackets, variables, or field names. The $ function is most useful when the data being searched is in an uncertain condition. Suppose you had to find an important name or term in a comment field of a .DBF file. A LIST command or a DO WHILE loop could be used with the $ function to display any fields containing the term in question. Technically, the $ is an operator rather than a function.

```
      . mtest = 'dBASE III PLUS'

dBASE III PLUS

      . mstring = 'III'

III

      . ? mstring $ mtest    <-- Object of search $ Text to search

.T.

      . ? 'XX' $ mtest

.F.
```

FIGURE 13.3 *Using the $ operator.*

The ASC() function will return the ASCII decimal equivalent of the leftmost character of the string argument. (Refer to Chapter 7 for an explanation of the hierarchy of the ASCII code.) This function may be useful in situations where you need to determine how characters will be evaluated in an IF/ENDIF condition, for example. Note that the function operates on only the leftmost character.

```
      . ? ASC('A')

65

      . ? ASC('AB')

65
```

FIGURE 13.4 *Using ASC().*

The CHR() function is the inverse of the ASC(). If you use a value between 0 and 255 as the argument, the function returns the symbol assigned to that value in the ASCII code. Appendix B contains a complete listing of the ASCII code. Not all values will display a symbol on the screen or printer. For example, CHR(7) will cause the computer's speaker to beep.

```
    . ? CHR(97)

a

    . ? CHR(197)

E
```

FIGURE 13.5   *Using CHR().*

The SPACE () function has appeared in other chapters as a means of initializing character variables to a specified number of blanks. There is an example in Figure 13.40.

The ISALPHA(), ISLOWER(), and ISUPPER() functions will all evaluate the first character of a string expression and return a logical .T. or .F. if the character is alphabetic, lowercase, or uppercase, respectively.

```
    . ? ISALPHA('A')
.T.

    . ? ISLOWER('A')
.F.

    . ? ISUPPER('A')
.T.
```

FIGURE 13.6   *Using ISALPHA(), ISLOWER(), and ISUPPER().*

When a string expression or variable and an integer are used as arguments in LEFT(), the leftmost number of characters specified is returned; you specify how many characters will be included. The RIGHT() function operates identically, except that it counts from the right. LEN() simply counts the number of characters in the string and returns the value.

```
    . ? LEFT('ASHTON-TATE',6)
ASHTON
    . company = 'ASHTON-TATE'

    . ? RIGHT(company,4)
TATE
    . ? LEN('ASHTON-TATE')
    11
```

FIGURE 13.7   *Using LEFT(), RIGHT() and LEN().*

Unwanted blanks are easily trimmed from the left or right of a string through the use of LTRIM() or RTRIM(). TRIM() is identical to RTRIM().

```
    . ? 'OVER ' + LTRIM('        HERE')
OVER HERE
    . ? RTRIM('OVER        ') + ' THERE'
OVER THERE
```

FIGURE 13.8 *Using LTRIM() and RTRIM().*

STUFF() will insert one string into another at any specified location. SUBSTR() is the inverse of STUFF(). It will remove a substring from another string. The AT() function will return the starting location of one string within another if you would prefer to have the computer do your counting for you. The value returned could then be used in the LEFT(), RIGHT(), STUFF(), or SUBSTR() function. If the string is not found, AT() returns 0.

```
    . ? STUFF( 'dBASE PLUS',7,0,'III ')
dBASE III PLUS
    . ? SUBSTR('dBASE III PLUS',7,3)
III
    . ? AT('I', 'dBASE III PLUS')
    7
```

FIGURE 13.9 *Using STUFF(), SUBSTR(), and AT().*

The first example in Figure 13.9 inserts the literal 'III', beginning at the seventh position of the literal 'dBASE PLUS', without replacing any characters. The second example displays the same literal by specifying three characters, starting at character 7. The AT() returns the first location of the character 'I'.

The SWITCH.PRG program which appears in Figure 13.10, makes liberal use of several string-handling functions. It will accept a person's first and last name in either order and in either case, then reverse the order and display the names in uppercase. A DO WHILE .T. is used so that the program can be repeated as often as the user wishes. Pressing Return at the GET block will cause the program to exit, since blanks will be stored in memname. The RTRIM() function is used to remove any trailing blanks from the string that might interfere with searches. Also, since the program will not operate properly if there is no blank between the two names, the $ operator is used in an IF/ENDIF to force the user to include one.

```
* SWITCH.PRG - exchanges the positions of two names in a string
*               based on a search for a blank.

SET TALK OFF
SET SCOREBOARD OFF
SET STATUS OFF

DO WHILE .T.
   CLEAR
   memname = SPACE(30)
   mblank = 0
   mfront = ''
   mback = ''
   mrev = ''

   @ 10,10 SAY 'Type your name in any order '
   @ 10,38 GET memname
   READ

   * Exit if all blanks
   IF memname = SPACE(30)
      CLEAR
      RETURN
   ENDIF

   * Trim trailing blanks
   memname = RTRIM(memname)

   * Check for no blank in name
   IF .NOT. ' ' $ memname
      @ 12,15 SAY 'Please include a blank'
      delay = 1
      DO WHILE delay < 25
         delay = delay + 1
      ENDDO delay < 25
      LOOP
   ENDIF .NOT. ' ' $ memname

   * Look for a blank
   mblank = AT(' ',memname)

   * Extract first section
   mfront = LEFT(memname, mblank-1)

   * Extract the second section
   mback = SUBSTR(memname, mblank+1, LEN(memname) - mblank)

   * Assemble the reversed name and print it upper case
   memrev = UPPER(mback + ' ' + mfront)

   @ 12,1 SAY 'Here is your name reversed in Caps * * '
   @ 12,42 SAY memrev

   @ 14,15 SAY 'Press any key to continue'
   WAIT ''

ENDDO .T.
```

```
        Type your name in any order Devere, Lenore

   Here is your name reversed in Caps * *   LENORE DEVERE,

                 Press any key to continue
```

FIGURE 13.10 *A program to demonstrate the use of functions.*

SWITCH.PRG uses several functions that base their actions on the location of the blank as a delimiter between the two names. The AT() function determines the location and stores it as a numeric value in mblank. The front part of the memname is extracted with the LEFT() function by specifying the location of the blank less one as the length to store in mfront. Although RIGHT() could have been used to extract the back part of the string, the SUBSTR() was used to demonstrate nesting of functions. In this case, the length of the string LEN() less the location of the blank is used to specify the length of the second name. The two parts of the name are then reassembled, separated by a blank as the argument of the UPPER() function, then displayed. The switching algorithm in SWITCH.PRG could be used with REPLACE to reverse the order of names previously stored in a .DBF file.

13.2 ARITHMETIC FUNCTIONS AND OPERATIONS

Computers are essential to the operation of all but the smallest businesses today. This is true for several reasons, including execution speed, vast and accurate memory capacity, and universal applications, among others. It is paradoxical that in spite of their power, computers are actually simple devices when they are defined in terms of the basic tasks they perform. They can perform complicated mathematical operations, but every expression must be broken down to the elementary step of combining two values and storing the result. This means that a fourth-grade multiplication problem such as 11×23 will be performed by adding 23 to an accumulating total 11 times. Of course, the computer has the advantage of electronic speed, which produces almost instantaneous results. A brief explanation of how numeric values and operations are stored and evaluated will be helpful to you when you are working with the arithmetic functions.

Nineteen bytes is the maximum size for a numeric field. Numeric accuracy is 15.9 digits, that is the standard set by the IEEE (Institute of Electrical and Electronic Engineers). You can depend on the first 15 digits. Since 13 digits are required to represent 1 trillion (1,000,000,000,000), you should rarely have the need for all 15.9 available positions. Accuracy is 13 for nonzero numbers.

The largest number is $1 \times 10 + 99$, and the smallest positive number is $1 \times 10 - 307$. They are either integer (no decimal places) or decimal. Results of calculations that are too large to display because of a numeric overflow are displayed in exponential format or scientific notation. This form is a convenient way to represent extremely large values. To convert to natural format, simply move the decimal point to the right the number of positions specified after the $+$ sign (or to the left for fractions that display a $-$ sign). Fill in zeros as needed.

```
      . ? 15 * 5
  75

      . ? 1*10^100

***************

      . ? 1* 10^98
 .999999999E+98
```

FIGURE 13.11 *Representing large numeric values.*

Numeric variables are treated differently by dBASE III PLUS than numeric constants. With expressed numeric values, only the required places of accuracy are used. When variables are used, all 15.9 places are used, that opens up the possibility of error in the very last positions after repeated operations. The first 13 significant digits of a number are considered when making comparisons of two fractional numbers. All 15.9 digits are used when comparing fractional numbers to zero.

```
      . A = 15
  15

      . B = 5
  5

      . ? A*B
                75
      . ? .999999999999999 > .999999999999998     (16 Places)
 .F.

      . ? .9999999999999 > .9999999999998     (14 Places)
 .F.

      . ? .999999999999 > .999999999998     (13 Places)
 .T.
```

FIGURE 13.12 *Accuracy in numeric variables and constants.*

```
. TYPE TEST_ACC.PRG
* TEST_ACC.PRG  To test numeric accuracy.

SET TALK OFF
STORE .00 TO memtotal
STORE 1 TO memcount

DO WHILE memcount < 100
    memtotal = memtotal + .10000000000000
    memcount = memcount + 1
ENDDO
```

FIGURE 13.13   *A program to test numeric accuracy.*

```
      . DO TEST_ACC

      . DISPLAY MEMORY

MEMTOTAL  priv  N      9.899999999999983  (            9.90000000)
MEMCOUNT  priv  N      100  (           100.00000000)
```

FIGURE 13.14   *Results of TEST_ACC.PRG.*

In the case of MEMTOTAL, 9.899999999999983 is the value that will display as the program demonstrates. The value as it is actually stored is (9.90000000).

The arithmetic operators and their meanings are listed in Figure 13.15.

( )	Parentheses for grouping
** or ^	Exponentiation
*	Multiplication
/	Division
+	Addition
−	Subtraction

FIGURE 13.15   *The arithmetic operators.*

Figure 13.16 on the following page lists numeric operations in their order of precedence. A numeric expression is scanned by dBASE III PLUS for each of these operations in the indicated order. This means that each expression will be evaluated from left to right five times, that will reduce it to a single numeric value.

1. Assign negative or positive values.
2. Functions.
3. Exponentiation.
4. Multiplication and division.
5. Addition and subtraction.

FIGURE 13.16   *Hierarchy of operations.*

If it is necessary to defeat the order of precedence, parentheses can be used, as in Figure 13.17. This concept is consistent with mathematics and with other programming languages. The SET DECIMAL TO command can be useful if you have to display a certain number of decimal positions. Study the expressions in Figure 13.17 and experiment with your own examples to become familiar with this concept.

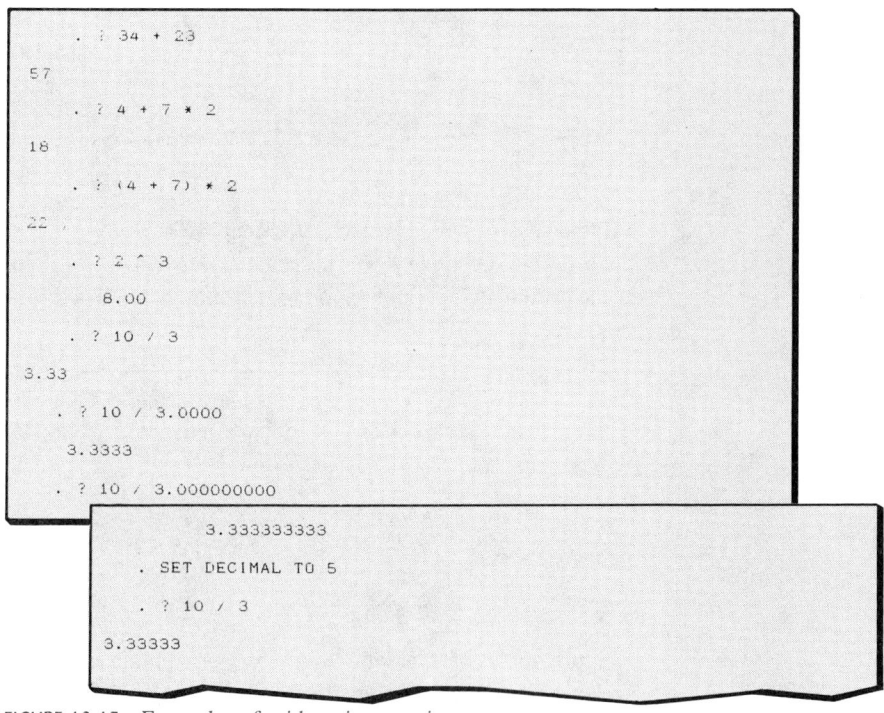

FIGURE 13.17   *Examples of arithmetic operations.*

The arithmetic functions included in dBASE III PLUS are certainly sufficient for dealing with typical business problems, but they are not designed to handle sophisticated applications such as those found in engineering. Experiment with these functions at the dot prompt, as you did with the string functions.

ABS() returns the absolute value of a numeric expression. This means that the number will be expressed as positive regardless of the stated sign of the value.

```
    . ? ABS(-154)

154
```

FIGURE 13.18   *Using ABS().*

EXP() returns the natural, or Napierian exponent of the numeric argument. It is based on the approximate value of *e*, 2.718282, rather than 2, which is used in binary arithmetic.

```
        . ? EXP(10.00000)

22026.4658
        . ? EXP(1.000000)

  2.718282
```

FIGURE 13.19   *Using EXP().*

INT() truncates any value to the right of the decimal point, producing an integer, or whole number. The real mathematical integer is the first integer greater than the argument, so negative values may not round up as might be expected.

```
        . ? INT(6.7)

  6

        . ? INT(-6.2)

  -6

        . ? INT(-6.7)

  -6
```

FIGURE 13.20   *Using INT().*

LOG() returns the natural logarithm of the numeric argument on the basis of the value of *e*, as in the EXP() function. The base 10 log can be calculated as in Figure 13.21.

```
    . ? LOG(20)
 3.00
      . ? LOG(2.71828)
1.00000
      . ? LOG(2.71828)/LOG(10)
   0.43429
```

FIGURE 13.21   *Using LOG().*

MAX() will return the highest of two values included in the argument. MIN() will return the lowest of any two values.

```
    . ? MAX(5,10)
  10
    . ? MIN(5,10)
  5
```

FIGURE 13.22   *Using MAX() and MIN().*

MOD() will return the remainder of a division operation expressed as a whole number. It is used in MODulo arithmetic.

```
    . ? MOD(10,4)
  2
```

FIGURE 13.23   *Using MOD().*

ROUND() establishes the number of decimal places to be recognized in an operation and rounds to that value.

```
        . ? ROUND(10/3,4)
 3.3333
        . ? ROUND(5.43,2)
  5.43
        . ? ROUND(5.43,1)
 5.40                          ƒ
        . ? ROUND(5.47,1)
 5.50
```

FIGURE 13.24   *Using ROUND().*

SQRT() will return the square root of the argument.

```
      . ? SQRT(16)
 4.00
```

FIGURE 13.25   *Using SQRT().*

VAL() will convert an alphanumeric number to a numeric value. STR() converts numeric values to strings. You must include the number of digits and the number of decimal places in the argument. The STR() function can be used to produce a single dollar sign in a screen or printer display. Combining VAL() with @ SAY will allow the user to determine the position of a display.

```
        . ? VAL('98.6 DEGREES') + 3
          101.60
        . ? STR(98.6+3,3,2) + ' DEGREES'
        101.60 DEGREES
 * Place a single dollar sign before a value
     . membal = 100
        . @ 15,15 SAY '$' + STR(membal,6,2)
            $100.00
 * Place a character at a selected location.
        . @ 10 + VAL(memchoice), 15 SAY '#'
```

FIGURE 13.26   *Using VAL() and STR().*

13.3 DATE FUNCTIONS AND OPERATIONS

Dates are stored as character strings in a set format that allows maximum use of the data in comparisons and ordering operations. The format YYYYMMDD ("19881225") arranges the units of time from largest to smallest so that conversions are made at the display level. This format permits the user to add and subtract dates with ease. Accounts can be aged, and compliance with time schedules can be monitored.

Dates are assumed to be in the twentieth century (19XX) unless the command SET CENTURY ON is activated. This requires the user to include the full four digits of the year instead of just the last two. Therefore, when the century changes in a few short years, dBASE III PLUS programs will not be obsolete. The YEAR() function will display the full year, which will indicate the correct century.

```
        . SET CENTURY ON

        . future = CTOD('01/01/2001')
01/01/2001

        . SET CENTURY OFF

        . ? future
01/01/01

        . ? YEAR(future)

  2001
```

FIGURE 13.27   *Using SET CENTURY ON.*

As mentioned earlier in this chapter, CDOW() will yield the day of the week for any date field expressed within the parentheses. CMONTH() is similar in that it will return the name of the month.

```
        . ? CDOW(future)

Monday

        . ? CMONTH(future)

January
```

FIGURE 13.28   *Using CDOW() and DMONTH().*

CTOD() will convert a character expression to a date-type field that can then be used for date calculations, if the user so desires. Naturally, the character expression must be in the proper format (MM/DD/YY, or DD/MM/YY for European use). DTOC() does the reverse. It converts date-type fields to character strings.

```
    . ? DTOC(future) + ' is sooner than you think.'
01/01/01 is sooner than you think.
```

FIGURE 13.29   *Using DTOC().*

DATE() is useful because it contains the system date as set by DOS. Since many microcomputers maintain the date and time with a battery-operated clock-calendar device, this function is convenient for reports and date calculations.

The DOW(), DAY(), MONTH(), and YEAR() functions return the numeric equivalent of the day of the week, day of the month, month or year. Figure 13.30 shows how these functions can be used in calculations.

```
    . ? DATE()
01/01/88
    . ? DOW(DATE())
6
    . ? DOW(DATE()) + 1
7
    . ? DAY(DATE())
1
    . ? DAY(DATE()) + 2
3
    . ? MONTH(DATE())
1
    . ? MONTH(DATE()) +3
4
    . ? YEAR(DATE())
1988
    . ? YEAR(DATE()) +13
2001
```

FIGURE 13.30   *Performing arithmetic with the date functions.*

To convert the DATE() display from the 01/01/88 format to a form more appropriate for correspondence, use the following command.

```
. ? CDOW(DATE()) + ', ' + CMONTH(DATE()) + ' ' + STR(DAY(DATE()),2)
+ ', ' + STR(YEAR(DATE()),4)

Friday, January 1, 1988
```

FIGURE 13.31   *Producing a correspondence date.*

Date-type fields are stored in a special format that permits addition and subtraction. The reason is that the dates are converted to a Julian date representing the number of days since January 1, 4713 B.C., which has significance in astronomy. For your convenience, dates are automatically displayed in the typical format by dBASE III PLUS. If you wish to work with dates, you will have to convert from character to date (CTOD) and from date to character (DTOC) as Figure 13.32 illustrates.

```
. ? DATE()
01/01/88
. ? CTOD('12/25/88')-DATE()
359                      <-- Shopping days left
. dob = CTOD('05/10/54')
05/10/54
. AGE = (DATE()-dob)/365.25       <-- Calculate an age
33.12
. AGE = INT((DATE()-dob)/365.25)     <-- Integer of age
33
```

FIGURE 13.32   *More date arithmetic.*

To convert from:	To:	Use this function:
Character	Date	CTOD()
Date	Character	DTOC()
Numeric	String	STR()
String	Numeric	VAL()

FIGURE 13.33   *Conversion functions.*

13.4 UTILITY FUNCTIONS

Chapter 10 introduced &, which is the macro expansion or substitution function. It was used there with the FIND command and variables to extract the actual value stored in the variable rather than the name of the variable itself. It may be convenient to store lengthy command lines in a variable and execute them with the &. No space is permitted after the &. Also, the macro expansion character should not be used in a DO WHILE condition because it will not evaluate properly.

```
.  macro = '? DATE()'

.  &macro

01/01/88
```

FIGURE 13.34 *Using the macro expansion function.*

COL() and ROW() will return the current position of the cursor on the screen.

```
.  ? ROW()

21
```

FIGURE 13.35 *Using ROW().*

Several functions are valuable because they provide useful information that may not be immediately evident while you are working with a database. Some of this information can also be obtained with the DISPLAY STATUS command. The functions and the returned results are listed in Figure 13.36.

OS()	— Name of the current operating system.
VERSION()	— Version of dBASE III PLUS in use.
DISKSPACE()	— The number of bytes that are free on the currently active disk.
FILE()	— A logical .T. or .F., depending on whether or not the file specified as an argument exists.
DBF()	— The name of the .DBF currently in use.
RECCOUNT()	— The number of records listed in the structure in the currently active .DBF file.

FIGURE 13.36 *Utility functions (Part 1 of 2).*

LUPDATE() — A date-type field stored as the last last date on which the active .DBF file was updated in any way.

RECSIZE() — The record size in the current .DBF file.

FIELD() — The name of the field based on a number from 1 to 128 as an argument.

RECNO() — The record number relating to the current position of the record pointer.

DELETED() — A logical .T. or .F. depending on whether or not the record was deleted.

TYPE() — The data type C,N,L,M

FIGURE 13.36   *Utility functions (Part 2 of 2).*

Figure 13.37 provides examples of the functions described in Figure 13.36.

```
        . ? OS()
DOS 3.30
        . ? VERSION()
dBASE III PLUS  version 1.1
        . ? DISKSPACE()
  7421952
        . USE CITIES

        . ? FILE('C:CITIES.DBF')
.T.
        . ? DBF()
C:CITIES.dbf
        . ? RECCOUNT()
         11
        . ? LUPDATE()
01/27/87
        . ? RECSIZE()
        37
        . ? FIELD(2)
```

FIGURE 13.37   *Putting the utility functions into practice (Part 1 of 2).*

```
STATE

    .  DELETE RECORD 1

    1 record deleted

    .  ? RECNO()

        1

    .  ? DELETED()

.T.

    .  ? TYPE('STATE')

C
```

FIGURE 13.37   *Putting the utility functions into practice (Part 2 of 2).*

The REPLICATE() function permits the display of any ASCII character on the screen or dot matrix printer. Creative use of these symbols can be quite attractive.

```
        . TYPE REPLIC.PRG
row = 1
cnt = 176
DO WHILE cnt < 234
    @ row,1 SAY cnt
    @ row,10 SAY REPLICATE(CHR(cnt),60)
    row = row + 1
    cnt = cnt + 1
ENDDO cnt < 234
```

FIGURE 13.38   *A program using REPLICATE().*

Several functions are available for networking and more advanced programming. They will be discussed in Chapter 15.

13.5 WRITING A PROGRAM TO UPDATE FILES

Updating or modifying records is very similar to appending, because user input data must be written to the file. The difference is that the data must be retrieved from a specific record and displayed both to verify that the correct record has been found and to show the user the current contents.

```
Structure for database: C:client.dbf
Number of data records:      11
Date of last update    : 01/01/88
Field  Field Name  Type       Width   Dec
    1  LIST_NUM    Character     11
    2  LAST        Character     18
    3  FIRST       Character     20
    4  NUM         Character      6
    5  ST          Character     15
    6  CITY        Character     20
    7  ZIP         Character      5
    8  AGT         Character      4
    9  PRICE       Numeric        7
   10  LIST_DATE   Date           8
   11  CONT_DATE   Date           8
** Total **                     124
```

FIGURE 13.39 *Structure of CLIENT.DBF.*

Figure 13.40 presents the pseudocode for CHG_CLIE.PRG.

```
Set environment
Do while user wants to continue
    Initialize memory variables and open files
    Display screen
    Input listing number
    Exit if number is blank
    Loop if number does not exist
    Move present data to memory variables on screen
    Do while user wants to update
        Put updated data in memory variables
    End of update routine
    Replace fields with updated memory variables
End of routine
```

FIGURE 13.40 *Pseudocode for CHG_CLIE.PRG.*

```
* CHG_CLIE.PRG -  Update records in the CLIENT.DBF file

* Set Environment
PRIVATE ALL
SET HEADING OFF
SET TALK OFF
SET BELL OFF
SET STATUS OFF
SET SCOREBOARD OFF
SET SAFETY OFF
CLEAR ALL
```

FIGURE 13.41 *A program to update records (Part 1 of 3).*

```
* Initialization
USE CLIENT INDEX LIST_NUM

DO WHILE .T.
   CLEAR
   mlist_num = SPACE(11)
   mlast = SPACE(18)
   mfirst = SPACE(20)
   mnum =SPACE(6)
   mst =SPACE(15)
   mcity =SPACE(20)
   mzip =SPACE(5)
   mprice = 0
   magt =SPACE(4)
   mlist_date = CTOD('  /  /  ')
   mcont_date = CTOD('  /  /  ')

   * GET Listing Number and display screen
   @  2, 29  SAY "CLIENT ENTRY"
   @  4, 29  SAY "LIST #"
   @  4, 36  GET  mlist_num PICTURE 'AA-99999-99'
   @  6, 12  SAY "LAST"
   @  6, 38  SAY "FIRST"
   @  8, 19  SAY "NUMBER"
   @  8, 34  SAY "STREET"
```

```
   @ 10, 19  SAY "CITY"
   @ 10, 47  SAY "ZIP"
   @ 12, 15  SAY "PRICE"
   @ 12, 50  SAY "AGENT"
   @ 14,  9  SAY "LIST DATE"
   @ 16, 16  SAY "CONTRACT DATE"
   @  1,  5  TO 17, 72      DOUBLE
   READ

   * Check for blank Listing Number
   IF mlist_num = '            '
        CLEAR
        CLEAR ALL
        RETURN
   ENDIF mlist_num = '            '

   * Check if record exists
   SEEK mlist_num
   IF .NOT. FOUND()
        @ 5,30 SAY 'Listing Number Not on File'
        mpause = 0
        DO WHILE mpause < 25
             mpause = mpause + 1
        ENDDO mpause < 100
        @ 5,30 SAY SPACE(25)
```

```
        LOOP
   ENDIF .NOT. FOUND()

   * Move current data to variables
   STORE LAST TO mlast
   STORE FIRST TO mfirst
   STORE NUM TO mnum
   STORE ST TO mst
   STORE CITY TO mcity
   STORE ZIP TO mzip
   STORE AGT TO magt
   STORE PRICE TO mprice
   STORE LIST_DATE TO mlist_date
   STORE CONT_DATE TO mcont_date
```

FIGURE 13.41   *A program to update records (Part 2 of 3).*

```
* GET remaining fields
ok = .Y.
DO WHILE ok
    @  6, 17  GET  mlast PICTURE '@!'
    @  6, 44  GET  mfirst PICTURE '@!'
    @  8, 26  GET  mnum PICTURE '@9'
    @  8, 41  GET  mst PICTURE '@!'
    @ 10, 25  GET  mcity PICTURE '@!'
    @ 10, 51  GET  mzip PICTURE '@9'
    @ 12, 21  GET  mprice PICTURE '9,999,999' RANGE 1000,2000000
    @ 12, 56  GET  magt
    @ 14, 20  GET  mlist_date
    @ 16, 30  GET  mcont_date
    READ
    @ 16,40 SAY 'Any Changes? (Y/N) ' GET ok
    READ
ENDDO ok

* Move updated data to file
REPLACE LAST WITH mlast,FIRST WITH mfirst,;
    NUM WITH mnum, ST WITH mst,;
    CITY WITH mcity, ZIP WITH mzip,;
    AGT WITH magt, PRICE WITH mprice,;
    LIST_DATE WITH mlist_date, CONT_DATE WITH mcont_date
ENDDO .T.
```

FIGURE 13.41   *A program to update records (Part 3 of 3).*

CHG_CLIE.PRG uses a DO WHILE .T. loop to allow the user to update records until pressing Return at the GET for mlist_num, which will exit as result of the IF/ENDIF testing for blanks in that field. The routine begins by clearing the screen and initializing all memory variables in preparation for accepting changes to the existing data in each field. A series of @ SAYs displays the input screen titles, and one GET block is provided for mlist_num. The test to exit the program follows a READ. The next task is to use an indexed search to locate the record that matches the contents of mlist_num. An error routine will allow the user to reenter the number if the search fails. When an existing record is located, the current data is STOREd to the memory variables on the screen.

Once the screen has been filled with the current data, the user can scan the screen and employ full-screen editing to change any field except the listing number, which must be protected from accidental updating. The changes are made in a DO WHILE loop, which can be exited by changing the logical variable ok. Finally, the contents of the fields are REPLACEd with the updated memory variables.

The strategy for updating must attempt to maintain data integrity as much as possible by providing PICTURE clauses and protecting the key field. The concepts presented in the preceding chapter can be used to alter the design of the program in order to update multiple databases that are logically related.

CHAPTER SUMMARY

13.1

Functions are internal algorithms that will produce a variety of effects on data. The results of a function can be displayed or STOREd. Arguments, the data to be affected and other specifications, are placed in parentheses after the name of the function. Some of the available functions operate on character data or strings. Some string function effects shown as examples include changing case, trimming blanks, and extracting substrings.

13.2

Very large numbers can be stored by dBASE III PLUS, but there are limits on the accuracy of numeric values when they are used in operations or comparisons. The rules of precedence for evaluating arithmetic expressions are given. Examples of the arithmetic functions include INT(), MAX(), ROUND(), VAL(), and STR().

13.3

Dates are stored in a special format that permits arithmetic. The CTOD() and DTOC() functions convert dates and character data for the sake of convenience. All aspects of a date are accessible with date functions such as CMONTH(), CDOW(), DOW(), DAY(), MONTH(), and YEAR().

13.4

A number of convenient utility functions report on the status of the operating system, active disk, and .DBF file. These include OS(), DISKSPACE(), REC-COUNT(), and TYPE(). These functions are normally used in the interactive mode.

13.5

A program to update records is similar to appending. The record must be retrieved and displayed in a custom entry screen. The user can then edit the data, which is stored in memory variables. When the operation has been completed, the updated data is REPLACEd to the .DBF file.

KEY TERMS and COMMANDS

Function	ASC()	ISUPPER()
Algorithm	CHR()	LEFT()
Argument	SPACE()	RIGHT()
UPPER()	ISALPHA()	LEN()
LOWER()	ISLOWER()	LTRIM()

RTRIM()	VAL()	COL()
TRIM()	STR()	ROW()
STUFF()	SET CENTURY ON()	OS()
SUBSTR()	YEAR()	VERSION()
AT()	CDOW()	DISKSPACE()
SET DECIMAL TO()	CMONTH()	FILE()
ABS()	CTOD()	DBF()
EXP()	DTOC()	RECCOUNT()
INT()	DATE()	LUPDATE()
LOG()	DOW()	RECSIZE()
MAX()	DAY()	FIELD()
MIN()	MONTH()	RECNO()
MOD()	YEAR()	DELETED()
ROUND()	$	TYPE()
SQRT()	&	REPLICATE()

dBUG dBASE

- Avoid making your system *case-sensitive* by using uppercase as a standard and converting everything automatically so the user does not have to worry about Shift keys or the Caps Lock. For the sake of consistency, you can convert the contents of memory variables to uppercase, using the UPPER function as shown below.

```
memchoice = UPPER(memchoice)
```

- MESSAGE() displays the dBASE III PLUS error message of the most recently issued error code that can be displayed with ERROR().

SELF-CHECK QUESTIONS

1. What is a function?
2. How can the result or effect of a function be preserved for later use in a program?
3. What is an algorithm? What is an argument?
4. Why is it important to consider the case of character data?
5. Name a use for the $ operator.
6. What part does the ASCII code play in the use of functions?
7. What results do the ISALPHA(), ISLOWER() and ISUPPER() functions produce?

8. Suggest a function to perform each of the following tasks:
   a. Extract the first six characters of a string.
   b. Extract a person's middle name from his or her full name.
   c. Extract the last five characters of a string.
9. What happens if a calculation produces too large a result?
10. What is the greatest accuracy in a numeric field?
11. What is the precedence of operations?
12. What is evaluated first, multiplication or division?
13. What does the INT() function do?
14. How do you specify the number of decimal places to round in the ROUND() function?
15. What is the purpose of the two numeric arguments in STR()?
16. What does SET CENTURY ON do?
17. In what form are dates actually stored?
18. How can you determine the day of the week from a date field?
19. What function will display the record size of the active .DBF file?

TRY IT YOURSELF

1. Write a function to determine whether the letter z is not in a string.
2. Select a graphic character with an ASCII value above 128 and write a brief program to fill one line with the character.
3. Write three commands to extract each of the three names from msailor.

   msailor = 'John Paul Jones'

4. Insert ' Fitzgerald ' in mpres as the middle name.

   mpres = 'John Kennedy'

5. Display the length of the result of Exercise 4.
6. Display the location of the letter F in Exercise 4.
7. Display the answers to the following problems with the ? command.
   a. Add 6 to 12; then divide the total by 5.
   b. Divide 10 by 4 and add 2 to the quotient.
   c. Square the product of 3 × 4.
8. Display the integer of –7.8 and 9.25.
9. Round 5.677 to two decimal places.
10. Convert the numbers in mstreet to a numeric value, add 2, and display 125 Main St. (Hint: Two functions needed.)

    mstreet = '123 Main St.'

11. Store your birthday to a date-type variable.
12. Determine the day of the week on which you were born.
13. How many days have you been alive as of today?
14. Display the number of days until your next birthday.
15. Display the system date in correspondence format.
16. What version of DOS are you using?
17. Display the type of mcheck.

mcheck = 161

PROGRAMMING PROJECT

```
Structure for database: C:cust2.dbf
Number of data records:      14
Date of last update   : 01/01/88
Field  Field Name  Type        Width    Dec
    1  SAL_NUM     Character      11
    2  LAST        Character      18
    3  FIRST       Character      20
    4  PROP_NUM    Character       8
    5  PROP_ST     Character      20
    6  PROP_CITY   Character      20
    7  PROP_ZIP    Character       5
    8  CONT_DATE   Date            8
    9  LIST_AGT    Character       4
   10  SELL_AGT    Character       4
   11  SOURCE      Character      10
   12  FINC        Character       5
   13  PRICE       Numeric         7
   14  LIST_COMM   Numeric         8      2
   15  SELL_COMM   Numeric         8      2
   16  SETT_DATE   Date            8
** Total **                      165
```

Write a program to update the CUST.DBF file, using a custom screen. You will have to append some records and index on SAL_NUM.

1. The program will loop until a Return is pressed for the SAL_NUM field.
2. Establish as much data validation as you judge reasonable.
3. Allow the user to reenter the SAL_NUM if the record is not found.
4. Enter the user's edits to memory variables before passing the date to the file.
5. Test the program by updating several records, then LISTing from the dot prompt.

14

EFFICIENCY SKILLS

LEARNING OBJECTIVES

1. To learn techniques to optimize the performance of programs.
2. To use advanced interactive techniques.
3. To write a program for printing a report.

Chapter

14

EFFICIENCY SKILLS

When a program has been debugged and is working well, you might be tempted to say that it is complete. However, improvements in performance are almost always possible. This chapter offers some suggestions for optimizing your program's performance.

14.1 OPTIMIZING YOUR SYSTEM

This chapter is not concerned with the right or wrong way to program a task, but with the issues that will bear upon the way your code will perform when compared to other possible strategies. You encountered this issue in Chapter 8 when the sequential IF/ENDIF, nested IF/ENDIF, and DO CASE/ENDCASE were compared. Since the DO CASE demanded the execution of fewer lines of code, it was deemed the most efficient. This chapter contains a method for timing procedures so that you can make informed decisions when comparing other aspects of program logic. The user gains the ultimate benefit from these efforts in the form of a system that operates at maximum speed within the limits of the hardware and dBASE III PLUS.

Once a system or a program has been written and tested, the programmer has the responsibility to *optimize* the code for the best possible performance. This means that programs should execute in a minimum amount of time without sacrificing clarity or integrity. It may also refer to the economical use of memory and disk space. Although experience is the best teacher in this case, some strategies are available for improving the performance of your programs.

Optimization must never take precedence over clarity and the self-documentation of code. In an effort to increase speed, some programmers may reduce all dBASE III PLUS commands to the first four letters, remove all comment lines, and eliminate spaces whenever possible. The time savings from this practice usually amount to less than five percent. The amount of time that will be lost when others attempt to work with the code is much greater than the small performance benefit. A comparison of the "optimized" code in Figure 14.1 with the code in Figure 14.3 on the opposite page should suffice as evidence of this. Although the two programs function identically, the one in Figure 14.1 is extremely difficult to understand.

```
SET TALK OFF
c=0
f=0
RUN TIME=0
DO WHIL c<100
c=c+1
ENDD
f=TIME()
f=VAL(SUBS(f,1,2))*60+VAL(SUBS(f,4,2))+VAL(SUBS(f,7,2))/60
? f
```

FIGURE 14.1   *"Optimized" code.*

Another performance issue involves the use of subroutines. On occasion you will have to choose between including the code for a routine within the current program or calling another program. For example, the program PROP.PRG in Figure 14.23 on pages 314 and 315 calls TRAPPER.PRG under certain conditions. The code in TRAPPER.PRG could just as easily have been placed within PROP.PRG. In general, a long procedure is probably best placed in a separate file in order to minimize the size of the calling program. If only a few lines are involved, the procedure should be left in the program to avoid opening another file. Note that MODIFY COMMAND holds only 50 kilobytes, or about 180 lines of code.

The TIME() function displays the system time as a character string. Unfortunately, no functions are available to perform arithmetic operations with hours, minutes, and seconds. You can use the VAL() and SUBSTR() functions to extract the numeric value of the number of seconds as a means of testing a procedure, as shown in Figure 14.2 on the opposite page. The number of seconds could be calculated for two procedures performing the same task. Simple subtraction would yield the difference in efficiency. Try the TIME_IT program on your computer; then try it with a different procedure. RUN TIME will retrieve the current time setting from the operating system when the program is finished.

```
      .  RUN TIME = 0

      .  ? TIME()

00:00:11

       .RUN TIME

      .  ? TIME()

16:26:19
```

FIGURE 14.2 *Using the RUN command.*

The command RUN TIME is actually calling an external program, the DOS
time program, and initializing the system time to 0. The program was called again
and the time was set for 4:26 P.M. The TIME() function is also useful when you
have to time-stamp a report.

```
* TIME_IT.PRG - Demonstrates how to time a procedure to check
*                efficiency.
SET TALK OFF
check = 0
finish = 0

* Set system time at 0
RUN TIME = 0

* Do the procedure to be timed
DO WHILE check < 100
     check = check + 1
ENDDO check < 100
finish = TIME()

* convert the TIME() string to numeric seconds
finish = VAL(SUBSTR(finish, 1, 2)) * 60 + ;
         VAL(SUBSTR(finish, 4, 2)) + ;
         VAL(SUBSTR(finish, 7, 2)) / 60

? finish
```

FIGURE 14.3 *A program to time procedures.*

Arrays are a common feature of other programming languages, such as BASIC.
They are arrangements of data in some sort of indexing scheme that permits quick
access to the *elements*, or individual pieces of data. A .DBF file with an index
satisfies this definition, except that the required disk access is slow and the two open
files count against the fifteen-file limit. Arrays, on the other hand, are usually stored
in memory for rapid access. Accessing data in an array is sometimes called a table
look-up. The limit of 256 memory variables must be respected when this option is
being considered. The names of elements are usually established using subscripts,
as in NAME(4). Since dBASE III PLUS does not provide subscripts, you are limited to coding "pseudoarrays."

The simplest way to emulate an array is to establish a set of memory variables and save them to a file that can be retrieved and placed in memory when needed. This method is fine if the data is static, meaning that it rarely changes and there is no need to access all the elements sequentially. For instance, the names of the states can be placed in an array similar to what is shown in Figure 14.4. The full name of the state can be retrieved by specifying the abbreviation. The array is placed in the STATES-.MEM file, using the SAVE command. It may then be brought into memory at any time with the RESTORE command. The ADDITIVE option prevents the RESTORE from destroying any existing memory variables your program may be using.

```
.  SAVE TO STATES

.  RESTORE FROM STATES ADDITIVE

.  DISP MEMORY
AL              pub    C    "Alabama"
AK              pub    C    "Alaska"
AR              pub    C    "Arkansas"
AZ              pub    C    "Arizona"
    4 variables defined,        36 bytes used
  252 variables available,    5964 bytes available
```

FIGURE 14.4 *Emulating an array.*

Figure 14.5 shows how an array might be used. The ST_FILE example contains only the abbreviations for two states, but an actual file could have other data and many more records. The object is to print the full name of the state which corresponds to the abbreviation in the file. Once the array has been placed in memory, the & can be used to display the contents of the memory variable, as the following program illustrates.

```
.  USE ST_FILE

.  LIST

Record#  ST
      1  AK
      2  AZ

.  TYPE ST.PRG

USE ST_FILE
RESTORE FROM STATES ADDITIVE
DO WHILE .NOT. EOF()
    code = ST
    ? 'Full name of ' + code + ' is ' + &code
    SKIP
ENDDO .NOT. EOF()

.  DO ST

Full name of AK is Alaska
Full name of AZ is Arizona
```

FIGURE 14.5 *A program to emulate an array with SAVE.*

If an array must be loaded or accessed sequentially, the method shown in Figure 14.6 will produce pseudosubscripting. This allows a DO WHILE loop to use iteration to work with the array elements. The key to the program is the generation of the variable names with a counter. This process yields the names array1, array2, and so on. The incrementing value of the counter had to be changed to a character variable with the STR() function in order to combine with the prefix array. After removing any possible leading blanks converted from leading zeros, use the & function to combine the two parts of the name. The data to be stored is then assigned to the new variable name. For example, the same structure could be used to access the elements of the array by substituting an @ SAY for the array&x = ST command.

```
        . TYPE ARRAY.PRG

SET TALK OFF
cnt = 1
USE ST_FILE
DO WHILE .NOT. EOF()
     x= LTRIM(STR(cnt,2,0))
     array&x = ST
     cnt = cnt+1
     SKIP
ENDDO .NOT. EOF()
LIST MEMORY

        . DO ARRAY

CNT         priv  N        3
X           priv  C  "2"
ARRAY1      priv  C  "AK"
ARRAY2      priv  C  "AZ"
    4 variables defined,        20 bytes used
  252 variables available,    5980 bytes available
```

FIGURE 14.6 *A program to emulate an array using &.*

.DBF records are brought in as needed by dBASE III PLUS in sectors of 512 bytes. Because the greatest processing delay occurs during disk input/output, dramatically increased performance can be realized by including as many records as possible in a sector. This obviously means that the records must be as short as possible without sacrificing the needs of the user. An extra benefit is the saving in disk space, which can be significant in a large file.

Indexes can become a burden on the system's performance. Two methods are used to keep an index current. First, the index can be recreated at the conclusion of every append, update, or delete session in a batch mode. Although an index is not involved, the program in Chapter 8 employs this processing strategy. Another method is to have all the indexes active during the operations in order to keep them updated constantly. This method would be required for a *volatile* file, meaning a file in which data changes often and must be instantly available for retrieval. Since both methods are valid, performance is the criterion for deciding which one to use in a

Consider shortening the length of an index to improve performance. A name field is likely to have a length of 25 to 30 characters. You may be able to maintain the unique quality of the data with less in the index by using SUBSTR(). In a file of reasonable size, it is highly unlikely that two last names would be identical beyond ten characters. You would realize a savings of 15 to 20 characters on the last name and more on the first.

```
INDEX ON SUBSTR(name, 1, 10) + SUBSTR(first, 1, 5) to name
```

READKEY() will return the value of the key that was used to exit a READ. The value of the key will be increased by 256 if any of the previous GETs have been changed. The Esc key, for example, normally carries a value of 12. This would increase to 268 (256 + 12) if any of the previous GETs had been changed. This capability enables you to program the use of the Esc, Return, or Ctrl-End keys for the convenience of the user.

```
again = .T.
DO WHILE again
   DO CASE
      CASE READKEY() = 270      && Ctrl-End with data change
      *   Code to update record
          again = .F.           && exit loop
      CASE READKEY() = 12       && Esc with no change
          again = .F.           && exit loop
      ENDCASE
ENDDO again
```

FIGURE 14.7 *An example of READKEY().*

The section of code in Figure 14.7 shows how the READKEY() function might be used to perform actions on the basis of what key the user presses and whether GETs have been updated. The program will update the record in the file and will exit if the user presses Ctrl and End simultaneously, or will simply exit on the Esc key.

A number of alternatives other than the RETURN are available exiting structures. There may be occasions when a system's operation can be improved by passing control directly back to the first menu of a system instead of forcing the user to ''back out'' through several levels of submenus. Figure 14.8 on the opposite page displays the available options and their meanings.

Ways to terminate DO WHILE .T.

EXIT	Branch to statement after ENDDO.
LOOP	Branch to DO WHILE and allow condition to exit.
RETURN	Execute calling program or go to the dot prompt.
RETURN TO MASTER	Execute highest program in system.
CANCEL	Go to the dot prompt.
QUIT	Exit dBASE III PLUS to DOS.

FIGURE 14.8 *Ways to terminate DO WHILE .T.*

14.2 BECOMING A POWER USER

On occasion, working with data from the dot prompt may be more convenient than writing a program. This would be the case for example, if a piece of information was needed as a single event. Suppose a sales manager needed to know how many of her firm's clients lived in Texas in order to establish sales territories. To provide the answer, it would clearly be more efficient to issue two or three well-designed commands at the dot prompt than to write and debug a program. This section contains some ways to increase your ability to manipulate data through the use of interactive commands. Users and programmers who are skilled and efficient in command usage are popularly called power users.

A WHILE clause can be used with interactive dedicated commands such as SUM, COUNT, and REPORT. WHILE is more efficient than FOR, because it goes directly to the first matching record as long as the WHILE comparative expression is true. Also, the execution will cease as soon as the expression is no longer true. This eliminates unnecessary executions. The advantages of this technique are amplified when it is employed with an index.

The fastest interactive access technique involves using a FIND, then executing a LIST . . WHILE. A FIND and a DO WHILE/ENDDO in a PRG. file will take longer, because the DO WHILE/ENDDO must be executed once for each record. As you might expect, the slowest method is the LIST FOR, because the FOR option will access and check all the records in the database. The LIST . . WHILE technique is, of course, limited by the ability of the LIST command to display data. If a complex screen or printed report is required, the @ SAY, which is presented in Chapter 11, must be used. This will require the use of the FIND and DO WHILE/ENDDO techniques, since a block of several commands will be executed for each valid record. Both of these methods require an index, which must be maintained and stored.

```
. FIND 'SMITH'

. LIST WHILE name = 'SMITH'
```

FIGURE 14.9 *Using LIST WHILE.*

The FIND will establish the WHILE clause to be set to logical true so that the rest of the command can operate correctly. It is important to note that the LIST command will not execute if the FIND is not successful. If it ever becomes necessary to display all the records from the current location of the record pointer to the end of the file, the LIST REST can be used.

```
. FIND 'SMITH'
. LIST REST
```

FIGURE 14.10 *Using LIST REST.*

You can test to see if a file has no records by opening the file and seeing if EOF() is true. The ZAP command will remove all the records while retaining the structure.

```
. USE TESTFILE
. ZAP
. ? EOF()
.T.
```

FIGURE 14.11 *Using EOF().*

TRANSFORM will enable you to use the the template functions and symbols from Chapter 11 with LIST, DISPLAY, LABEL, and REPORT. Notice the quotes around the template.

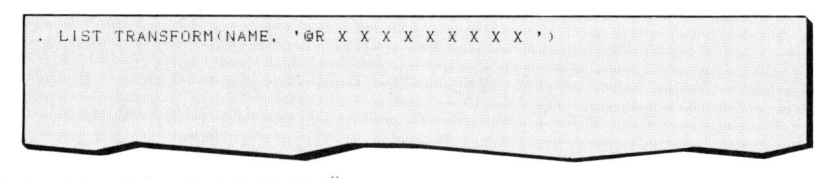

```
. LIST TRANSFORM(NAME, '@R X X X X X X X X X ')
```

FIGURE 14.12 *Using TRANSFORM().*

SET FILTER TO will store a FOR condition so that it can be assumed during interactive processing. Only those records which contain 'PA' in the state field will be recognized by LIST after the command in Figure 14.13 on the opposite page.

```
. SET FILTER TO state = 'PA'
```

FIGURE 14.13 *Using SET FILTER TO.*

SET FIELDS TO will perform the same function for a list of fields. Only city and pop_82 will be referenced with the command shown in Figure 14.14. The selected fields are marked with the > sign in the structure.

```
. USE CITIES
. SET FIELDS TO city, pop_82

. LIST STRUCTURE
Structure for database: C:CITIES.dbf
Number of data records:        11
Date of last update   : 01/01/88
Field  Field Name  Type       Width    Dec
    1  >CITY       Character      20
    2   STATE      Character       2
    3   POP_70     Numeric         7
    4  >POP_82     Numeric         7
** Total **                      37
```

FIGURE 14.14 *Using SET FIELDS TO.*

You are already aware of the convenience of using the up arrow key to retrieve previously issued commands from the HISTORY buffer. It is possible to edit a command line at the dot prompt using the keys shown in Figure 14.15. You can save many keystrokes and errors by retrieving commands and modifying instead of retyping.

Set insert on or off	Ins
Move to start of previous word	Home
Delete rest of line	^Y (Ctrl-Y)
Delete current character	Del
Delete current word	^T (Ctrl-T)
Move to start of next line	End
Delete current line	Esc

FIGURE 14.15 *Command line editing keys.*

SET ALTERNATE TO will establish a text file that can be opened with SET ALTERNATE ON. Any screen displays that do not utilize full-screen editing will echo to the file to produce a transcription of the work session on disk. The results of the file can be viewed with the TYPE command, MODIFY COMMAND, or an external word processor. If a printer is not currently available, processed data can be saved to a file for printing at a later time. The examples in this text were reproduced with the SET ALTERNATE TO command.

```
. SET ALTERNATE TO TEST
. SET ALTERNATE ON

. TYPE TEST.TXT

. USE CITIES
. LIST CITY
Record#   CITY
       1  *SAN FRANCISCO
       2   PHILADELPHIA
       3   DALLAS
       4   SAN DIEGO
       5   HOUSTON
       6   MIAMI
       7   CLEVELAND
       8   PITTSBURGH
       9   LOS ANGELES
      10   JACKSONVILLE
      11   COLUMBUS
. SET ALTERNATE OFF
```

FIGURE 14.16   *Using an ALTERNATE file.*

Experimentation and testing are the best tools for increasing your skills. Several journals and books that recommend timesaving procedures and strategies are widely available.

14.3 WRITING A PROGRAM TO PRINT A REPORT

Producing a report on the printer is different from displaying a screen in several important respects. Clearly, you will have to deal with a second piece of equipment, the printer. Printers vary greatly in their performance, limitations, and construction. Some critical concerns include the following:

1. How wide is the printer's carriage? 80 or 132 characters?
2. Can it print graphic characters like CHR(197)?
3. What are the special print codes for compressed print, expanded print, italics, etc.?

In addition, the user must be prompted for the operation of the printer. The program must control the length of each page, the formatting of the lines, EJECT-ing, and directing output to the correct device. It is clear from these facts that producing a custom printed report is more complicated than generating a screen display.

A program that can print a report will have to access data from records in the same manner that a screen report program does. Naturally, you must have the record access routine operating correctly before attempting to develop the report. A series of @ SAYs will be used to position the fields, but the similarity ends there. The printing program is responsible for controlling the printer's page handling. The page length must be monitored in order for page headings and EJECTs to occur at the right place. A memory variable can be incremented to serve as a line counter for page breaks, and a coordinate can be incremented for the @ SAY which reacts to the SET DEVICE TO command.

SET PRINT ON	— "Echo" print; ? and all display commands such as LIST go to both the screen and the printer.
SET DEVICE TO SCREEN	— All @ SAY and @ GET statements go to the screen only.
SET DEVICE TO PRINT	— All @ SAY statements go only to the printer (@ GET will not work).

FIGURE 14.17   *Printer usage commands.*

You can design a display on a coding form or graph paper first. Always be certain that the row and column values in the @ SAY statements are issued chronologically. You can't "back up" the printer by printing row 12 and then row 10; if you do, a page eject will occur. Also, you must issue an EJECT before printing the next page or you may lose the last line in the printer's buffer. Figure 14.18 demonstrates a strategy for printing headings and EJECTing pages on the basis of the value of a row counter.

```
row = 100
DO WHILE .NOT. EOF()
    IF row > 57
       EJECT
       row = 5
       *  print page heading
       row = 10
    ENDIF
    * print a record
    row = row + 1
       SKIP
ENDDO WHILE .NOT. EOF()
```

FIGURE 14.18   *Using a row counter.*

Before the printing routine executes, the program should prompt the user to check whether the printer is ready and the paper is set at the top-of-form. Force the user to respond with a keystroke to verify the printer's status.

```
* Check printer
@ 21, 15 SAY 'Turn on printer and adj paper'
@ 22, 15 SAY 'Press Esc to abort or any other key to print'

* Wait for a response
CLEAR TYPEAHEAD
ok = 0
DO WHILE ok = 0
   ok = INKEY()
ENDDO ok = 0

* Remove the message
@ 21, 0 CLEAR
IF ok <> 27
      @ 10,15 SAY 'PRINTING . . . Please be patient'

* Connect to printer
SET DEVICE TO PRINT
```

FIGURE 14.19 *Prompting the user for printer use.*

The ON ERROR command will circumvent the normal dBASE III PLUS error-handling procedure and will allow the programmer to execute a custom routine that might be more friendly and might prevent the program from being canceled. The command should be placed at the start of the program or wherever you expect an error to occur. The TRAPPER.PRG program tests the value of the ERROR() function, which will contain a numeric value representing a specific error condition. Errors 125 and 126 indicate an unconnected or off-line printer.

```
ON ERROR DO TRAPPER   <-- Placed at the start of the program

* TRAPPER.PRG Trap for printer errors
      IF ERROR() = 125 .OR. ERROR() = 126
                SET DEVICE TO SCREEN
                SET COLOR TO B+*/W,,
                @ 12,15 SAY 'THE PRINTER IS NOT READY'
                WAIT 'Ready to try again? (Y/N)' to fixit
                IF UPPER(fixit) = 'Y'
                     SET COLOR TO GR+/B,,B
                     CLEAR
                     RETRY
                ELSE
                     SET COLOR TO GR+/B,,B
                     SET DEVICE TO SCREEN
                     CLEAR
                     SET ESCAPE ON
                     CLEAR ALL
                     CANCEL
                ENDIF UPPER(fixit) = 'Y'
      ENDIF ERROR() = 125 .OR. ERROR() = 126
      RETURN
```

FIGURE 14.20 *A program to trap printer errors.*

If an ON ERROR command has been issued, the program in Figure 14.20 will test for either of the two printer error messages. Instead of subjecting the user to a cancel of the program and a dBASE III PLUS error message, the program displays a custom message in a blinking color and permits a second chance to print the report.

The structure for CLIENT.DBF is displayed in Figure 14.21.

```
. USE CLIENT

. LIST STRUCTURE

Structure for database: C:client.dbf
Number of data records:        15
Date of last update    : 01/01/88
Field  Field Name  Type       Width    Dec
     1  LIST_NUM    Character     11
     2  LAST        Character     18
     3  FIRST       Character     20
     4  NUM         Character      6
     5  ST          Character     15
     6  CITY        Character     20
     7  ZIP         Character      5
     8  AGT         Character      4
     9  PRICE       Numeric        7
    10  LIST_DATE   Date           8
    11  CONT_DATE   Date           8
** Total **                      123
```

FIGURE 14.21   *Structure for CLIENT.DBF.*

The program in Figure 14.23 on pages 314 and 315 prints a report for your study using the ideas presented in this section as an example.

```
Set environment
Initialize files and variables
Set error routine
Prompt user to check printer
If not escape key
   Clear the prompt and display working message
   Connect program to printer
   Print header on first page
   Do if not at end of file
        If end of page
           New page
           Reset counter
        Endif
        Print a record
        Skip and increment counter
   Enddo
   Print footer and eject
   Print summary report and eject
Endif
Close and return
```

FIGURE 14.22   *Pseudocode for PROP_LIST.PRG.*

```
* PROP_LIST.PRG -  Report of current listings by street name.

* Set Environment
PRIVATE ALL
SET HEADING OFF
SET TALK OFF
SET BELL OFF
SET STATUS OFF
SET SCOREBOARD OFF
SET ESCAPE OFF
SET SAFETY OFF
SET COLOR TO GR+/B,,B
CLEAR ALL

* Initialization
CLEAR
USE CLIENT INDEX ST
row =  1
ok = 0
tot = 0
cnt = 1
ON ERROR DO TRAPPER
* Check printer
@ 21, 15 SAY 'Turn on printer and adjust paper'
@ 22, 15 SAY 'Press Esc to abort or any other key to print'
```

```
* Wait for a response
CLEAR TYPEAHEAD
ok = 0
DO WHILE ok = 0
   ok = INKEY()
ENDDO ok = 0

* Remove the message
@ 21, 0 CLEAR
IF ok <> 27
      @ 10,15 SAY 'PRINTING . . . Please be patient'

      * Connect to printer
      SET DEVICE TO PRINT

      * Begin printing
      row = 1
      @ row, 15 SAY ' SUMMARY OF LISTINGS BY STREET ADDRESS'
      @ row, 60 SAY 'AS OF'
      @ row, 65 SAY DATE()
      row = row + 3

      * Print the records
      DO WHILE .NOT. EOF()
         IF row > 55
```

```
               EJECT
               row = 1
            ENDIF
            @ row,1 SAY NUM
            @ row,8 SAY ST
            @ row,30 SAY LIST_NUM
            @ row,43 SAY LAST
            @ row,63 SAY AGT
            @ row,68 SAY LIST_DATE
            row = row + 1
            @ row , 10 SAY PRICE  PICTURE '9,999,999'
            @ row,68 SAY CONT_DATE
            tot = tot + PRICE
            cnt = cnt + 1
            row = row + 2
            SKIP
         ENDDO WHILE .NOT. EOF()
```

FIGURE 14.23 *A program to print a summary report (Part 1 of 2).*

```
        * Print footer on last page
        @ row, 1 SAY 'END OF LISTING'
        EJECT

        * Print Totals
        @ 5, 15 SAY 'PRODUCTIVITY AS OF '
        @ 5, 35 SAY DATE()
        @ 7, 10 SAY 'Number of Properties'
        @ 7, 32 SAY cnt PICTURE '999'
        avg = tot/cnt
        @ 9, 10 SAY 'Average price of property'
        @ 9, 40 SAY avg PICTURE '999,999'
        EJECT
ENDIF ok # 27


SET DEVICE TO SCREEN
CLEAR
SET ESCAPE ON
CLEAR ALL
RETURN


* TRAPPER.PRG Trap for printer errors
      IF ERROR() = 125 .OR. ERROR() = 126
            SET DEVICE TO SCREEN
                     SET COLOR TO B+*/W,,
                     @ 12,15 SAY 'THE PRINTER IS NOT READY'
                     WAIT 'Ready to try again? (Y/N)' to fixit
                     IF UPPER(fixit) = 'Y'
                          SET COLOR TO GR+/B,,B
                          CLEAR
                          RETRY
                     ELSE
                          SET COLOR TO GR+/B,,B
                          SET DEVICE TO SCREEN
                          CLEAR
                          SET ESCAPE ON
                          CLEAR ALL
                          CANCEL
                     ENDIF UPPER(fixit) = 'Y'
            ENDIF ERROR() = 125 .OR. ERROR() = 126
            RETURN
```

FIGURE 14.23   *A program to print a summary report (Part 2 of 2).*

The environment settings for PROP_LIST.PRG are typical except for SET ESCAPE OFF. The Esc key will be employed to allow the user to abort the printing routine and return to the calling menu program without the system "crashing." Since the status of the printer is critical, the user must check it before continuing with the program. The CLEAR TYPEAHEAD will ensure that the user's next keystroke is captured by the INKEY() function and stored in ok as a result of the DO WHILE ok loop. Since 27 is the ASCII code for the Esc key and because of the IF ok < > 27 statement, the printing routine will execute only if the Esc has *not* been pressed.

A message is displayed while the printing routine operates. The SET DEVICE TO PRINT command will direct all @ SAYs to the printer. If a problem with the printer has generated an error code, the ON ERROR DO TRAPPER will pass control to that program. However, if the printer is properly set, a page heading that includes the date is printed and row is incremented. A DO WHILE .NOT. EOF()

loop will access all the records in the database which are indexed by the street name. The check for the end of the page, which will EJECT and reset row, appears at the top of the loop. The selected fields are positioned with the @ SAY, using the current value of row. Note that each record uses two lines to print, with a blank line between each record and the next. Before advancing to the next record, a counter variable, "cnt", is incremented and the value in the PRICE field is accumulated in the variable "tot". These two values will be used for a productivity report at the end of the listing report. When all the records have been accessed, a footer is printed to assure the user that the report is complete.

The productivity report appears on a new page. After a heading, the total number of properties is printed from the variable "cnt". The total dollar value of all properties is divided by the number of properties to produce an average price. This is displayed with a PICTURE clause and the page is EJECTed. It is important to issue a SET DEVICE TO SCREEN command for the next screen display. Also, the Esc key must be reactivated.

Report programs are as diverse as the needs of business. Gaining experience with the strategies and procedures explained in this section will contribute a great deal to your ability to produce attractive and meaningful reports.

CHAPTER SUMMARY

14.1

Optimization is the improving of the performance of code in speed and storage. Efforts should be made to optimize code after it operates correctly but not at the expense of clarity or integrity. When procedures become too large, they should be placed in another module. The TIME() function is useful for testing the performance of structures and procedures. Performance can be improved by using arrays to store frequently accessed static data in memory. Arrays can be simulated by using SAVE to store a set of variables or by generating unique variable names with a counter and a DO WHILE loop. Shortening record length and index keys will improve performance. The READKEY() function can test the user's use of specific keys to determine alternative actions.

14.2

You can improve your capability with interactive commands in several ways. Using a FIND and an index with the LIST . . WHILE command provides rapid access of data. TRANSFORM() will permit the use of template functions with LIST. SET FIELDS and SET FILTER conveniently store specifications with the LIST as well. Interactive commands will respond to editing keys. SET ALTERNATE TO/ON will store all screen displays to a .TXT file.

14.3

Programs for printing reports must address many details. Among these are checking the status of the printer, advancing pages, and formatting the report. A row counter is used to monitor the progress of the page and to position the print head. A series of IF/ENDIFs and nested DO WHILEs must be established to control the process. An error-trapping routine is useful for helping the user work with the printer. The ON ERROR command and the ERROR() function can be used to test for a specific error code for this purpose. INKEY() is used to test for an exit key.

KEY TERMS

optimization   element
array   volatile

COMMAND SUMMARY

TIME() — Display the system time.

VAL() — Convert character digits to numeric values.

SUBSTR() — Identifies substrings.

RUN — Execute external programs.

SAVE — Save memory variables to a .MEM file.

RESTORE — Restore memory variables.

READKEY() — Capture a keystoke after a READ.

EXIT — Branch to statement after ENDDO.

RETURN TO MASTER — Execute highest program in system.

CANCEL — Go to the dot prompt.

TRANSFORM() — Use template functions in a command line.

SET FILTER TO — Establish a condition.

SET FIELDS TO — Limit display to specified fields.

SET ALTERNATE TO — Open an alternate file.

SET DEVICE TO PRINT — Direct @ SAY commands to printer.

EJECT — Advance a page on the printer.

ON ERROR — Trap error conditions.

ERROR() — Returns the number of an error.

SET ESCAPE OFF — Disable the Escape key.

dBUG dBASE

- PCOL() and PROW() will return the position of the printer's print head when debugging a program to print a report.
- ISCOLOR() will return .T. or .F., depending on whether a color card and monitor are installed on the system. This is useful for determining how to set displays. You might provide separate routines for monochrome and color displays in your programs.
- FKLABEL() will return the label of the Function key that corresponds to the number supplied as an argument. This function and FKMAX(), which returns the number of Function keys available on the system, are more valuable in hardware environments external to the IBM-PC world. GETENV() will display the current setting for the DOS SET commands commonly found in the CONFIG.SYS and AUTOEXEC.BAT files.
- INKEY() returns the ASCII value of the most recent keystroke in the TYPEAHEAD buffer on a first in – first out basis. If the TYPEAHEAD buffer is set to 0 to eliminate its effect, the immediate response of the keyboard can be captured and tested with ON KEY for progamming.
- READKEY() is similar to INKEY() except that it captures the full-screen editing keystrokes, such as how the user has exited from a GET block after a READ. The fact that a different value is returned for each keystroke, depending on whether an update has occurred, permits you to program for any situation the user might present while working with your append and edit screens.

SELF-CHECK QUESTIONS

1. What is optimization? How is it accomplished?
2. What is the criterion for deciding whether or not to place a procedure in a separate file?
3. What does RUN TIME do?
4. What is an array? Why are arrays useful?
5. Why is it important to limit record length?
6. What command would you use to exit to the dot prompt from a program?
7. Why is the WHILE more efficient than the FOR?
8. For what purpose could a file generated by SET ALTERNATE TO be used?
9. Name three responsibilities that must be addressed in a report printing program.

TRY IT YOURSELF

1. Write a program similar to TIME_IT.PRG and test the performance of a DO WHILE loop with and without a nested comment line.
2. Use the RUN command to change the DOS date.
3. Save the names of the last four U.S. presidents to an array similar to the one shown in Figure 14.4. Use the initials of the presidents as variable names. Test the access, using an accept command to prompt the initials from the user, then return the full name.
4. Create a pseudoarray name using the &, as shown in Figure 14.6. Store a value in the variable and display the contents.
5. Write a short DO WHILE .T. loop and experiment with the methods illustrated in Figure 14.8. Note the results for future use.
6. Use LIST WHILE and LIST REST with an indexed .DBF file, as shown in Figures 14.9 and 14.10.
7. Use TRANSFORM() to display data in uppercase.
8. Use SET FILTER TO and SET FIELDS TO with the CITIES.DBF file, as in Figures 14.13 and 14.14, then type a LIST.
9. Type a long command at the dot prompt and experiment with the editing keys, as described in Figure 14.5.
10. Open an alternate file; SET ALTERNATE ON; display some data on the screen; close the file; and view the contents with the TYPE command.

PROGRAMMING PROJECT

Write a program to generate a report, using CLIENT.DBF from Figure 14.21. Include an error checking program.

15

ADVANCED TOPICS

LEARNING OBJECTIVES

1. To examine the advantages of using dBASE III PLUS on LANs.
2. To transfer data to and from .DBF files.
3. To compare the advantages and disadvantages of compilers and program generators.
4. To survey security concerns and future trends for dBASE III PLUS.

Chapter

ADVANCED TOPICS

There are thousands of users of dBASE III PLUS all over the world. The environment that supports the dBASE community is dynamic and is growing rapidly. Driven by this growth and by the increasing rate of hardware development, the marketplace has responded with a range of useful development tools. Local area networks (LANs) are allowing people to work together in a powerful new environment. Shortcomings of dBASE III PLUS are being met by compilers which speed execution considerably. The future holds the promise of enhanced capacities and the use of artificial intelligence or expert systems. These areas and others are discussed in this chapter. The capability you have developed from working with this text will serve you well as you participate in this exciting and rewarding technological evolution.

15.1 NETWORKING AND FILE TRANSFER

A *local area network (LAN)* is a group of two or more personal computers, with or without printers and other peripheral devices, that are connected with cable, twisted wire, or fiber optics. Each computer, or *workstation*, has a circuit board installed and has access to software that allows the transfer of data throughout the network. One computer is designated as the *file server*. It is usually a powerful PC with a high capacity hard disk that is shared by others on the network. The file server processes requests for the use of shared files and peripherals. In most networks, the file server can still function as a normal PC while the network is in operation. Other workstations have the option of working on the network or functioning as a freestanding

PC as well. The file server is a *critical node*, since all network operations are dependent on its status. If it should "crash," network operations would cease.

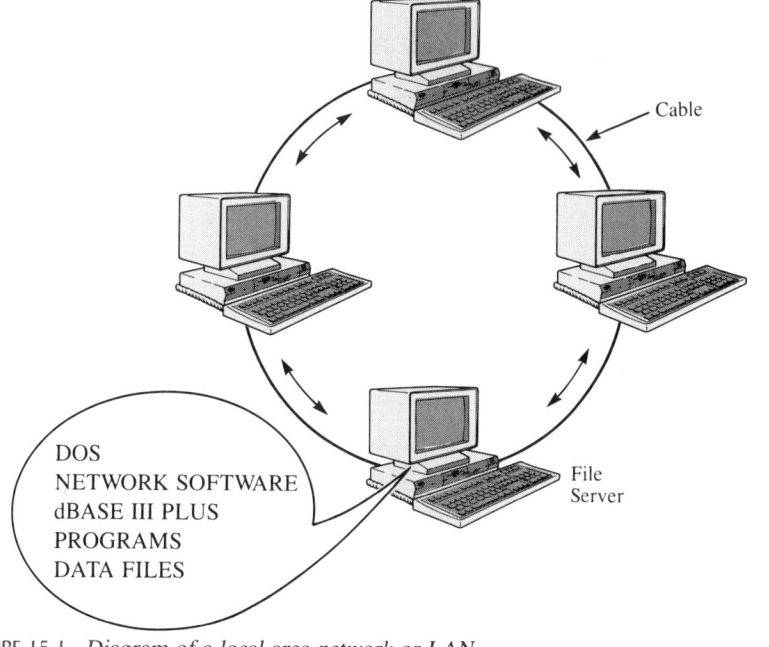

FIGURE 15.1   *Diagram of a local area network or LAN.*

The hard disk of the file server is partitioned into private directories and one shared directory that contains all the shared files accessible by the other workstations. The users who have signed on to the network can work with the shared files as if they were stored on their own disks. Programs that are installed on the file server are available to all network users.

A separate version of dBASE III PLUS is provided for local area network use. The multiuser version of dBASE III PLUS is designed to run on the Novell Advanced Netware/86, Version 1.01, or the IBM-PC Network Program, Version 1.0. The files contained on the two Administrator disks must reside on the hard disk of the file server. Each user must have a copy of the ACCESS.COM file in order to use the network version of dBASE III PLUS.

The shared disk on the file server contains data files that can be accessed by all users simultaneously. For example, a telemarketing business can provide several operators with workstations that are networked together. Network dBASE III PLUS, an application program, and data files can all reside on the file server's hard disk, which makes them available to all the operators. Orders could be taken and placed in an order file by all the operators. This is an example of a *real-time* or an *on-line* *system*.

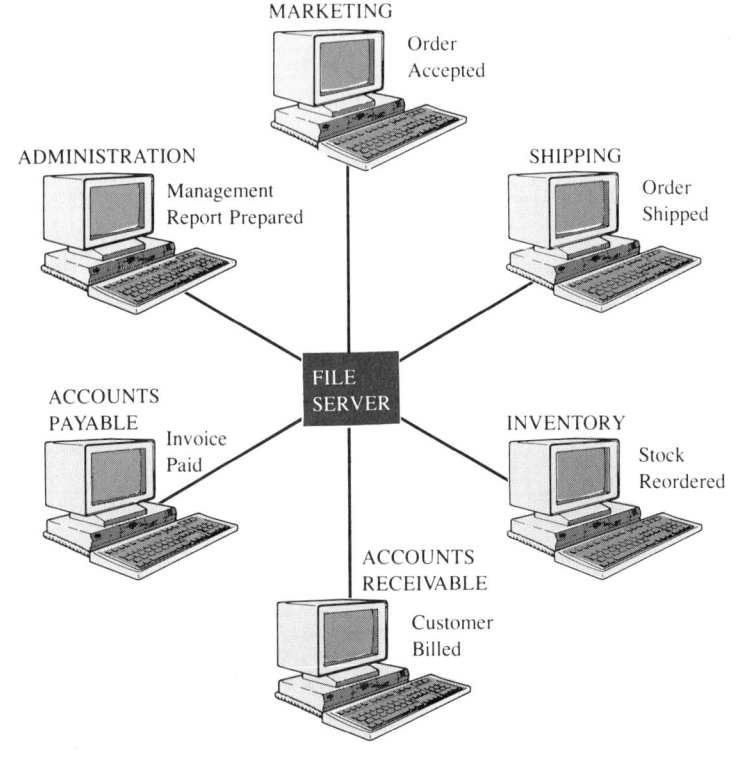

FIGURE 15.2   *Typical Usage of a Local Area Network.*

Programmers can use a local area network to develop a system as a team, sharing system parameters, development rules and procedures, and the various sub-parts of the system on which they are working, all in real time. Ordinarily they might have to work in isolation, getting information only at intervals. Another advantage of LANs is the sharing of devices such as printers, plotters, and hard disks. Such sharing can be very useful.

Many users can access centralized files
Users can communicate in path files
Expensive devices can be shared
Data is more secure
Software costs can be reduced through licensing

FIGURE 15.3   *Advantages of a Local Area Network.*

To avoid a situation in which two users attempt to change the same record or file at the same time, the Network version of dBASE III PLUS provides several *locking* commands. .DBF files are opened in the *exclusive* mode, meaning that requests to use the file by other users will be denied. After the file has been closed by the original user, it becomes available to others. The SET EXCLUSIVE OFF command allows several users to open and use the same file at the same time. The EDIT command allows the viewing, but not the changing, of data in this mode. To allow changes, any user can EDIT a record and lock it with Ctrl-O. Pressing Ctrl-O again will unlock the record and save the changes. Some commands, such as APPEND and COPY, automatically lock the file until the operation is complete, since their purpose is to make changes.

```
. USE VENDOR
File is in use by another.
            ?
USE VENDOR
Do you want some help? (Y/N) No
```

FIGURE 15.4 *Effect of SET EXCLUSIVE ON.*

Programming in the network environment makes use of special commands for handling locking and unlocking. The FLOCK() function will both lock and test a file. If the lock is successful, a .T. is returned; if not, an .F. is returned. The UNLOCK command is used to release any lock on the file. Records can be locked and unlocked in a similar manner, using RLOCK() and UNLOCK. The @ GET/ READ and the REPLACE commands require that records be locked in order to operate. Other users will not be able to move the record pointer to a locked record.

```
. SET EXCLUSIVE OFF
. USE VENDOR
.    FLOCK()
.T.

. REPLACE COMP WITH 'IBM'
Record is not locked.

. REPLACE COMP WITH 'IBM'
Do you want some help? (Y/N) No

. RLOCK()
. REPLACE COMP WITH 'IBM'
    1 record replaced
```

FIGURE 15.5 *Using FLOCK() and RLOCK().*

Electronic spreadsheets such as Lotus 1-2-3 are another very powerful type of business software. These application programs enable a user to display and manipulate rows and columns of numbers in a convenient way. Since projections can be assembled easily which allows a "what if" analysis, spreadsheets are popular with business managers. Because Lotus 1-2-3 includes a limited database capability, people sometimes face the decision whether to use Lotus 1-2-3 or dBASE III PLUS in a given situation. Each program has relative strengths and weaknesses, although there are many information problems that could be solved with dBASE III PLUS as well as with the database features of Lotus 1-2-3.

dBASE III PLUS	**LOTUS 1-2-3**
Programming language	Limited programming with macros
Very large capacity	Capacity limited to 8000 rows
Limited math functions	Variety of powerful math functions
No graphics feature	Excellent graphics
Strong database functions	Limited database functions
Limited math modeling potential	Excellent for math modeling

Examples

Client file	Loan amortization
Inventory system	Comparisons
Order and Billing	Budget projections

FIGURE 15.6   *Comparison of dBASE III PLUS and Lotus 1-2-3.*

Many microcomputer users will work with both products in order to take advantage of desired features and then transfer information between the two programs. In summary, information that is best represented as records, meaning many repetitive pieces of information, is probably best handled by dBASE III PLUS. Lotus 1-2-3 is the best choice for information that is essentially mathematical in nature and is best represented in a matrix (rows and columns).

In a business environment, it is sometimes necessary to transfer data from one software product to another. This is often the case with spreadsheet applications, such as Lotus 1-2-3. Figure 15.7 on the following page shows the result in Lotus 1-2-3 when the WKS extension is used with the COPY command. Rearranging the columns to produce a usable spreadsheet is a simple matter.

```
. USE CITIES
. COPY TO CITY123 WKS
     11 records copied

     CITY              STPOP_70 POP_82
     SAN FRANCISCO     CA715674 691637
     PHILADELPHIA      PA**************
     DALLAS            TX844401 943848
     SAN DIEGO         CA697471 915956
     HOUSTON           TX**************
     MIAMI             FL334859 382726
     CLEVELAND         OH750879 558869
     PITTSBURGH        PA520089 414936
     LOS ANGELES       CA**************
     JACKSONVILLE      FL504265 556370
     COLUMBUS          OH540025 570588

     CITY              STATE    POP_70    POP_82
     SAN FRANCISCO     CA        715674    691637
     PHILADELPHIA      PA       1949996   1665382
     DALLAS            TX        844401    943848
     SAN DIEGO         CA        697471    915956
     HOUSTON           TX       1233535   1725617
     MIAMI             FL        334859    382726

     CLEVELAND         OH        750879    558869
     PITTSBURGH        PA        520089    414936
     LOS ANGELES       CA       2811801   3022247
     JACKSONVILLE      FL        504265    556370
     COLUMBUS          OH        540025    570588
```

FIGURE 15.7 *COPYing a file to Lotus 1-2-3.*

Data files are stored in a variety of formats, which are determined by the choice of software. Some examples follow:

1. Delimited files use commas between fields and use quotation marks around character data. BASIC data files are stored this way.

```
"Ann Boline","492 Port Ave.","Seattle"
```

2. SDF files (System Data Format) use fixed-length records, without delimiters. Fields are determined by length.

```
Ann Boline       492 Port Ave.       Seattle
```

3. In .DBF files, data is stored as one block, which is then partitioned through the use of the specifications in the header or the structure of the file.

The APPEND command can be used to transfer data files from one form to a .DBF file, as follows:

```
APPEND FROM filename SDF
APPEND FROM delimited file
APPEND FROM WKS Lotus 1-2-3 worksheet
APPEND FROM DIF Visicalc worksheet
APPEND FROM SYLK Multiplan worksheet
```

The COPY TO command transfers .DBF files to other forms as follows:

```
COPY TO filename SDF
COPY TO delimited file
COPY TO WKS Lotus 1-2-3 worksheet
COPY TO DIF Visicalc worksheet
COPY TO SYLK Multiplan worksheet
```

PFS files can be IMPORTed and EXPORTed as follows:

```
USE MYFILE
IMPORT FROM filename TYPE PFS

EXPORT TO filename TYPE PFS
```

The dCONVERT utility is provided in order to translate dBASE II files to dBASE III PLUS. This is necessary because of the significant changes in the file structures and the language elements.

15.2 COMPILERS — A SPEEDY ALTERNATIVE

Because each statement must be retrieved and evaluated separately, using a process called *parsing*, dBASE III PLUS is referred to as an *interpreted* language. After parsing, the command is translated into machine or *assembly language*, which the computer can execute. Since this process must be repeated for each command, it is relatively slow. The alternative is to reduce all the instructions to a form that can be executed by the computer immediately, in one step. This is exactly what *compiled* languages do. COBOL and FORTRAN programmers must first write a *source* program, then use the compiler to produce an *object file* that can then be executed. The extra steps impede program development, but the overwhelming speed of object programs more than compensates for the extra effort in large-scale systems. Recognizing this need on the part of dBASE III PLUS programmers, software companies have released several compatible compilers. Three popular examples are: Clipper, by Nantucket Corp.; FoxBASE+, by Fox Software; and Quicksilver, by Wordtech Systems. Figure 15.8 on the following page shows some of the advantages of using a compiler.

Advantages of Compilers

Additional Features — The following features may be found on compilers: windowing; multiple SET RELATION TO; increased size limits; array memory variables; extra functions; user-defined functions; improved use of memo fields.

Protection of Source Code — Since the object code is all that is required to run the program, the developer can keep the source code for copy protection.

Speed of Execution — By nature, object code will run faster than an interpreter. The differences in speed are constantly in dispute among the software vendors. Because different types of tasks produce a variety of comparison factors, it is difficult to make a blanket statement. However, it is reasonable to expect compilers to perform between two to six times faster than dBASE III PLUS.

FIGURE 15.8 *Advantages of compilers.*

Incompatibility is the greatest disadvantage of compilers. You must realize that because you are programming with another product, not everything will be the same. Index files may not be constructed in the same way. Several commands and functions are different, while others are absent. Compiled files can become quite large, because they carry the overhead of the compiled commands as well as your programs; altogether they can create a burden on memory. The lack of interactive debugging and the delay of the compiling process slow down program development considerably.

The complexity and expense of a compiler may be avoidable if performance can be improved by upgrading the hardware. For example, moving a dBASE III PLUS application to an IBM-AT or to a Personal System/2 Model 80 from an IBM-PC will produce results that are comparable to compiling the same application on the PC. Figure 15.9 shows how a Clipper session would work.

A Clipper Session

```
A:CLIPPER C:MENU.PRG
```

While the file is compiled, line numbers are monitored and errors are displayed on the screen. Piping the output to a file as shown below makes it more convenient to study the errors.

```
A:CLIPPER C:NEWFILE > ERR
```

You would then debug the source code in dBASE III PLUS and rerun the compiler until the code was error free. The resulting .OBJ file must be linked with the linker file.

```
A:PLINK86 FILE C:NEWFILE C:PROG
```

After a long delay, a large .EXE file will be produced which can be executed from DOS by specifying the file name.

FIGURE 15.9 *A Clipper session.*

RUNTIME+ is included with the complete dBASE III PLUS package. It is comprised of dBRUN, dBCODE and dBLINKER. You can use dBCODE to encrypt and reduce your program files to a form only dBASE III PLUS or dBRUN can execute. It also removes all extra space and comments, and condenses the code to an encrypted form. This protects the original programs from modification. You can link your coded program files into one file with dBLINKER if you choose. If you use dBRUN, it will run only those files that have been processed with dBLINKER. Since RUNTIME+ was designed for software developers, Ashton-Tate will sell dBRUN to users of your system who do not own dBASE III PLUS. Some programming limitations occur when these products are used.

Program generators are programs that "write" other programs. The applications generator, for instance, is included with the dBASE III PLUS package. It uses menus to prompt the user for typical functions such as CREATE DATABASE, in addition to AUTOMATIC APPLICATION GENERATOR and ADVANCED APPLICATION GENERATOR. A complete set of files must be in place before the generator can be used. You will be prompted for file names and other specifications. A menu program will be produced with a set of procedures that utilize the interactive commands such as APPEND, EDIT, and BROWSE. It is a superficial way to organize these procedures under a menu for the sake of convenience.

GENIFER is a more sophisticated program generator from Bytel Corp. It has multiple-file capability, a powerful report generator, and data validation. File names and specifications must be entered first; then all screens, reports, and menus must be designed; and finally, the programs are produced. GENIFER makes extensive use of PROCEDUREs, a way of linking files together in one file. The code that is produced can become quite complex and may be difficult for less experienced programmers to modify.

15.3 SECURITY AND ADMINISTRATION

In the event of a disaster such as a building or office fire, data is the most vulnerable portion of a business computer system. The hardware and software can be reinstalled within a day, but the data may never be recovered. Losses can result from less violent causes as well, such as an accidental formatting of the hard disk or the ZAPping of a .DBF file.

Data can be protected in a number of ways. The most important form of protection is backup. It may seem obvious that copies of important data files should be made and stored in a safe location on a regular basis, but it is surprising how many businesses do not follow this procedure. You may have to reestablish the file and input the data from paper forms. The frequency of data backup varies with the volume of transactions. .DBF files *must* be backed up with reasonable frequency, .PRG files must have one current backup, and .NDX files can be regenerated. The appropriate question is: How much unprotected data can the business afford to lose? Backups might need to be made once a day or once a month, depending on the level of activity. Figure 15.10 lists various ways in which data can be lost.

Causes of Data Loss

1. Accidental formatting of the disk.
2. Power failure while a .DBF file is open.
3. A DOS DEL *.* command.
4. A DELETE ALL/PACK or ZAP command.
5. Removal of a floppy before closing a .DBF file.
6. Physical disasters such as fire.

FIGURE 15.10   *Causes of data loss.*

The more informed and well-trained the users of a system are, the safer the data is. Persons who are unaware of what can go wrong may inadvertently damage the data. The old saying "A little learning is a dangerous thing" holds true here. Many files have been damaged by curious but untrained users.

With dBASE III PLUS, some security is provided in the form of encryption, which is the scrambling or coding of data to prevent access by unauthorized individuals. The PROTECT utility permits an administrator to use pull-down menus in order to determine which users have access to several levels of system use. Note that this utility operates only within a network. Once the system is installed, all users must log in, providing from three to five identifiers that consist of a group name, a log in name, and a password. An account name and an access level may also be required.

Log in name	— Usually the user's first name.
Password	— Selected by the user for privacy from other users.
Group name	— Used to organize access to files that are related to an employee's department or division.
Account	— Used to document system use and accountability.
Access	— Determines the amount of access privileges from level 1 to 8.

FIGURE 15.11   *Aspects of the PROTECT utility.*

15.4 PRESENT PERSPECTIVE AND FUTURE DIRECTIONS

Much of the power of dBASE III PLUS is drawn from its design, which incorporates concepts and techniques that were developed on mainframe computers. The similarity in design places dBASE III PLUS in the same category as SQL and other fourth generation languages. Figure 15.12 suggests a view of the hierarchy of some widely used languages. The lower a language is on the scale, the closer the commands affect minute aspects of machine operation, which increases efficiency. Unfortunately, these lower languages are not English-like and are difficult to use. The higher languages are more like natural language and contain powerful features. The figure illustrates the position of dBASE III PLUS in the business software world.

Hierarchy of Languages

KEE, PROLOG	(5GL) — Include AI
dBASE III PLUS, SQL, QBE, NOMAD	(4GL) — Query Languages
BASIC, COBOL, PASCAL	(HOL) — High-Order Languages
C, ASSEMBLY LANGUAGE	— Low-Level Languages
MACHINE CODE	

FIGURE 15.12 *Hierarchy of languages.*

The table in Figure 15.13 demonstrates some of the similarities and differences among some popular languages and DBMSs by comparing several critical commands. Notice the strong similarities between SQL and dBASE III PLUS. Also, some commands are missing from BASIC and COBOL because no single command exists for the function in question. For example, although the GET in BASIC will retrieve a record from a disk file, the only criterion for selecting a specific record is the record number, which is of little use. A substantial amount of programming would be required to find a particular Social Security number, for example.

Comparison of Commands

	Establish a file	Add	Retrieve	Delete	Modify
BASIC	OPEN/FIELD	PUT	(GET)		LET
COBOL	OPEN/SELECT	WRITE			MOVE
SQL	CREATE	INSERT	SELECT	DELETE	UPDATE
dBASE III PLUS	CREATE	APPEND	FIND	DELETE	REPLACE
QBE		I.	P.	D.	U.

FIGURE 15.13 *Comparison of commands.*

Another reason dBASE III PLUS is in the same category as the SQL standard is that it contains all the essential features of a full DBMS. The chief difference lies in the hardware environment of each. Because of its advanced set of file-managing commands and other features, dBASE III PLUS has obvious advantages over BASIC and other high-order languages (HOLs). This suggests that dBASE III PLUS will enjoy continued expansion of its user base, especially in the corporate environment where its powers can be utilized to their full potential.

The community of dBASE III PLUS users and programmers represents a wide variety of occupations. Managers find dBASE III PLUS ideal for handling many aspects of a business environment. Accountants can write their own applications or can modify existing accounting systems that are written in dBASE III PLUS. The ability to develop systems for managing and reporting data is naturally a highly valued skill in the job marketplace. Many small consulting firms across the country are prospering because of the need for the support and development of dBASE III PLUS custom applications.

There will certainly be future revisions of dBASE III PLUS. Since many dBASE III PLUS users work in the corporate world, future enhancements may include stronger connections among dBASE III PLUS and mainframe programs like SQL; the ability to run under other operating systems, such as UNIX; and faster execution of programs to compete with compilers. A future version entitled dBASE IV may also take full advantage of the speed and capacity of the IBM Personal System/2 Model 80. It is probable that future versions will occupy much more disk space and memory as well.

Dramatic improvement in computer performance will undoubtedly result from recent breakthroughs in the field of superconductivity. Computers will store more information and will process information faster. Size and cost will continue to decrease. Programs like dBASE III PLUS and their logical antecedents, artificial intelligence and expert systems, naturally will benefit from these improvements, because their power is always constrained by the limits of the computer. The next generation of DBMSs will probably include a more natural language-user interface, along with aspects of artificial intelligence and expert systems. (These characteristics are sometimes used to describe fifth generation languages, or 5GL.) In conclusion, the future holds much promise for continued improvement in the dBASE III PLUS environment. The skills you have acquired while working with this text will become more valuable as these improvements are realized.

CHAPTER SUMMARY

15.1

A local area network links computers together to share files and peripherals. The file server stores the files and programs which the workstations access and update. Collisions are avoided by locking files and records through the use of SET

EXCLUSIVE ON, FLOCK(), and RLOCK(). Files from a variety of software products, such as Lotus 1-2-3, can be transferred in and out of .DBF files.

15.2

With dBASE III PLUS you are using an interpreter as opposed to a compiler. Compilers reduce programs to the computer's native code, which executes rapidly. Several dBASE III PLUS compilers are available which include some useful features but may not be compatible. RUNTIME + and the applications generator are included with dBASE III PLUS to speed up, protect, and write programs.

15.3

The backup of data files is critical to system security. Data loss can result from natural disasters or operator error. Users should be trained to protect data. Access security is provided through the PROTECT utility, which limits access to authorized users at several levels.

15.4

The characteristics of dBASE III PLUS place it in the same category as the most powerful fourth generation languages, such as SQL. It has several advantages over high-order languages like BASIC, and it has a large and varied base of users. Future versions may connect easily to mainframe environments and take advantage of hardware developments. Aspects of artificial intelligence and expert systems may be included.

KEY TERMS

local area network	machine language	PROTECT
workstation	assembly language	Fourth-generation languages
file server	compiler	SQL
critical node	source file	High-order language (HOL)
real-time	object file	UNIX
on-line system	RUNTIME +	superconductivity
locking	encryption	artificial intelligence
SDF	program generator	expert system
interpreter	back up	Fifth generation languages
parsing		

COMMAND SUMMARY

SET EXCLUSIVE OFF — Open files to all network users.
FLOCK() — File locking function.
UNLOCK — Unlock a network file.
RLOCK() — Record locking function.

SELF-CHECK QUESTIONS

1. What are LANs? Why are they useful?
2. Where are shared files and programs stored in a network?
3. What is meant by a real-time or an on-line system? Where would it be useful?
4. How are data collisions between users handled by dBASE III PLUS?
5. Why would it be useful to transfer .DBF records to Lotus 1-2-3?
6. Name three software products that support file transfer with dBASE III PLUS.
7. What is the difference between an interpreter and a compiler?
8. What are the advantages and disadvantages of using a compiler?
9. Judging from the description in Chapter 15, would you call RUNTIME+ a compiler? Why?
10. What is a disadvantage of using a program generator?
11. How often should a business back up its data files?
12. What are some precautions against data loss?
13. Under what circumstances would it be beneficial to use the PROTECT utility?
14. Why is development of programs faster in dBASE III PLUS than in high-order languages?
15. What improvements would you recommend for the next version of dBASE III PLUS?

CASE STUDY

PURITY REALTY

CASE STUDY

Purity Realty is a medium sized brokerage of approximately 30 agents. The owner, Dan Zucco is an excellent manager but is too occupied with his duties to design and control the work flow in the office. This responsibility belongs to Jennifer Rollings who maintains the office records and prepares the documents which are associated with the selling and buying of properties. Because the firm is enjoying substantial growth Jennifer's workload has become overwhelming. The problem had become so critical that Dan decided to purchase a computer system to give Jennifer some relief.

The salesman who sold the computer to Purity included the MS-DOS operating system and a word processing program. Since Jennifer had acquired some computer background through a course at a local college, she was able to begin using the computer to handle the office correspondence more efficiently. In discussing how the computer might improve the flow of information in the firm, Jennifer discovered that Dan, like most new users, had many mistaken preconceptions. Dan said, "I expect all of our essential client and customer information to be safely stored in the computer and I want accurate and timely reports of several aspects of the business." Jennifer began constructing a word processing file of 180 records which looked like the example below.

```
Shugart, Jerry and Kim
896 Leader Avenue
Philadelphia, PA
$89000
Agent - Steve Huntzinger
May 4, 1988
```

When the list was printed and presented to Dan, he was pleased that the data was stored and available for use. He then made the following requests:

1. Print the list in alphabetical order.
2. Provide a total of all sales for each agent.
3. Include the commission paid to the agent.

Dan had additional requests but these were enough to convince Jennifer that the word processing software was not the tool for the job. Since the file she had created was a simple list of data there was no way to select the names and alphabetize them.

The prices could not be totaled because the data were just symbols, not numeric fields. Adding an additional line of data to each of the 180 records would have been a time-consuming, frustrating task.

Dan's impression of how the computer and the software should operate is quite common among new users. Jennifer knew that the word processing program would not be enough to do the job. She remembered that a fellow student, Eric Allen, had established a consulting business after graduation. Jennifer arranged a meeting between herself, Dan, and Eric. During the meeting Eric explained how dBASE III PLUS could provide Dan with the record keeping and reporting functions he required. Since Jennifer was already computer literate it was agreed that Eric would sell and install dBASE III PLUS, set up some database files, and train Jennifer to manage the system and run reports.

Eric spent the next few days asking many questions around the office to evaluate the information needs of Purity Realty. He discovered that files were being kept for both clients (people who had listed their houses for sale with the agency) and for customers (people who had purchased homes). In addition there was an agent list and information on commissions. When an agent needed information about a transaction, a card file was used to retrieve the number of the file in the cabinet. Agents would frequently interrupt Jennifer's work to find misplaced files.

While he continued to gather information about the files, Eric decided to set up a database for agent information. Since this data did not change very often and did not include critical financial fields, it was a convenient way to introduce dBASE III PLUS to the office environment without great risk. The agent data was being kept on a list which was updated and photocopied occasionally:

NAME
AGENT #
ADDRESS
CITY ST ZIP
HOME PHONE
OFFICE PHONE

Meanwhile, Eric was planning the structure for the files which would hold the customer and client data. Eric had assembled all the information which would be included in a typical record folder from the file cabinet. The following is a list of some fields he found in a client file:

Name
Property address
    City, State, Zip
Date of contract
Price of property
Office file number
Central Listing number (from a realtor's listing service)
Agent number

Customer files looked like this:

Name
Current address
    City, State, Zip
Property address
    City, State, Zip
Contract date
Settlement date
Price
Listing agent
Selling agent

After reviewing the fields to be included with Dan and Jennifer, Eric determined how each field would be represented in dBASE III PLUS. All fields which contain alphabetic data such as name or city would obviously be character type, as well as some fields containing only numbers but not used for calculations (zip). Only the appropriate length and a meaningful field name had to be chosen. Here are the structures that Eric established:

```
Structure for database: C:AGENT.dbf
Number of data records:        0
Date of last update   : 01/01/88
Field  Field Name  Type       Width    Dec
    1  NAME        Character     25
    2  ADDRESS     Character     25
    3  CITY        Character     15
    4  STATE       Character      8
    5  AGENT_NUM   Character      4
    6  HOME        Character      8
    7  OFFICE      Character      8
** Total **                      94

Structure for database: C:CUST.dbf
Number of data records:        0
Date of last update   : 01/01/88
Field  Field Name  Type       Width    Dec
    1  SAL_NUM     Character     11
    2  LAST        Character     18
    3  FIRST       Character     20
    4  CURR_NUM    Character      8
    5  CURR_ST     Character     20
    6  CURR_CITY   Character     20
    7  CURR_ZIP    Character      5
    8  PROP_NUM    Character      8
    9  PROP_ST     Character     20
   10  PROP_CITY   Character     20
   11  PROP_ZIP    Character      5
   12  CONT_DATE   Date           8
   13  LIST_AGT    Character      4
```

```
14   SELL_AGT    Character        4
15   PRICE       Numeric          7
16   ML_NUM      Character        5
*Total**                        184
```

```
Structure for database:  C:CLIENT.dbf
Number of data records:        0
Date of last update   : 01/01/88
Field   Field Name  Type        Width    Dec
    1   LIST_NUM    Character      11
    2   ML_NUM      Character       5
    3   LAST        Character      18
    4   FIRST       Character      20
    5   NUM         Character       6
    6   ST          Character      15
    7   CITY        Character      20
    8   ZIP         Character       5
    9   AGT         Character       4
   10   PRICE       Numeric         7
   11   LAST_DATE   Date            8
**  Total  **                    120
```

Jennifer learned to use the Assistant feature to APPEND, EDIT, and DELETE records as the roster of agents changed. She also began to develop reports using CREATE/MODIFY REPORT. One day Dan asked for a list of properties in a certain zip code that were priced above $100,000. Eric wrote the following program to provide the list, but Jennifer noticed that it would not be useful criteria for other than those already in the program.

```
* CUST1.PRG - Displays Selected Records in the CUST.DBF file

SET TALK OFF
USE CUST
DO WHILE .NOT. EOF()
    IF PRICE > 100000 .OR. PROP_ZIP = '55677'
        ? PROP_NUM, PROP_ST, PROP_CITY, PROP_ZIP, PRICE
    ELSE
        ? PROP_NUM, PROP_ST, 'Not Selected'
    ENDIF PRICE > 100000
SKIP
ENDDO .NOT. EOF()
CLEAR ALL
```

Occasionally individuals other than Jennifer needed to add records to the two files. Eric wrote two programs to automate the APPEND process for those who did not know how to use dBASE III PLUS.

```
* ADD_CLIE.PRG - Add Records to CLIENT.DBF
CLEAR
USE CLIENT
DO WHILE .T.
STORE ´ ´ TO OK
CLEAR
@ 2, 25  SAY "NEW RECORD? (Q to quit)"
@ 0, 22  TO  3, 53    DOUBLE
@ 2,49 GET OK
READ
IF OK = ´Q´ .OR. OK = ´q´
    CLEAR ALL
    DO IT
ENDIF
APPEND BLANK
CLEAR
@ 2, 29  SAY "CLIENT ENTRY"
@ 4, 15  SAY "CURR/SOLD"
@ 4, 25  GET  C_S
@ 4, 29  SAY "LIST #"
@ 4, 36  GET  LIST_NUM
@ 4, 49  SAY "M/L #"
@ 4, 55  GET  ML_NUM
@ 6, 12  SAY "LAST"
@ 6, 17  GET  LAST
@ 6, 38  SAY "FIRST"
@ 6, 44  GET  FIRST
@ 8, 19  SAY "NUMBER"
@ 8, 26  GET  NUM
@ 8, 34  SAY "STREET"
@ 8, 41  GET  ST
@ 10, 19  SAY "CITY"
@ 10, 25  GET  CITY
@ 10, 47  SAY "ZIP"
@ 10, 51  GET  ZIP
@ 12, 15  SAY "PRICE"
@ 12, 21  GET  PRICE
@ 12, 30  SAY "PRICE CHANGE (C)"
@ 12, 47  GET  PC
@ 12, 50  SAY "AGENT"
@ 12, 56  GET  AGT
@ 14,  9  SAY "LIST DATE"
@ 14, 20  GET  LIST_DATE
@ 14, 31  SAY "EXP. DATE"
@ 14, 42  GET  EXP_DATE
@ 14, 52  SAY "EXTENSION (X)"
@ 14, 66  GET  EXT
@ 16, 16  SAY "CONTRACT DATE"
@ 16, 30  GET  CONT_DATE
@ 16, 42  SAY "SOURCE"
@ 16, 50  GET  SOURCE
@ 17, 72  TO 17, 72    DOUBLE
@  1,  5  TO 17, 72    DOUBLE
READ
ENDDO
```

```
* ADD_CUST.PRG - Add Customers to CUST.DBF
CLEAR
USE CUST
DO WHILE .T.
STORE ' ' TO OK
CLEAR
@  2, 25  SAY "NEW RECORD? (Q to quit)"
@  0, 22  TO  3, 53    DOUBLE
@  2,49 GET OK
READ
IF OK = 'Q' .OR. OK = 'q'
    CLEAR ALL
    DO IT
ENDIF
APPEND BLANK
CLEAR
@  1,  4  SAY "P/S"
@  1,  8  GET  P_S
@  1, 31  SAY "CUSTOMER ENTRY"
@  3,  4  SAY "SALE #"
@  3, 12  GET  SAL_NUM
@  3, 25  SAY "LAST"
@  3, 30  GET  LAST
@  3, 49  SAY "FIRST"
@  3, 55  GET  FIRST
@  5, 34  SAY "CURRENT"
@  6,  4  SAY "NUM."
@  6,  9  GET  CURR_NUM
@  6, 16  SAY "STREET"
@  6, 23  GET  CURR_ST
@  6, 40  SAY "CITY"
@  6, 45  GET  CURR_CITY
@  6, 66  SAY "ZIP"
@  6, 70  GET  CURR_ZIP
@  8, 34  SAY "PROPERTY"
@  9,  4  SAY "NUM."
@  9,  9  GET  PROP_NUM
@  9, 16  SAY "STREET"
@  9, 23  GET  PROP_ST
@  9, 40  SAY "CITY"
@  9, 45  GET  PROP_CITY
@  9, 66  SAY "ZIP"
@  9, 70  GET  PROP_ZIP
@ 12,  4  SAY "CONTRACT DATE"
@ 12, 18  GET  CONT_DATE
@ 12, 30  SAY "M.L.#"
@ 12, 36  GET  ML_NUM
@ 12, 45  SAY "SELL AGT"
@ 12, 54  GET  SELL_AGT
@ 12, 62  SAY "LIST AGT"
@ 12, 71  GET  LIST_AGT
@ 15, 15  SAY "PRICE"
@ 15, 21  GET  PRICE
@ 15, 30  SAY "COMM"
@ 15, 35  GET  COMM
@ 15, 45  SAY "CO.$"
@ 15, 50  GET  CO_DOLL
@ 17, 20  SAY "REF.FEE"
@ 17, 28  GET  REF_FEE
@ 17, 37  SAY "REF"
@ 17, 41  GET  REF
@ 19, 18  SAY "SOURCE"
@ 19, 25  GET  SOURCE
@ 19, 40  SAY "FINANCING"
@ 19, 51  GET  FINC
@  0,  2  TO 20, 76    DOUBLE
READ
ENDDO
```

As the files began to grow, updating became quite inconvenient since EDIT requires the record number. Jennifer suggested that Eric write a program to retrieve records by the listing number in order to update. The following program demonstrates an improvement in Eric's programming skill:

```
* CHG_CLIE.PRG - Update records in the CLIENT.DBF file

* Set Environment
PRIVATE ALL
SET HEADING OFF
SET TALK OFF
SET BELL OFF
SET STATUS OFF
SET SCOREBOARD OFF
SET SAFETY OFF
CLEAR ALL

* Initialization
USE CLIENT INDEX LIST_NUM

DO WHILE .T.
   CLEAR
   mlist_num = SPACE(11)
   mlast = SPACE(18)
   mfirst = SPACE(20)
   mnum =SPACE(6)
   mst =SPACE(15)
   mcity =SPACE(20)
   mzip =SPACE(5)
   mprice = 0
```

```
   magt =SPACE(4)
   mlist_date = CTOD( '01/01/88')
   mcont_date = CTOD( '01/01/88')

   * GET Listing Number and display screen
   @  2, 29   SAY "CLIENT ENTRY"
   @  4, 29   SAY "LIST #"
   @  4, 36   GET  mlist_num PICTURE 'AA-99999-99'
   @  6, 12   SAY "LAST"
   @  6, 38   SAY "FIRST"
   @  8, 19   SAY "NUMBER"
   @  8, 34   SAY "STREET"
   @ 10, 19   SAY "CITY"
   @ 10, 47   SAY "ZIP"
   @ 12, 15   SAY "PRICE"
   @ 12, 50   SAY "AGENT"
   @ 14,  9   SAY "LIST DATE"
   @ 16, 16   SAY "CONTRACT DATE"
   @  1,  5   TO 17, 72     DOUBLE
   READ

   * Check for blank Listing Number
   IF mlist_num = '
      CLEAR
      CLEAR ALL
```

```
         RETURN
      ENDIF mlist_num = '

   * Check if record exists
   SEEK mlist_num
   IF .NOT. FOUND()
         @ 5,30 SAY 'Listing Number Not on File'
         mpause = 0
         DO WHILE mpause < 25
               mpause = mpause + 1
```

```
     ENDDO mpause < 100
     @ 5,30 SAY SPACE(25)
     LOOP
ENDIF .NOT. FOUND()

* Move current data to variables
STORE LIST_NUM TO mlist_num
STORE LAST TO mlast
STORE FIRST TO mfirst
STORE NUM TO mnum
STORE ST TO mst
STORE CITY TO mcity
STORE ZIP TO mzip
STORE AGT TO magt
STORE PRICE TO mprice
STORE LIST_DATE TO mlist_date
STORE CONT_DATE TO mcont_date

* GET remaining fields
ok = .Y.
DO WHILE ok
   @  6, 17  GET  mlast PICTURE '@!'
   @  6, 44  GET  mfirst PICTURE '@!'
   @  8, 26  GET  mnum PICTURE '@9'
   @  8, 41  GET  mst PICTURE '@!'
```

```
   @ 10, 25  GET  mcity PICTURE '@!'
   @ 10, 51  GET  mzip PICTURE '@9'
   @ 12, 21  GET  mprice PICTURE '9,999,999' RANGE 1000,2000000
   @ 12, 56  GET  magt
   @ 14, 20  GET  mlist_date
   @ 16, 30  GET  mcont_date
   READ
   @ 16,40 SAY 'Any Changes? (Y/N) ' GET ok
   READ
ENDDO ok

* Move updated data to file
REPLACE LIST_NUM WITH mlist_num, LAST WITH mlast,;
   FIRST WITH mfirst, NUM WITH mnum, ST WITH mst,;
   CITY WITH mcity, ZIP WITH mzip,;
   AGT WITH magt, PRICE WITH mprice,;
   LIST_DATE WITH mlist_date, CONT_DATE WITH mcont_date
ENDDO .T.
```

Since the update program worked so well Eric rewrote the original append program and made it more convenient for Jennifer to use. He wrote a similar program for the customer data and grouped them together in a menu-driven system.

```
* MENU.PRG - Menu for System
      CLEAR ALL
      SET BELL OFF
      SET COLOR TO W/B,,G
      CLEAR
      SET TALK OFF
      STORE " " TO CHOICE
      @  2, 28  SAY "PURITY REALTY CO."
      @  4, 24  SAY "1 - ADD TO CUSTOMER FILE (SALES)"
      @  6, 24  SAY "2 - ADD TO CLIENT FILE (LISTINGS)"
      @  8, 24  SAY "3 - EXIT" .
      @ 11, 24  SAY "ENTER CHOICE"
      0, 18  TO 13, 62    DOUBLE
      @ 11,37 GET CHOICE
      READ
      DO CASE
        CASE CHOICE = '1'
          DO ADD_CUST
        CASE CHOICE = '2'
          DO ADD_CLIENT
        CASE CHOICE = '3'
          CLEAR ALL
          CLEAR
          QUIT
      ENDCASE
```

```
* ADD_CLIE.PRG -   Add records to the CLIENT.PRG file

* Set Environment
PRIVATE ALL
SET HEADING OFF
SET TALK OFF
SET BELL OFF
SET STATUS OFF
SET SCOREBOARD OFF
SET SAFETY OFF
CLEAR ALL

* Initialization
USE CLIENT INDEX LIST_NUM

DO WHILE .T.

   MLIST_NUM = SPACE(11)
   MLAST = SPACE(18)
   MFIRST = SPACE(20)
   MNUM =SPACE(6)
   MST =SPACE(15)
   MCITY =SPACE(20)
   MZIP =SPACE(5)
   MPRICE = 0
```

```
   MAGT =SPACE(4)
   MLIST_DATE = CTOD('01/01/88')
   MCONT_DATE = CTOD('01/01/88')

   * GET Listing Number and display screen
   @  2, 29  SAY "CLIENT ENTRY"
   @  4, 29  SAY "LIST #"
   @  4, 36  GET   MLIST_NUM PICTURE  AA-99999-99
   @  6, 12  SAY "LAST"
   @  6, 38  SAY "FIRST"
   @  8, 19  SAY "NUMBER"
   @  8, 34  SAY "STREET"
   @ 10, 19  SAY "CITY"
   @ 10, 47  SAY "ZIP"
   @ 12, 15  SAY "PRICE"
```

```
@ 12, 50   SAY "AGENT"
@ 14,  9   SAY "LIST DATE"
@ 16, 16   SAY "CONTRACT DATE"
@ 17, 72   TO 17, 72    DOUBLE
@  1,  5   TO 17, 72    DOUBLE
READ

* Check for blank Listing Number
IF MLIST_NUM = '               '
     CLEAR
     CLEAR ALL
     RETURN
ENDIF MLIST_NUM = '

* Check if record already exists
SEEK MLIST_NUM
IF FOUND()
     @ 5,30 SAY 'Listing Number on File'
     mpause = 0
     DO WHILE mpause < 25
         mpause = mpause + 1
     ENDDO mpause < 100
     @ 5,30 SAY SPACE(25)
     LOOP
ENDIF FOUND()
```

```
* GET remaining fields
ok = .Y.
DO WHILE ok
@  6, 17   GET   MLAST PICTURE '@!'
@  6, 44   GET   MFIRST PICTURE '@!'
@  8, 26   GET   MNUM PICTURE '@9'
@  8, 41   GET   MST PICTURE '@!'
@ 10, 25   GET   MCITY PICTURE '@!'
@ 10, 51   GET   MZIP PICTURE '@9'
@ 12, 21   GET   MPRICE PICTURE '9,999,999' RANGE 1000,2000000
@ 12, 56   GET   MAGT
@ 14, 20   GET   MLIST_DATE
@ 16, 30   GET   MCONT_DATE
READ
@ 16,40 SAY 'Any Changes? (Y/N) ' GET ok
READ
ENDDO ok
APPEND BLANK
REPLACE LIST_NUM WITH MLIST_NUM, LAST WITH MLAST,;
   FIRST WITH MFIRST, NUM WITH MNUM, ST WITH MST,;
   CITY WITH MCITY, ZIP WITH MZIP,;
   AGT WITH MAGT, PRICE WITH MPRICE,;
   LIST_DATE WITH MLIST_DATE, CONT_DATE WITH MCONT_DATE
CLEAR GETS
ENDDO .T.
```

Jennifer and Dan were so pleased with the new programs that Eric was asked to make similar improvements for the reports. He wrote the program for a list by seller's name first, and then completed an improved version of the list by street name. Finally, he added a menu to link the programs conveniently.

```
* SELLER.PRG - List Properties by Seller's Name
SET DEVICE TO SCREEN
CLEAR
SET ESCAPE ON
CLEAR ALL
RETURN
CLEAR
ACCEPT 'When Printer is Ready and Paper is Adjusted Press Return' TO OK
USE CLIENT INDEX LAST
SET DEVICE TO PRINT
ROW = 1
@ ROW, 30 SAY ' SUMMARY OF LISTINGS BY SELLER'
@ ROW, 65 SAY DATE( )
ROW = ROW + 2
DO WHILE .NOT. EOF( )
        IF ROW > 55
                EJECT
                ROW = 1
        ENDIF
        IF C_S = 'S'
                SKIP
        ENDIF
        @ ROW,1 SAY LAST
        @ ROW,20 SAY LIST_NUM
        @ ROW,34 SAY NUM
        @ ROW,41 SAY ST
                @ ROW,57 SAY AGT
                @ ROW,62 SAY LIST_DATE
                @ ROW,72 SAY EXP_DATE
                ROW = ROW + 1
                @ ROW,10 SAY PRICE
                ROW = ROW + 2
                SKIP
        ENDDO
        @ ROW, 1 SAY 'END OF LISTING'
        EJECT
        SET DEVICE TO SCREEN
        CLEAR
        CLOSE DATABASES
        RETURN
```

```
* PROP_LIST.PRG -  Report of current listings by street name.

* Set Environment
PRIVATE ALL
SET HEADING OFF
SET TALK OFF
SET BELL OFF
SET STATUS OFF
SET SCOREBOARD OFF
SET ESCAPE OFF
SET SAFETY OFF
SET COLOR TO GR+/B, ,B
CLEAR ALL

* Initialization
CLEAR
USE CLIENT INDEX ST
row =  1
ok = 0
tot = 0
cnt = 1
ON ERROR DO TRAPPER
* Check printer
@ 21, 15 SAY 'Turn on printer and adjust paper'
@ 22, 15 SAY 'Press Esc to abort or any other key to print'
```

```
* Wait for a response
CLEAR TYPEAHEAD
ok = 0
DO WHILE ok = 0
   ok = INKEY( )
ENDDO ok = 0

* Remove the message
@ 21, 0 CLEAR
IF ok <> 27
     @ 10,15 SAY 'PRINTING . . . Please be patient'

     * Connect to printer
     SET DEVICE TO PRINT

     * Begin printing
     row = 1
     @ row, 15 SAY ' SUMMARY OF LISTINGS BY STREET ADDRESS'
     @ row, 60 SAY 'AS OF'
     @ row, 65 SAY DATE( )
     row = row + 3

     * Print the records
     DO WHILE .NOT. EOF( )
        IF row > 55
           EJECT
           row = 1
        ENDIF
           @ row,1 SAY NUM
           @ row,8 SAY ST
           @ row,30 SAY LIST_NUM
           @ row,43 SAY LAST
           @ row,63 SAY AGT
           @ row,68 SAY LIST_DATE
           row = row + 1
           @ row , 10 SAY PRICE PICTURE '9,999,999'
           @ row,68 SAY CONT_DATE
           tot = tot + PRICE
           cnt = cnt + 1
           row = row + 2
           SKIP
     ENDDO WHILE .NOT. EOF( )

     * Print footer on last page
     @ row, 1 SAY 'END OF LISTING'
     EJECT

     * Print Totals
     @ 5, 15 SAY 'PRODUCTIVITY AS OF'
     @ 5, 35 SAY DATE( )
     @ 7, 10 SAY 'Number of Properties'
     @ 7, 32 SAY cnt PICTURE '999'
     avg = tot/cnt
     @ 9, 10 SAY 'Average price of property'
     @ 9, 40 SAY avg PICTURE '999,999'
     EJECT
ENDIF ok # 27
```

```
* TRAPPER.PRG - Trap for printer errors
    IF ERROR() = 125 .OR. ERROR() = 126
            SET DEVICE TO SCREEN
            SET COLOR TO B+*/W,,
            @ 12,15 SAY 'THE PRINTER IS NOT READY'
            WAIT 'Ready to try again? (Y/N)' to fixit
            IF UPPER(fixit) = 'Y'
                SET COLOR TO GR+/B,,B
                CLEAR
                RETRY
            ELSE
                SET DEVICE TO SCREEN
                SET COLOR TO GR+/B,,B
                CLEAR
                SET ESCAPE ON
                CLEAR ALL
                CANCEL
            ENDIF UPPER(fixit) = 'Y'
    ENDIF ERROR() = 125 .OR. ERROR() = 126
```

```
* REPORT.PRG - Menu for Report Programs
  CLEAR ALL
  SET BELL OFF
  SET COLOR TO W/B,,G
  CLEAR
  SET TALK OFF
  STORE " " TO CHOICE
  @  2, 28  SAY "PURITY REALTY CO."
  @  4, 24  SAY "1 - LISTINGS BY PROPERTY"
  @  6, 24  SAY "2 - LISTINGS BY NAME"
  @  8, 24  SAY "3 - RETURN TO MAIN MENU"
  @ 12, 24  SAY "ENTER CHOICE"
  @  0, 18  TO 14, 62    DOUBLE
  @ 11,37 GET CHOICE
  READ
  DO CASE
     CASE CHOICE = '1'
          DO PROP
     CASE CHOICE = '2'
          DO NAME
     CASE CHOICE = '3'
          CLEAR ALL
  ENDCASE
  RETURN
```

APPENDICES

COMMANDS AND FUNCTIONS

dBASE III PLUS COMMANDS BY PURPOSE

File Commands

CLEAR ALL	JOIN
CLOSE	MODIFY COMMAND
COPY	MODIFY FILE
COPY FILE	MODIFY FILE ASCII
COPY STRUCTURE	MODIFY LABEL
COPY STRUCTURE EXTENDED	MODIFY QUERY
CREATE	MODIFY REPORT
CREATE FROM	MODIFY SCREEN
CREATE LABEL	MODIFY STRUCTURE
CREATE QUERY	MODIFY VIEW
CREATE REPORT	REINDEX
CREATE SCREEN	RENAME
CREATE VIEW	SAVE TO
CREATE VIEW FROM	SELECT
DELETE FILE	SET ALTERNATE TO
ERASE	SET CATALOG TO
EXPORT TO PFS	SORT
IMPORT FROM PFS	TOTAL
INDEX	USE

Data Commands

? and ??	CHANGE
@	CLEAR GETS
APPEND	CONTINUE
APPEND BLANK	COUNT
APPEND FROM	DELETE
AVERAGE	DISPLAY
BROWSE	DISPLAY MEMORY

EDIT
FIND
GET
GO/GOTO
INSERT
LABEL FORM
LIST
PACK
READ
RECALL

REPLACE
REPORT FORM
SEEK
SET DEVICE TO
SET PRINT
SKIP
SUM
TYPE
UPDATE
ZAP

Programming Commands

&
&&
*
=
ACCEPT
AVERAGE
CALL
CANCEL
CASE
CLEAR ALL
CLEAR MEMORY
COUNT
DIR
DISPLAY FILES
DISPLAY HISTORY
DISPLAY MEMORY
DISPLAY STATUS
DISPLAY STRUCTURE
DO
DO...WITH
DO CASE
DO WHILE
ELSE
ENDCASE
ENDDO
ENDIF
ENDTEXT
EXIT
GET
IF

INPUT
LIST FILES
LIST HISTORY
LIST MEMORY
LIST STATUS
LIST STRUCTURE
LOAD
LOOP
M->
NOTE
ON ERROR
ON ESCAPE
ON KEY
OTHERWISE
PARAMETER
PRIVATE
PROCEDURE
PUBLIC
QUIT
READ
RELEASE
RELEASE MODULE
RESTORE
RESUME
RETRY
RETURN
RETURN TO MASTER
RUN or !
SAVE
SET DEBUG

SET HISTORY
SET PROCEDURE TO
SET STEP
SET TALK
STORE

SUM
SUSPEND
TEXT
WAIT

Utility Commands

ASSIST
CLEAR
CLEAR FIELDS
CLEAR GETS
CLEAR TYPEAHEAD
EJECT
SET ALTERNATE
SET BELL
SET CARRY
SET CATALOG
SET CENTURY
SET COLOR
SET CONFIRM
SET CONSOLE
SET DATE
SET DEBUG
SET DECIMALS
SET DEFAULT TO
SET DELETED
SET DELIMITERS
SET DEVICE TO
SET DOHISTORY
SET ECHO
SET ESCAPE
SET EXACT
SET FIELDS
SET FILTER TO
SET FIXED

SET FORMAT TO
SET FUNCTION TO
SET HEADING
SET HELP
SET HISTORY
SET INDEX TO
SET INTENSITY
SET MARGIN TO
SET MEMOWIDTH TO
SET MENU
SET MESSAGE TO
SET ORDER TO
SET PATH TO
SET PRINT
SET PRINTER TO
SET PROCEDURE TO
SET RELATION TO
SET SAFETY
SET SCOREBOARD
SET STATUS
SET STEP
SET TALK
SET TITLE
SET TYPEAHEAD TO
SET UNIQUE
SET VIEW TO
SET VIEW TO ?
USE ?

String Functions

$
ASC()
AT()
CHR()
ISALPHA()

ISLOWER()
ISUPPER()
LEFT()
LEN()
LOWER()

LTRIM()
REPLICATE()
RIGHT()
SPACE()

STUFF()
SUBSTR()
TRIM()
UPPER()

Numeric Functions

ABS()
EXP()
IIF()
INT()
LOG()
MAX()
MIN()

MOD()
ROUND()
SQRT()
STR()
TRANSFORM()
VAL()

Date Functions

CDOW()
DMONTH()
CTOD()
DATE()
DAY()

DOW()
DTOC()
MONTH()
YEAR()

Utility Functions

BOF()
COL()
DBF()
DELETED()
DISKSPACE()
EOF()
ERROR()
FIELD()
FILE()
FKLABEL()
FKMAX()
FOUND()
GETENV()
INKEY()
ISCOLOR()

LUPDATE()
MESSAGE()
NDX()
OS()
PCOL()
PROW()
READKEY()
RECNO()
RECOUNT()
RECSIZE()
ROW()
TIME()
TYPE()
VERSION()

NETWORK FUNCTIONS and COMMANDS

ACCESS()   RLOCK()
DISPLAY USERS   SET ENCRYPTION ON
FLOCK()   SET EXCLUSIVE ON
LOCK()   UNLOCK
LOGOUT   USE EXCLUSIVE

dBASE III PLUS COMMANDS AND FUNCTIONS

$ — Evaluate presence of substring.

& — Macro expansion function.

&& — In-line comment.

* — Comment line.

= — STORE operator.

? and ?? — Display expressions.

@ — Position cursor for SAY or GET.

ABS() — Absolute value.

ACCEPT — Store user input data to variable.

ACCESS() — User access for PROTECT utility.

APPEND — Add new record to .DBF file.

APPEND BLANK — Add record with no screen.

APPEND FROM — Add data from another file.

ASC() — ASCII code of character.

ASSIST — Call the assistant feature.

AT() — Determine position of substring.

AVERAGE — Compute average of numeric fields.

BOF() — Beginning of file.

BROWSE — View and edit several records.

CALL — Execute binary file.

CANCEL — Return to dot prompt.

CASE — One condition in a DO CASE.

CDOW() — Character day of week.

CHANGE — Edit fields and records.

CHR() — Display ASCII character.

CLEAR — Clear the screen.

CLEAR ALL — Close files and release variables.

CLEAR FIELDS — Clear SET FIELDS status.

CLEAR GETS — Release GET variables.

CLEAR MEMORY — Release variables.

CLEAR TYPEAHEAD — Clear typeahead buffer.

CLOSE — Close files.

COL() — Cursor column position.

CONTINUE — Move to next record after LOCATE.

COPY — Copy .DBF file.

COPY FILE — Copy any file.

COPY STRUCTURE — Copy .DBF structure only.

COPY STRUCTURE EXTENDED — Copy structure to .DBF file.

COUNT — Count records satisfying a condition.

CREATE — Create new .DBF file.

CREATE database FROM structure extended file.

CREATE LABEL — Generate a label-printing file.

CREATE QUERY — Store a filter condition.

CREATE REPORT — Generate a report-printing file.

CREATE SCREEN — Generate a screen-display file.

CREATE VIEW — Store file relations.

CREATE VIEW FROM ENVIRONMENT — Store working environment.

CTOD() — Convert character string to date.

DATE() — The system date.

DAY() — Numeric day of month.

DBF() — Name of current .DBF file.

DELETE — Mark a record for deletion.

DELETE FILE — Remove a file from the disk.

DELETED() — Deletion status of record.

DIR — Display disk directory.

DISKSPACE() — Amount of free disk space.

DISPLAY — Display active .DBF fields.

DISPLAY FILES — Display files on active disk.

DISPLAY HISTORY — Display recently issued commands.

DISPLAY MEMORY — Show contents of memory.

DISPLAY STATUS — Display report of system status.

DISPLAY STRUCTURE — Display .DBF structure.

DISPLAY USERS — Display users on network.

DO — Execute a program file.

DO CASE — Structure for selecting among options.

DO WHILE — Structure for repetition.

DO...WITH — Execute a program file with parameters.

DOW() — Day of week as a numeric value.

DTOC() — Convert a date to a character string.

EDIT — Change contents of a record.

EJECT — Advance paper in printer.

ELSE — Alternative action in IF/ENDIF.

ENDCASE — Closing statement for DO CASE.

ENDDO — Closing statement for DO WHILE.

ENDIF — Closing statement for IF.

ENDTEXT — Closing statement for TEXT.

EOF() — Indicates end of file.

ERASE — Deletes a file.

ERROR() — Numeric code of error condition.

EXIT — Branch out of a DO WHILE.

EXPORT TO — Transfer data to PFS file.

EXP() — Exponential value.

FIELD() — Field name of specified field.

FILE() — Indicate existence of file.

FIND — Indexed search for a value.

FKLABEL() — Function key names.

FKMAX() — Number of function keys.

FLOCK() — Lock a network file.

FOUND() — Indicate success of FIND or SEEK.

GET — Accept user input data to custom screen.

GETENV() — Display DOS status.

GO/GOTO — Move record pointer.

IF — Structure for conditional branching.

IIF() — Immediate IF.

IMPORT FROM PFS — Transfer a PFS file.

INDEX — Establish index file on key.

INKEY() — Code of user's last keystroke.

INPUT — Accept user input data to variable.

INSERT — Insert a blank record.

INT() — Integer of a value.

ISALPHA() — Determine if character is alphabetic.

ISCOLOR() — Determine if color monitor is in use.

ISLOWER() — Determine if letter is lowercase.

ISUPPER() — Determine if letter is uppercase.

JOIN — Combine two databases.

LABEL FORM — Print labels using LABEL file.

LEFT() — Extract left-most characters of string.

LEN() — Length of a string.

LIST — Display fields from .DBF file.

LIST FILES — Display names of files on disk.

LIST HISTORY — Display recently executed commands.

LIST MEMORY — Display memory variables.

LIST STATUS — Display report of system status.

LIST STRUCTURE — Display .DBF structure.

LOAD — Load a binary file for execution.

LOCK() — Lock a network file for update.

LOGOUT — Sign off network.

LOG() — Logarithm of value.

LOOP — Return to DO WHILE.

LOWER() — Change to lowercase.
LTRIM() — Remove leading blanks.
LUPDATE() — Date of last file update.
MAX() — Greater of two values.
MESSAGE() — Message of current error.
MIN() — Lesser of two values.
MODIFY COMMAND — Enter text editor for .PRG file.
MODIFY FILE — Enter text editor for ASCII file.
MODIFY LABEL — Update .LBL file.
MODIFY QUERY — Update .QRY file.
MODIFY REPORT — Update .FRM file.
MODIFY SCREEN — Update .SCR/.FMT file.
MODIFY STRUCTURE — Change .DBF structure.
MODIFY VIEW — Update .VUE file.
MOD() — MODulus of a value.
MONTH() — Numeric value of month.
M→ — Reference memory variable.
NDX() — Names of active .NDX files.
NOTE — Comment line.
ON ERROR — Execute error-handling routine.
ON ESCAPE — Execute on Escape key.
ON KEY — Execute if any key pressed.
OS() — Name of operating system.
OTHERWISE — Alternative clause for DO CASE.
PACK — Remove deleted records.
PARAMETER — Pass variables to another program.
PCOL() — Location of printer column.
PRIVATE — Restricts variable use.
PROCEDURE — Combines .PRG files.
PROW() — Location of printer row.
PUBLIC — Establish global variable.
QUIT — Quit dBASE III PLUS, return to DOS.
READ — Store values in GET blocks.
READKEY() — Value of key after READ.
RECALL — Remove deletion mark from record.
RECNO() — Number of current record.
RECOUNT() — Number of records in file.
RECSIZE() — Size of current record.
REINDEX — Recreate active indexes.
RELEASE — Clear memory variables.
RELEASE MODULE — Clear a LOADed binary file.
RENAME — Change file name.
REPLACE — Change value in field.
REPLICATE() — Repeat a character.

REPORT FORM — Establish an .FRM file.

RESTORE — Read a .MEM file into memory.

RESUME — Continue program execution after SUSPEND.

RETRY — Reexecute an error-trapped statement.

RETURN — Pass control to a higher program.

RETURN TO MASTER — Pass control to first .PRG file.

RIGHT() — Extract right-most characters.

RLOCK() — Lock a network record for update.

ROUND() — Round value.

ROW() — Position of cursor row.

RUN or ! — Execute outside program.

SAVE — Place variables and values in file.

SEEK — Do an indexed search for a value.

SELECT — Open a work area.

SET — Set system control parameters.

SET ALTERNATE TO/ON — Open .TXT file.

SET BELL — Control speaker beep.

SET CARRY — Carry data to new record.

SET CATALOG — Open .CAT file to group related files.

SET CENTURY — Display full year.

SET COLOR — Change screen colors.

SET CONFIRM — Control skipping to next field in screens.

SET CONSOLE — Turn off monitor display.

SET DATE — Control date format.

SET DEBUG — Send ECHO output to printer.

SET DECIMALS — Control decimal positions.

SET DEFAULT TO — Change active disk drive.

SET DELETED — Hide deleted records.

SET DELIMITERS — Specify screen-editing delimiters.

SET DEVICE TO — Control output device SCREEN/PRINT.

SET DOHISTORY — Control HISTORY feature.

SET ECHO — Display program commands as they execute.

SET ESCAPE — Control Escape key.

SET EXACT — Exact matches for comparisons.

SET EXCLUSIVE ON — Lock network files.

SET FIELDS — Restrict display of fields.

SET FILTER TO — Control conditions for display of records.

SET FIXED — Control number of decimal places.

SET FORMAT TO — Open .FMT file.

SET FUNCTION TO — Control function key values.

SET HEADING — Control field name display in LIST.

SET HELP — Control HELP prompt on error.

SET HISTORY — Control number of commands in HISTORY.

SET INDEX TO — Open .NDX files.

SET INTENSITY — Control enhanced display.

SET MARGIN TO — Control printer margin.

SET MEMOWIDTH TO — Control memo field width.

SET MENU — Control screen navigation menu.

SET MESSAGE TO — Control custom message on screen.

SET ORDER TO — Establish controlling index file.

SET PATH TO — Set directory path for file search.

SET PRINT — Echo print of screen displays.

SET PRINTER TO — Redirect to printing device.

SET PROCEDURE TO — Open procedure file.

SET RELATION TO — Chain .DBF files on key.

SET SAFETY — Prompt for file overwrite.

SET SCOREBOARD — Control scoreboard display.

SET STATUS — Control status line display.

SET STEP — Pause program after each command.

SET TALK — Display command results.

SET TITLE — Prompt for inclusion in .CAT file.

SET TYPEAHEAD TO — Control typeahead buffer size.

SET UNIQUE — Restrict indexing to unique records.

SET VIEW TO — Open .VUE file.

SKIP — Move record pointer.

SORT — Rewrite .DBF file in order.

SPACE() — Fill with spaces.

SQRT() — Square root of value.

STORE — Establish a memory variable.

STR() — Convert a numeric value to a string.

STUFF() — Insert a substring into another string.

SUBSTR() — Extract a substring from another string.

SUM — Total numeric fields.

SUSPEND — Pause program execution.

TEXT — Display page of text.

TIME() — Display system time.

TOTAL — Create a .DBF file with totals.

TRANSFORM() — Use PICTURE formats.

TRIM() — Remove trailing blanks.

TYPE — Display an ASCII file.

TYPE() — Display type of field.

UNLOCK — Remove LOCK on network data.

UPDATE — Batch mode updating of .DBF file.

UPPER() — Convert letters to uppercase.

USE — Open a .DBF file.

USE EXCLUSIVE — LOCK network files.

VAL() — Convert character numerals to numeric value.

VERSION() — Display version of dBASE III PLUS.

WAIT — Pause for key input by user.
YEAR() — Numeric value of year in date.
ZAP — Remove all records from .DBF file.

COMMANDS NOT IN dBASE III

@ DOUBLE
CALL
CLEAR FIELDS
CLEAR TYPEAHEAD
CREATE QUERY
CREATE SCREEN
CREATE VIEW
CREATE VIEW FROM ENVIRONMENT
DISPLAY HISTORY
EXPORT TYPE PFS
IMPORT FROM TYPE PFS
LIST HISTORY
LOAD
MODIFY QUERY
MODIFY SCREEN
MODIFY VIEW
ON ERROR/ESCAPE/KEY
RESUME

RETRY
SET CATALOG ON
SET CATALOG TO
SET CENTURY
SET DATE
SET DOHISTORY
SET FIELDS
SET FIELDS TO
SET HISTORY
SET HISTORY TO
SET MESSAGE TO
SET ORDER TO
SET PRINTER TO
SET STATUS
SET TITLE
SET TYPEAHEAD TO
SET VIEW TO
SUSPEND

MODIFIED COMMANDS

APPEND FROM
BROWSE
CLOSE ALL
INDEX (UNIQUE)
READ [SAVE]

REPORT FORM (SUMMARY)
SELECT /?
SET COLOR (BACKGROUND)
SET FILTER TO (FILE)
SET MENUS

ASCII CODES

ASCII VALUE	CHARACTER	CONTROL CHARACTER	ASCII VALUE	CHARACTER	CONTROL CHARACTER
000	(null)	NUL	038	&	
001	☺	SOH	039	'	
002	●	STX	040	(	
003	♥	ETX	041	)	
004	♦	EOT	042	*	
005	♣	ENQ	043	+	
006	♠	ACK	044	,	
007	(beep)	BEL	045	-	
008	◘	BS	046	.	
009	(tab)	HT	047	/	
010	(line feed)	LF	048	0	
011	(home)	VT	049	1	
012	(form feed)	FF	050	2	
013	(carriage return)	CR	051	3	
014	♫	SO	052	4	
015	☼	SI	053	5	
016	►	DLE	054	6	
017	◄	DC1	055	7	
018	↕	DC2	056	8	
019	‼	DC3	057	9	
020	¶	DC4	058	:	
021	§	NAK	059	;	
022	▬	SYN	060	<	
023	↨	ETB	061	=	
024	↑	CAN	062	>	
025	↓	EM	063	?	
026	←	SUB	064	@	
027	→	ESC	065	A	
028	(cursor right)	FS	066	B	
029	(cursor left)	GS	067	C	
030	(cursor up)	RS	068	D	
031	(cursor down)	US	069	E	
032	(space)	SP	070	F	
033	!		071	G	
034	"		072	H	
035	#		073	I	
036	$		074	J	
037	%		075	K	

ASCII VALUE	CHARACTER	CONTROL CHARACTER	ASCII VALUE	CHARACTER	CONTROL CHARACTER
076	L		126	~	
077	M		127	⌂	
078	N		128	Ç	
079	O		129	ü	
080	P		130	é	
081	Q		131	â	
082	R		132	ä	
083	S		133	à	
084	T		134	å	
085	U		135	ç	
086	V		136	ê	
087	W		137	ë	
088	X		138	è	
089	Y		139	ï	
090	Z		140	î	
091	[		141	ì	
092	\		142	Ä	
093	]		143	Å	
094	^		144	É	
095	_		145	æ	
096	`		146	Æ	
097	a		147	ô	
098	b		148	ö	
099	c		149	ò	
100	d		150	û	
101	e		151	ù	
102	f		152	ÿ	
103	g		153	Ö	
104	h		154	Ü	
105	i		155	¢	
106	j		156	£	
107	k		157	¥	
108	l		158	Pt	
109	m		159	ƒ	
110	n		160	á	
111	o		161	í	
112	p		162	ó	
113	q		163	ú	
114	r		164	ñ	
115	s		165	Ñ	
116	t		166	ª	
117	u		167	º	
118	v		168	¿	
119	w		169	⌐	
120	x		170	¬	
121	y		171	½	
122	z		172	¼	
123	{		173	¡	
124	|		174	«	
125	}		175	»	

ASCII VALUE	CHARACTER	CONTROL CHARACTER	ASCII VALUE	CHARACTER	CONTROL CHARACTER
176	░		226	Γ	
177	▒		227	π	
178	▓		228	Σ	
179	│		229	σ	
180	┤		230	μ	
181	╡		231	τ	
182	╢		232	Φ	
183	╖		233	Θ	
184	╕		234	Ω	
185	╣		235	δ	
186	║		236	∞	
187	╗		237	Ø	
188	╝		238	∈	
189	╜		239	∩	
190	╛		240	≡	
191	┐		241	±	
192	└		242	≥	
193	┴		243	≤	
194	┬		244	⌠	
195	├		245	⌡	
196	─		246	÷	
197	┼		247	≈	
198	╞		248	°	
199	╟		249	●	
200	╚		250	•	
201	╔		251	√	
202	╩		252	ⁿ	
203	╦		253	²	
204	╠		254	■	
205	═		255	(blank 'FF')	
206	╬				
207	╧				
208	╨				
209	╤				
210	╥				
211	╙				
212	╘				
213	╒				
214	╓				
215	╫				
216	╪				
217	┘				
218	┌				
219	█				
220	▄				
221	▌				
222	▐				
223	▀				
224	α				
225	β				

ERROR MESSAGES

ALIAS name already in use (24) — LIST STATUS to see file usage.

ALIAS not found (13) — LIST STATUS to see file usage.

Beginning of file encountered (38) — Check record pointer position.

Cannot erase a file which is open (89) — Close the file first.

Cannot write to a read-only file — Change file status from DOS.

CONTINUE without LOCATE (42) — Issue a LOCATE.

Cyclic Relation (44) — Evaluate SET RELATION TO commands.

Database in encrypted (131) — Secure access through PROTECT.

Database is not indexed (26) — Establish index to use SEEK or FIND.

Data type mismatch (9) — Evaluate type of data.

.DBT file cannot be opened (41) — Check memo field status.

Disk full when writing file: (56) — Acquire more disk space.

End-of-file encountered (4) — Check .DBF or .NDX status.

*** Execution error on + : Concatenated string too large, shorten string.

Field name already in use — Use another name.

File already exists (7) — Use another name.

File does not exist (1) — Check file name.

Index file does not match database (19) — Use correct .NDX file.

Insufficient memory — Check CONFIG.SYS, increase memory.

Mismatched DO WHILE and ENDDO (96) — Check program logic.

No database in USE. Enter file name: (52).

Not a dBASE database (15) — Use dCONVERT, check header.

Not enough disk space for SORT — Acquire disk space.

Printer not ready (125) — Check printer settings.

Record is in use by another (109) — Unlock network record.

Record is not in index (20) — Reindex the file.

Record is out of range (5) — Reindex the file.

Syntax error (10) — Check syntax and typing.

Syntax error in ... expression — Fix form specification.

Too many files are open (6) — Check CONFIG.SYS, reduce files.

Unable to load COMMAND.COM (92) — Check disk contents.

Unauthorized access level (133) — Gain access through PROTECT.

Unauthorized log in (132) — Gain access through PROTECT.

Unbalanced parentheses (8) — Check expression.

∗∗∗ Unrecognized command verb (16) — Check command syntax.

Unrecognized phrase/keyword in command (36) — Check command syntax.

Unterminated string (35) — Check quotation marks.

Variable not found (12) — Check variable name.

Wrong number of parameters (94) — Compare DO WITH and PARAMETERS.

-> — arrow prefix to identify SELECTed files.

Accumulator — a memory variable used to accumulate an arithmetic total.

Action diagrams — the bracketing of control structures for clarity.

Algorithm — a logical series of steps to solve a problem.

Alphanumeric — any character-type symbol.

Alphanumeric constant — a specific piece of character-type data.

Alphanumeric literal — a specific piece of character-type data.

Archive — to place records in an inactive file.

Argument — the data affected by a function.

Array — a group of elements sharing a common name.

ASCII — a standard code used to represent data in a computer system.

Assembly language — a low-level language using native machine instructions.

Backup — to make a copy of a file to prevent data loss.

BASIC — a common third-generation language.

Batch mode — processing transactions as a group.

Boyce-Codd Normal Form — an arrangement of data to reduce redundancy.

Buffer — a portion of memory reserved for file transfer.

Byte — the amount of storage required for one character of data.

Called program — a subprogram activated by another program.

Calling program — a program that activates a subprogram.

Chaining — establishing indexed links among files.

Character — one symbol such as 7 or z.

COBOL — a third-generation language used on mainframe computers.

Coding — writing instructions using a programming language.

COMMAND.COM — a file containing a portion of MS-DOS.

Compiler — a program used to reduce source code to machine code.

Concatenation — the combining of two strings with a + sign.

Condition — a logical test comparing two data items.

CONFIG.DB — a file containing dBASE III PLUS settings.

CONFIG.SYS — a file containing DOS settings.

Counter — a memory variable incremented to count.

CPU — the central processing unit.

Critical node — a vital station in a local area network.

Data — information represented in a computer system.

Data integrity — using programming to ensure that data are correct.

Database — an organized collection of data.

Database management system — a program to store and organize data.

DBMS — a database management system.

Dijkstra Structures — the three primary control structures.

Element — one item in an array.

Encryption — a method of scrambling data for security.

Field — a piece of data representing one entity, such as a name.

File — a collection of records.

File name — a name assigned to a file by the user.

File server — the central computer in a local area network.

Flat file — an unorganized list of data.

FORTRAN — a third-generation language.

Full-screen editing — the use of blocks and editing keys on the screen.

Function — a means of converting or viewing data in a more useful way.

Function key — ten or twelve software assigned keys.

Functional decomposition — the process of top-down design.

Functional dependency — a type of file redundancy reduced with normalization.

Header — the beginning section of a .DBF file.

Hierarchical — a type of DBMS used on mainframe systems.

High-order language (HOL) — languages that are English-like.

I-P-O chart — an input-processing-output chart.

If-then-else — a decision making control structure.

In-line code — including functions within the program, instead of modules.

Interactive — programs that respond to user input.

Internal memory — circuits that hold data temporarily.

Interpreter — a program that processses lines of code individually.

Iteration — the repeating of a section of code.

Key field — the field used in an index.

Kilobyte — 1,024 bytes of data.

LAN — local area network.

Local area network — a means of communicating and sharing data among PCs.

Locking — restricting file usage on a network.

Machine language — native instrutions to the CPU.

Many-to-many — a look-up relationship involving multiple occurrences.

Megahertz — millions of cycles per second.

Menu-driven — systems controlled with menu selections, not commands.

Modules — separate programs performing a function in a system.

MS-DOS — the disk operating system used with dBASE III PLUS.

Mutually exclusive — when only one option is logically possible in a set.

Nesting — the placing of one control structure within another.

Normalization — the process of eliminating redundancy in files.

Null string — a character literal containing no data.

Numeric constant — a specific numeric value.

Numeric literal — a specific numeric value.

Object file — the executable file produced by a compiler.

One-to-many — a file relationship with multiple occurrences in one file.

One-to-one — a file relationship with single occurrences in each file.

Operating system — a set of programs essential to basic system operations.

Optimization — improving the performance of programs.

Parsing — scanning lines of code for execution.

Program generator — a program that writes code.

PROTECT — a utility to provide file security.

Pseudocode — brief statements outlining program functions.

Query — a request for data from a system.

Reasonableness — testing whether data is within acceptable limits.

Record — a collection of fields.

Scope — specifies the number of records affected by a command.

Selection — using a control structure to select records.

Self-documenting — including comments and indention in programs.

Source file — code to be processed by a complier.

SQL — a standard used in DBMS languages.

String — a set of aphanumeric characters.

Structure — the format for a .DBF file.

Structure diagram — a means of outlining system relationships.

Subprograms — modules within a system.

Subroutine — a subprogram.

Syntax — the rules of a language.

Table — an arrangement of data in rows and columns.

Third normal form — data that has been normalized to reduce redundancy.

Transparent — processes that are not evident to the user.

Value — a numeric literal.

Volatile — data that is subject to frequent change.

Work area — a section of memory assigned to one .DBF file.

Workstation — one computer in a local area network.

BIBLIOGRAPHY

Codd, E. F. 1970, June. A Relational Model of Data for Large Shared Databanks. *Communciations of the ACM*, Vol. 13 (6).

Date, C. J. 1982. *An Introduction to Database Systems*. Reading, MA: Addison-Wesley

Dijkstra, E. W., Dahl, O. J., & Hoare, D. A. R. 1972. *Structured Programming*. Academic Press.

Fagin, R. 1979, May. Normal Forms and Relational Database Operations. *Proceedings ACM SIGMOND*.

Kernighan, B. W., & Plauger, P. J. 1978. *The Elements of Programming Style*. New York: McGraw-Hill.

Knuth, D. E. 1973. *The Art of Computer Programming, Volume 3: Sorting and Searching*. Reading, MA: Addison-Wesley.

Lammers, S. 1986. Interviews. *Programmers at Work*. Redmond, WA: Microsoft Press.

Martin, J. 1977. *Computer Database Organization*. Englewood Cliffs, NJ: Prentice-Hall.

Martin, J., & McClure, C. 1985. *Action Diagrams*. Englewood Cliffs, NJ: Prentice-Hall.

Pratt, P. J., & Adamski, J. J. 1987. *Database Systems: Management and Design*. Boston, MA: Boyd & Fraser Publishing Co.

Weinberg, G. M. 1971. *The Psychology of Programming*. New York: Van Nostrand Reinhold

Yourdon, E., & Constantine, L. L. 1979. *Structured Design*. Englewood Cliffs, NJ: Prentice-Hall.

JOURNALS

Data Based Advisor, Data Based Solutions, San Diego, CA.

PC TECH JOURNAL, Ziff-Davis Publishing, Boulder, CO.

Technotes, Ashton-Tate, Escondido, CA.